JOURNAL FOR THE STUDY OF THE OLD TESTAMENT
SUPPLEMENT SERIES
322

Sheffield Academic Press

The Conceptual Coherence of the Book of Micah

Mignon R. Jacobs

Journal for the Study of the Old Testament
Supplement Series 322

Copyright © 2001 Sheffield Academic Press

Published by
Sheffield Academic Press Ltd
Mansion House
19 Kingfield Road
Sheffield S11 9AS
England

www.SheffieldAcademicPress.com

Typeset by Sheffield Academic Press
and
Printed on acid-free paper in Great Britain
by Biddles Ltd

British Library Cataloguing-in-Publication Data

A catalogue record for this book is available
from the British Library

ISBN 1-84127-176-4

CONTENTS

Part III
DISCERNING CONCEPTUALITY

ACKNOWLEDGMENTS

The process of completing this work has been a rewarding one thanks to several groups of people. This is slightly revised version of my 1997 Claremont Graduate University dissertation. I owe special thanks to the members of my committee: Dr Rolf P. Knierim, my advisor and chair of my committee, for his guidance and insight throughout my doctoral studies; Dr James A. Sanders and Dr Marvin A. Sweeney.

Thanks to Paul Luna and Josephine Floridez who encouraged and supported me as I completed this work.

My brother Carlos probably knows the story of how each chapter took shape. I thank him for his love, care and wisdom.

Thanks to the people at Sheffield Academic Press for all their work in preparing my manuscript for publication.

My deepest thanks go to God.

January 2000

ABBREVIATIONS

ABD	David Noel Freedman (ed.), *The Anchor Bible Dictionary* (New York: Doubleday, 1992)
AJSL	*American Journal of Semitic Languages and Literatures*
AnBib	Analecta biblica
ATR	*Anglican Theological Review*
BDB	Francis Brown, S.R. Driver and Charles A. Briggs, *A Hebrew and English Lexicon of the Old Testament* (Oxford: Clarendon Press, 1907)
Bib	*Biblica*
BKAT	Biblischer Kommentar: Altes Testament
BR	*Bible Review*
BZAW	Beihefte zur *ZAW*
CAT	Commentaire de l'Ancien Testament
CBQ	*Catholic Biblical Quarterly*
DJD	Discoveries in the Judean Desert
EBib	Etudes bibliques
FzB	Forschung zur Bibel
FOTL	The Forms of the Old Testament Literature
GKC	*Gesenius' Hebrew Grammar* (ed. E. Kautzsch, revised and trans. A.E. Cowley; Oxford: Clarendon Press, 1910)
HAR	*Hebrew Annual Review*
ICC	International Critical Commentary
IDB	George Arthur Buttrick (ed.), *The Interpreter's Dictionary of the Bible* (4 vols.; Nashville: Abingdon Press, 1962)
Int	*Interpretation*
ISBE	Geoffrey Bromiley (ed.), *The International Standard Bible Encyclopedia* (4 vols.; Grand Rapids: Eerdmans, rev. edn, 1979–88)
JAOS	*Journal of the American Oriental Society*
JBL	*Journal of Biblical Literature*
JSOT	*Journal for the Study of the Old Testament*
JSOTSup	*Journal for the Study of the Old Testament*, Supplement Series
KAT	Kommentar zum Alten Testament
KB	Ludwig Koehler and Walter Baumgartner (eds.), *Lexicon in Veteris Testamenti libros* (Leiden: E.J. Brill, 1953)
NICOT	New International Commentary on the Old Testament

OBO	Orbis biblicus et Orientalis
OTL	Old Testament Library
RB	*Revue biblique*
ResQ	*Restoration Quarterly*
RevSém	*Revue sémitique*
SBLDS	SBL Dissertation Series
SBLMS	SBL Monograph Series
SBT	Studies in Biblical Theology
SEÅ	*Svensk exegetisk årsbok*
SJLA	Studies in Judaism in Late Antiquity
SJT	*Scottish Journal of Theology*
ST	*Studia theologica*
TDOT	G.J. Botterweck and H. Ringgren (eds.), *Theological Dictionary of the Old Testament*
THAT	Ernst Jenni and Claus Westermann (eds.), *Theologisches Handwörterbuch zum Alten Testament* (Munich: Chr. Kaiser, 1971–76)
ThWAT	G.J. Botterweck and H. Ringgren (eds.), *Theologisches Wörterbuch zum Alten Testament* (Stuttgart: W. Kohlhammer, 1970–)
TTZ	*Trierer theologische Zeitschrift*
TWOT	R. Laird Harris, Gleason L. Archer, Jr and Bruce K. Waltke (eds.), *Theological Wordbook of the Old Testament* (2 vols.; Chicago: Moody Press, 1980)
VT	*Vetus Testamentum*
VTSup	*Vetus Testamentum*, Supplements
WBC	Word Biblical Commentary
ZAW	*Zeitschrift für die alttestamentliche Wissenschaft*

INTRODUCTION

Early research on the book of Micah focused on the disunity of the book through analysis of its 'inconsistencies'. The main focus of present research on the book of Micah, however, is the question of the book's 'unity/coherence'. The question itself has been in large part the problem faced by the methods employed to answer it. For while the fundamental issue has been the coherence of the book, the lack of clarity in the formulation of the question has been a deterrent to discerning the coherence of the whole.

The various proposals of the book's structure are the clearest indicators of the variety of views concerning the book's coherence. An understanding of the conceptuality of its parts and their interrelationship within the whole is fundamental to discerning the book's coherence. In spite of this, each proposal simply presupposes an understanding of the conceptuality, and therefore characterizes the units of the book in accordance with the presuppositions about its conceptuality. Thus, the concern to discern the conceptuality of the book has remained a secondary concern, and at times an optional element in the attempts to discern the book's coherence. Furthermore, the various attempts have succumbed to the ambiguities that are characteristic of the absence of clear definitions of their key terms, that is, those terms used in the formulation of their questions and in their analyses of the book. In light of these and other limitations of past research, the present study proposes to define and carry out the task of discerning the conceptual coherence of the book through a sustained analysis of the text.

The thesis of the present study is that the final form of the book of Micah exhibits a conceptual coherence discernible through its structure and generated by its conceptuality. Therefore, analysis of the structure and the conceptuality is fundamental to the task of discerning the coherence of the book. Towards the accomplishment of this overall task, three parts are propsed to reflect the various aspects of the task. Part I consists of Chapters 1 and 2. Chapter 1 provides the context for the present study through a review of the history of research. It examines the ways in which previous studies have dealt with issues of the book's coherence, that is, as evident in their proposals concerning its structure. It also attempts to identify the previous studies' criteria for discerning coherence.

Chapter 2 provides the theoretical basis for the study. It has the two-fold task of defining the proposed method, thus providing an understanding of its task, and defining the key terms and presuppositions of the study, for example, coherence, conceptuality, theme. With regards to presuppositions, it will examine the following questions: What is coherence? How is it related to conceptuality? How is it related to structure? Are there different types of coherence? And how is coherence to be discerned?

Part II consists of Chapters 3, 4 and 5. Chapter 3 examines the coherence of the book through a structural analysis of the final form. This chapter attempts to demonstrate how structure, as an essential aspect and indicator, contributes to the discerning of coherence.

The focus of Chapters 4 and 5 will be a unit-by-unit exposition of the book with the aim of identifying the conceptuality of the constitutive units (as identified in the structural analysis). It will include a discussion of the interrelationship of the various conceptual levels in order to discern the conceptuality and hence the conceptual coherence of the whole.

Part III consists of Chapters 6 and 7. Chapter 6 will then evaluate the various concepts as they function within the whole. It will also look at the contextual aspects of the book of Micah and specifically at the extent that these and other intertextual aspects contribute to the understanding of the place of the concept in the coherence of the book. It is here that the proposal concerning the conceptual coherence of the book will be articulated.

Chapter 7 will conclude the study with a synthesis of the previous chapters. It will also incorporate two aspects: an evaluation of the present study's contribution to research on the book of Micah and consideration of the implications of this study for future studies on conceptual coherence.

Part I

HISTORY AND METHOD

Chapter 1

HISTORY OF RESEARCH ON THE BOOK OF MICAH

Introduction

Over the last two centuries, several challenges have confronted scholars in their interpretation of the extant form of the book of Micah. Included among these challenges are questions about the 'the authenticity of the hope oracles', the arrangement of the extant form of the book, and 'the nature and interpretation of the difficult passages'.[1] While these challenges have contributed to multiple proposals concerning the book's[2] unity or lack thereof, recently (from the 1960s up to the present), a trajectory constituted by analyses of the book's unity/coherence has emerged into the foreground primarily with questions of 'literary coherence'. This trajectory raises other challenges, the most significant being the need to define what is meant by coherence and the need to move beyond attempts to discern the literary integrity[3] of the text to the analysis of its conceptuality which gives rise to the literary integrity.

It must be said at the outset that the challenge of identifying the coherence of the book of Micah has been addressed through various

---

1. For discussion of the history approached from this perspective see: John T. Willis, 'Fundamental Issues in Contemporary Micah Studies', *ResQ* 13.2 (1970), pp. 77-90. An attempt to up-date Willis's survey of Micah studies was made by Knud Jeppesen, 'New Aspects of Micah Research', *JSOT* 8 (1978), pp. 3-32; *idem*, 'How the Book of Micah Lost its Integrity', *ST* 33 (1979), pp. 101-31.

2. In the present discussion the 'book of Micah' and 'the book' are used to refer to the extant form of the MT now designated as מיכה. These designations are not used of the person Micah or to either confirm or deny that the extant text was written or spoken by the person Micah.

3. Although it is often used interchangeably with the term 'cohesion', the use of the designation 'literary coherence' at this point, simply reflects its use in the history of research on the book of Micah. See Chapter 3 below for the present author's discussion of 'cohesion'.

methods including: traditio-historical criticism,[4] literary criticism,[5] text criticism,[6] form criticism,[7] historical critical,[8] redaction criticism[9] and rhetorical criticism.[10] As evidenced by the various proposals concerning the macro-structure, the particular method does not seem to influence the outcome of the investigation.[11] No one methodological approach leads

4.   Walter Beyerlin, *Die Kulttraditionen Israels in der Verkündigung des Propheten Micha* (Göttingen: Vandenhoeck & Ruprecht, 1959).

5.   B. Renaud, *Structure et Attaches littéraires de Michée IV-V* (Paris: J. Gabalda, 1964); *idem, La Formation du Livre de Michée: Tradition et Actualisation* (Paris: J. Gabalda, 1977); T.K. Cheyne, *Micah: With Notes and Interpretation* (The Cambridge Bible for Schools and Colleges; Cambridge: Cambridge University Press, 1893); J.M.P. Smith, *Micah, Zephaniah, Nahum, Habakkuk, Obadiah, and Joel* (ICC; Edinburgh: T. & T. Clark, 1911); Conrad von Orelli, *The Twelve Minor Prophets* (Edinburgh: T. & T. Clark, 1897); *idem,* 'Micah', in *ISBE*, III, pp. 2046-47; John T. Willis, 'The Structure, Setting, and Interrelationships of the Pericopes in the Book of Micah' (unpublished PhD dissertation, Vanderbilt University, 1966). He combines the literary approach with form-critical observations and redaction-critical analysis; David Hagstrom, *The Coherence of the Book of Micah: A Literary Analysis* (SBLDS, 89; Atlanta: Scholars Press, 1988).

6.   Paul Haupt, 'Critical Notes on Micah', *AJSL* 26 (1910), pp. 201-52; *idem,* 'The Book of Micah', *AJSL* 27 (1911), pp. 1-63.

7.   Johannes Lindblom, *Micha literarisch untersucht* (Acta Academiae Aboensis: Humaniora, 6.2; Äbo: Äbo Akademi, 1929); Artur Weiser, *Das Buch der zwölf kleinen Propheten* (Göttingen: Vandenhoeck & Ruprecht, 1963), pp. 228-90; *idem, The Old Testament: Its Formation and Development* (trans. D.M. Barton; New York: Association Press, 1961); Gary Stansell, *Micah and Isaiah: A Form and Tradition Historical Comparison* (SBLDS, 85; Atlanta: Scholars Press, 1988).

8.   Leslie C. Allen, *The Books of Joel, Obadiah, Jonah and Micah* (NICOT; Grand Rapids: Eerdmans, 1976); James L. Mays, *Micah: A Commentary* (OTL; Philadelphia: Westminster Press, 1976); Kenneth H. Cuffey, 'The Coherence of Micah: A Review of the Proposals and a New Interpretation' (unpublished PhD dissertation, Drew University, 1987).

9.   L.M. Luker, 'Doom and Hope in Micah: The Redaction of the Oracles Attributed to an Eighth-Century Prophet' (unpublished PhD dissertation, Vanderbilt University, 1985); H.W. Wolff, *Micah: A Commentary* (trans. G. Stansell; Minneapolis: Augsburg, 1990); T. Lescow, 'Redaktionsgeschichtliche Analyse von Micha 1-5', *ZAW* 84 (1972), pp. 46-85; *idem,* 'Redaktionsgeschichtliche Analyse von Micha 6-7', *ZAW* 84 (1972), pp. 182-212.

10.   Charles S. Shaw, *The Speeches of Micah: A Rhetorical-Historical Analysis* (JSOTSup, 145; Sheffield: JSOT Press, 1993).

11.   See Table 2 in Chapter 3 of this study for further information on the proposals of the various scholars.

to a consensus. Thus, for example, a redactional analysis is not the common denominator among those who propose a three-part structure of the book. Rather, the decisive elements in the proposed structure and coherence are the presuppositions about the book's conceptuality—that is, that which governs what is said. It is therefore necessary that these presuppositions are identified in the discussions of the structure of the book and the criteria for coherence. Notably, however, the means by which scholars have dealt with the book are in part based on their presuppositions concerning the 'formation' of the book.[12]

The following discussion is not intended to identify every author who has written on parts or all of the book of Micah.[13] The aim here is to represent the main views about the book of Micah that have been formulated over the last two centuries. The focus will be two interrelated aspects: (a) structure as an indicator of the scholars' view of the book's coherence; and (b) the criteria for discerning coherence—as argued by the various scholars and observed in their proposals concerning the book's structure.

Review of Research

1. *Nineteenth Century CE*

Prior to the nineteenth century, the authenticity of the book of Micah was virtually unquestioned; thus, the coherence of the book of Micah was undisputed. The nineteenth century, however, brought a significant change by questioning the unity of the book. During this time, the studies of the book of Micah took as their point of departure the observation that there are many inconsistencies in the final form of the book that confirm its incoherence. The main trends of scholarship were concerned not so much with defending the coherence of the book as much as with delineating its inconsistencies by using literary and historical criteria of consistency. Toward this goal scholarly investigations focused on questions of authenticity. In these instances, the inconsistencies were most often seen as differences in authorship, and inconsistencies were interpreted as evidence of incoherence. Accordingly, the basic criterion for

12.   Willis, 'Structure, Setting', pp. 45-46.

13.   A close approximation of such a survey may be found in Willis, 'Structure, Setting'. Cf. Cuffey, 'Coherence of Micah'. Others such as Hagstrom, *The Coherence*, also acknowledge the breadth of Willis's survey and do not repeat the presentation of it.

the coherence of the book of Micah was consistency—that is, consistency itself being variously defined to include issues of authorship, historical provenance of the oracles and substantive continuity. Consequently, to the extent that consistency and authenticity were deemed the same and questionable, to this extent coherence was also questionable. Two scholars exemplified the research in this period.

a. *G.H. von Ewald (1876)*

Ewald[14] proposes that the book of Micah is a complete unit consisting of chs. 1–5.[15] The unit is comprised of three portions distinguished from each other by their tone and character, namely, chs. 1, 2–3 and 4–5. He argues that 'each of the [three sections] differs from the others with respect to its entire tone and character, so much so that the structure of the strophes takes in each case a peculiar form; and yet the *same fundamental thought* connects them indissolubly together'.[16] Their distinctions, however, are bound together by a common historical context similar to that of Isaiah—that is, the reign of Hezekiah.[17]

One the basis of the same criteria of style and historical context, Ewald attributes chs. 6–7 to an anonymous prophet, stating that the 'form and art of [the] piece is also so essentially different that on that account alone we can hardly suppose that we have the same author' as in chs. 1–5.[18] He further argues that the similarities of chs. 6–7 to certain Psalms, Jeremiah, Habakkuk, and other literature of the seventh century BCE further suggest a historical gap between it and the preceding chapters.

As to how the two distinct units came to be juxtaposed, Ewald, on the basis of style, discounts the argument that chs. 6–7 are Micah's words written later in the life of the prophet. He notes that chs. 6–7 are dramatic in style and originated as literary rather than as oral units concluded that the unit was accidentally joined to the book of Micah (that is, chs. 1–5).[19]

---

14. *The Commentary on the Prophets of the Old Testament* (trans. J.F. Smith; 5 vols.; London: Williams & Norgate, 1876).

15. Ewald, *Commentary on the Prophets*, p. 324.

16. Ewald, *Commentary on the Prophets*, p. 292, my emphasis.

17. Ewald, *Commentary on the Prophets*, p. 293.

18. Ewald, *Commentary on the Prophets*, p. 325.

19. Ewald, *Commentary on the Prophets*, p. 326.

Ewald does not deny the coherence of either chs. 1–5 or 6–7. Instead, his proposal is built on the presupposition of the coherence of the two distinct units vis-à-vis each other. What he contests is the coherence of the whole constituted by these distinctive units, that is, chs. 1–5 and 6–7. It may then be observed that for Ewald, the basic criteria for coherence are common historical context and stylistic features. Thus Ewald's views may be summarized as follows: the presence of stylistic inconsistencies may distinguish units; but the place of the units in the thought progression of the larger unit determines the coherence of the whole.

b. *B. Stade (1881 and 1883)*

Stade[20] argues that the genuine Mican oracles are chs. 1–3, minus 2.12-13 who he sees as a later addition that interrupts the thought progression of chs. 1–3. This unit constitutes a coherent whole whose focus is judgment—ch. 1 proclaims the judgment while the unit constituted by chs. 2–3 gives the reasons for the judgment. His basis for dating chs. 1–3 to the eighth century BCE is the similarities of the Mican oracles to Isaiah.[21] Much like Ewald, Stade questions the authenticity of the book of Micah, but he went beyond Ewald in proposing that chs. 4–5 are not from the same historical time as chs. 1–3. On the basis of various similarities, he notes parallels between chs. 4–5 (postexilic) and Deutero-Zechariah (Zech. 12–14) and between chs. 1–3 (exilic) and Isaiah 1–39. Likewise, he notes that chs. 4–5 present a message that is opposed to the message of doom in chs. 1–3[22] and concludes that the coherence of the unit (chs. 4–5) consists of the theme (of the nations) and its consistent style.[23] In following Wellhausen,[24] Stade proposes that 7.7-20 originated in a different historical context (postexilic) than the preceding verses, that is, 6.1–7.6 (seventh century BCE).[25]

---

20.   B. Stade, 'Bemerkungen über das Buch Micha', *ZAW* 1 (1881), pp. 161-72.

21.   Stade, 'über das Buch Micha', pp. 162-65.

22.   Stade, 'über das Buch Micha', pp. 165-69. He suggested that without the addition of this counterbalance the book of Micah may not have been included in the canon.

23.   B. Stade, 'Weitere Bemerkungen zu Micha 4.5', *ZAW* 3 (1883), pp. 1-16

24.   F. Bleek, *Einleitung in das Alte Testament* (ed. J. Wellhausen; Berlin: Georg Reimer, 4th edn, 1878), p. 425. He proposed that 7.7-20 is separated from 7.1-6 by about a century. Contrary to Ewald who had proposed a seventh-century BCE date for chs. 6–7 as a unit, Wellhausen proposed an exilic date.

25.   B. Stade, 'Streiflichter auf die Entstehung der jetzigen Gestalt der alttestamentlichen Prophetenschriften', *ZAW* 23 (1903), pp. 153-71.

According to Stade, the coherence of units such as chs. 1–3 is not disputed. The dispute is over the coherence of the whole whose constitutive parts originated in different historical times—for example, chs. 1–3, eighth century BCE; 4–5, exilic to postexilic; 6.1–7.6, seventh century BCE; and 7.7-20, postexilic—were composed by different authors, and have different messages. Stade's understanding is that the message of chs. 1–3 is judgment. In his opinion, the heterogeneity of chs. 4–5 also shows the incoherence of the whole which itself is constituted by the juxtaposition of the two units, chs. 1–3 and 4–5. The joining of these units while not accidental, as believed by Ewald, is the result a deliberate effort to counteract the message of judgment.[26] Notably, Stade's criteria for coherence include a common 'explicit' message and shared historical setting.[27]

2. *Twentieth Century CE*

a. *1900–1950*
The tone set by the works of Ewald and Stade continued into this early twentieth century in the works of those who sought to further distinguish the origins of the units and sub-units of the text.[28] While attention to inconsistencies remained in critical studies of the book of Micah, the focus on authenticity was paired with questions concerning the arrangement of the final form of the book. At issue was the coherence of a unit consisting of materials from different historical contexts. While in the previous century scholars were content to explain the incoherence as the juxtaposition of historically different materials, a trend developed during this time that sought to resolve the incoherence of the book.

26. Stade, 'Weitere Bemerkung', pp. 7-8.

27. The present writer says 'explicit' for reasons that will become clear in the following chapters. Here let it be said that Stade's attention was to the immediately apparent message without further analysis to find the common denominator among the diverse messages.

28. See Karl Marti, *Das Dodekapropheton* (KHAT, 13; Tübingen: J.C.B. Mohr, 1904), pp. 258-64. He proposed that the final form of the book came about through a long process extending through to the second century BCE. The book consists of three sections: chs 1–3, 4–5 and 6–7. The pre-exilic pericope, 4.1-4, was added to chs. 1–3 to counteract the threat. During the fifth century BCE 6.1-8 was added. The other units in chs. 4–7 were added later. Cf. Albin van Hoonacker, *Les douze petits prophètes* (EBib; Paris: J Gabalda, 1908).

J. Halévy (1904 and 1905). Halévy[29] defends the authenticity of the book of Micah by arguing that the source of the incoherence is not the inauthenticity of the material nor the inherent incoherence of the units, but rather the arrangement of these units. The extant form of the book is attributed to compilers who, in attempting to make sense of the disjointed pericopes,[30] altered the original arrangement of the material. Since the incoherence of the extant form is due to the inconsistencies resulting from a loss of the original arrangement of the book, he proposes that any inconsistency may be resolved through a rearrangement of the text units. Coherence is then achieved by a restoration of the original authorial order,[31] vis-à-vis the extant redactional order.

The work of Halévy prompts some of the questions that presently challenge any analysis of the coherence of a work. Is original arrangement determinative of coherence? In light of the various redactional elements, by what criteria is the originality of the final arrangement to be determined? If coherence is only possible with the original arrangement of the material there can be no decisive statement made about the coherence of this or any other text, to the extent that the original context of a text may be inaccessible due both to the challenges of transmission of the text and more specifically the redactional aspects of the text. Furthermore, even with an original arrangement, one may still be unable to discern the coherence of the text. For coherence is more than literary arrangement (though this arrangement may or may not be indicative of a coherence) or even the original authorial order of materials.

A very significant oversight is committed by Halévy. This has to do with the intention and more precisely the needs of the community for whom possibly this text is being preserved. Halévy does not address the issue of the deliberate rearrangement of the text for the purpose of communicating a particular message. He assumes that the original order was being sought by the redactors. If the redactors who were close to the material gave it an incoherent arrangement, how can one so far removed as Halévy presume to know the original coherence? What advantage does he have over the past redactors? By what criteria can

29.   J. Halévy, 'Le Livre de Michée', *RevSém* 12 (1904), pp. 97-117, 193-216, 289-312; *idem*, 'Le Livre de Michée', *RevSém* 13 (1905), pp. 1-22.

30.   Halévy, 'Michée' (1905), p. 2.

31.   Halévy 'Michée' (1904), p. 215. The arrangement he proposes is as follows: 1.1–2.5, 6, 11, 7, 10; 3.1-12; 4.8-10; 2.12-13; 4.4-6, 11-13; 5.1-5, 14, 7-13, 6; 4.1-5; 6.1-12; 4.14; 6.13-16; 7.13; 7.1-12, 14-20.

one begin to responsibly discern coherence if not by the indicators in the extant form?

Halévy acknowledges that the order that was given to the text by the redactors resulted in inconsistencies. Is this order incoherent by virtue of not being original? Wherein lie the inconsistencies? On what basis are inconsistencies identified? Is inconsistency the criterion of incoherence as seen earlier in the works of Ewald and Stade? If so, what types of inconsistencies are and are not significant? Are they all determinants of coherence such that the presence of any type or quantity is indicative of incoherence?

Finally, if the coherence of the extant form is so different from that of the original—presumably the result of imposing a foreign order onto the material—does not Halévy's rearrangement run the same risk of imposing a foreign coherence?

Coherence is not only a product of the order of the text but its contents. Thus, there may be materials that are by literary standards disorderly but nonetheless coherent. By the same token, there may be incoherent materials that are orderly by literary standards. Therefore, neither order nor content is the exclusive determinant of coherence. The use and reuse/resignification of older materials as well as the redactional modification of a text may result in inconsistencies of style, historical contexts and even competing concepts. However, if the preservation and more specifically the redaction is believed and assessed to be deliberate, can the resulting coherence be any less deliberate? It is, therefore, not so much a question of whether or not there is coherence in any given text, but a question of the nature and extent of that coherence. Even Halévy acknowledges the existence of a type of coherence prior to his rearrangement of the pericopes—not every unit and sub-unit was rearranged. Those that were allowed to remain in their extant position are assessed by Halévy to be coherent. Consequently, Halévy, on the basis of the content of the materials, argues implicitly in favor of the existence of coherence within a diverse whole. So, for example, Halévy presented the following as the original arrangement: 1.1–2.5, 6, 11, 7-10; 3.1-12; 4.8-10.[32]

P. Haupt (1910 and 1911). Haupt[33] makes the similar historical context of texts the criterion for coherence. On this basis, he argues that the

---

32. Halévy, 'Michée' (1904).
33. Haupt, 'Critical Notes', pp. 201-52; *idem*, 'The Book of Micah', pp. 1-63.

extant form of the book of Micah is incoherent in that its compositional history, ranging from 702–100 BCE, is not properly grouped together. Coherence in this respect is achieved by rearranging the materials to reflect their chronological order. Thus, in this scheme the text would be ordered as follows: 3.9-10; 3.2-3; 3.5-7 (702 BCE); 3.12 (701 BCE); 6.2-4a (168 BCE).

Haupt not only presumes his ability to date the units to the smallest components, but also to restore a logic to the text. It is to his credit that Haupt, for all his conjectures, recognizes coherence within units of the same time period. This is in no way to say that similarity of historical context is the sole determinant of coherence or even necessary to coherence. Thus, it may be said that Haupt sees a diachronic coherence but denies any synchronic aspects of that coherence.

J.M.P. Smith (1911). Smith[34] proposes that the book of Micah consists of three sections that are differentiated from each other in tone, content and perspective: chs. 1–3; 4–5; 6–7.[35] Of these, chs. 1–3 (eighth century BCE) are original to Micah the prophet and chs. 4–7 are later (chs. 4–5 exilic; chs. 6–7 postexilic). In their style and language chs. 1–3 are direct and forceful while chs. 4–6 exhibit a less forceful and reflective poetic style. As to content, the differences are observable: chs. 1–3, denunciation and judgment; chs. 4–5, hope and promises of salvation; chs. 6–7, a combination of doom and hope.

Smith states, however, that the unit consisting of chs. 4–5 lacks logical continuity and is most likely a collection of miscellaneous fragments.[36] The same applies to the unit chs. 6–7 which consists of seven sections none of which are closely connected (6.1-5, 6-8, 9-16; 7.1-6, 7-10, 11-13, 14-20). Of these 6.9-16 and 7.1-6 are Mican; 6.6-8; 7.7-10, 14-20 are postexilic. Smith therefore concludes that the unit consisting of chs. 6–7 is also a collection of miscellaneous fragments from approximately four authors from various periods.[37]

For Smith the criteria of coherence include similarity of style and common historical context. At points, however, his use of his criteria is inconsistent. Proposing that chs. 6–7 constitute a unit, he further argues that the unit has no coherence. Why argue for chs. 6–7 as an independent

34. Smith, *Micah, Zephaniah.*
35. Smith, *Micah, Zephaniah,* p. 8.
36. Smith, *Micah, Zephaniah,* pp. 12-16.
37. Smith, *Micah, Zephaniah,* p. 117.

unit if it shows no coherence? The very argument that these chapters form a unit presupposes some sort of unifying aspect.

Smith also employes this 'content' criterion inconsistently. If a division is to be made between chs. 3 and 4 on the basis of content, then it seems that a division for the macro-structure is also to be made between 7.6 and 7.7 and between 2.11 and 2.12-13. Why maintain a section of doom alone but also one mixed with both hope and doom? (While I am not necessarily proposing that a division be made at 7.7 on the macro-structural level, the objection is intended to illustrate Smith's inconsistent application of his criteria.) As a result of his inconsistency, this view does not explain the place of 2.12-13.

J. Lindblom (1929). Lindblom's basic assumption is that the final form of the book of Micah is accidental and as such incoherent.[38] His form-critical analysis focuses on the detailed delimitation of each pericope, their generic classifications, and the determination of the *Sitz im Leben* of each. His observation of the distinctive pericopes and their discon-nectedness from each other leads Lindblom to conclude that the result of any attempt to discern coherence of the book will result in failure.[39] He maintains, however, the generic integrity of such passages as 2.6-11 (disputation) and 6.1-8 (covenant lawsuit).[40]

He also insists that the interpreter is responsible for explaining the compositional history of the book, a history which encompasses at least three editions: the first consisting of 1.2-7; 6.9-11 (pre-722 BCE); 1.8-16 (711 BCE); 2.1-4, 6-11; 3.1-12; 4.9-10, 14 (701 BCE);[41] the second during the time of Manasseh includes all materials from the first edition plus 4.11-13; 5.8; 6.1-8; 7.1-4, 13;[42] and the third edition which developed over a long period of time. Yet the necessity of identifying the compositional history for Lindblom had more to do with ascertaining how the pericopes are connected than identifying the extent of the coherence resulting from those connections. He attributes these connections mainly to redactors.

38. Lindblom, *Micha literarisch untersucht*, p. 9.
39. Lindblom, *Micha literarisch untersucht*, p. 82.
40. Lindblom, *Micha literarisch untersucht*, pp. 122, 166. These two passages record conversations: 2.6-11 between Micah and his opponents; and 6.1-8 the lawsuit in vv. 1-5 is responded to by the people (vv. 6-7).
41. Lindblom, *Micha literarisch untersucht*, p. 161.
42. Lindblom, *Micha literarisch untersucht*, p. 162.

Lindblom's denial of the existence of the coherence of the whole does not hold true with respect to the pericopes. For him coherence of the units is not indicative of the coherence of the whole. Likewise for him the coherence of a unit is compromised by the presence of distinctive genres in as much as coherence is consistency of genre.

b. *1960–1970*

A. *Weiser (1961 and 1963)*. Weiser's proposal concerning the extant arrangement of the book differs significantly from that of Lindblom. Unlike Lindblom, he maintains that the extant form of the book is the result of purposeful redaction.[43] He further argues that the cult is the primary setting of the book as intended by the redactor[44] who gave the book its four-part arrangement of alternation between threats and promises: chs. 1–3 (doom); chs. 4–5 (promise); 6.1–7.6 (threat); 7.8-20 (promise).[45]

For Weiser redactional intentionality defines the coherence of the whole in spite of the presence of different genres. He therefore assumes a conceptuality of the final form of the book—a conceptuality consistent with the intentions of the final redactor.

B. *Renaud (1964 and 1977)*. Renaud attributes chs. 4–5 to the early fifth century BCE and proposes that the overall theme of this unit is messianic. It is an eschatological strand used to contemporize the message to the disenchanted Israel. The unit itself is a collection of pericopes organized to exhibit a clear structure: A, 4.1-4; B, 4.6-7; C, 4.8-14; C', 5.5.1-5; B', 5.6-7; A', 5.8-14.[46] The relationship of the pericopes is based on their common theme, for example, 4.1-4 and 5.8-14 are concerned with the theme of the destiny of the nations.

In his 1977 study, Renaud[47] maintains his arguments concerning chs.

43. Artur Weiser, *Das Buch*; *idem*, *The Old Testament*, p. 255.

44. Weiser, *The Old Testament*, pp. 232, 254, 263, 283; particularly 4.1-5; 6.9-16; 7.8-20.

45. Weiser, *The Old Testament*, pp. 231-32. For other studies published in the 1950s see Eduard Nielson, *Oral Tradition* (SBT; London: SCM Press, 1954), pp. 84-85. He presents his analysis of chs. 4-5 as a distinctive unit marked off from chs. 1–3 and 6–7. Chapters 4–5 consists of the units: 4.1-4, 6-8, 9-14; 5.1-5, 6-7, 9-14. Cf. Beyerlin, *Die Kulttraditionen Israels*.

46. Renaud, *Structure*.

47. Renaud, *La Formation*.

4–5 while presenting a redactional analysis of the entire book of Micah. Accordingly, he proposes a purposeful redaction of the book that took place in several stages: (a) the original Mican core (chs. 1–3 and 6.9-15); (b) the exilic additions (6.2-8; 7.1-6) concerned with the denunciation of sins; (c) the postexilic additions to 1.1-2; chs. 1–3; 6.1–7.7. Chapters 4–5 and 7.8-20 were added in order to neutralize the threats of the other passages.[48] He proposes that the book of Micah was at this point arranged into two parts: chs. 1–5 and 6–7. This arrangement was later changed with the relocation of 2.12-13 from its original place between 4.7 and 8 to its current position. The result is the present arrangement: chs. 1–2; 3–5; 6–7. The coherence of the book according to Renaud's argument is the product of the redactional activity.

J.T. Willis (1966). Willis, who authored several studies in the 1960s,[49] presents in his 1966 dissertation the first comprehensive study on the coherence of the book of Micah. His basic intention is 'to defend the thesis that the book of Micah in its present form exhibits a type of coherence'.[50] This coherence is the result of purposeful redaction and may to be discerned by analysis of literary signals as well as content. The aim of such redaction was to apply Micah's oracles to a particular historical situation. According to Willis, the redactors' organization of the traditional materials can be determined only by analyzing the book, not by superimposing preconceived modern Western standards onto the ancient work.[51]

Willis addresses several aspects in attempting to support his thesis. First, in his review of scholarship, he classifies the scholars according to their explanations of the final form of the book. These explanations include: rearrangement theory, disconnected pericope theory, compilation theory, literary development theory and and chronological theory.[52]

48. Renaud, *La Formation*, p. 403.

49. Willis, 'Structure, Setting'; *idem*, 'Micah IV 14—V 5: A Unit', *VT* 18 (1968), pp. 529-47; *idem*, 'A Note on ויאמר in Micah 3.1', *ZAW* 80 (1968), pp. 50-54; *idem*, 'The Structure of Micah 3–5 and the Function of 5.9-14 in the Book', *ZAW* 81 (1969), pp. 191-214; *idem*, 'The Structure of the Book of Micah', *SEÅ* 34 (1969), pp. 5-42.

50. Willis, 'Structure, Setting', p. 104.

51. Willis, 'Structure, Setting', p. 299.

52. Willis, 'Structure, Setting', pp. 45-92, classifies these explanations into five categories all of which reflect various understandings of the nature of the materials in the book of Micah. The categories facilitate understanding of the many positions

Second, he presents his proposal of the structure and the interrelationship of the parts. This takes the form of a critique of previous proposals, including the proposals for dividing the book into: chs. 1–3; 4–5; 6.1-6(7); 7.7(8)-20; and chs. 1–3; 4–5; 6–7.[53] Instead he proposes that the book exhibits an A-B-A pattern exemplified by content, length and theme. This pattern, he concludes, is the most 'natural' representation of the structure of the book (namely, chs. 1–2; 3–5; 6–7).[54]

Willis further argues that the pattern is signaled by the summons to hear (שמעו) in 1.2, 3.1 and 6.1. Each section begins with an oracle of doom (1.2–2.11; 3.1-12; 6.1–7.6) and ends with an oracle of hope (2.12-13; 4–5; 7.7-20). This pattern is the work of a sixth-century BCE redactor who adapted the materials to a liturgical setting which is evident in

of scholars over the last century. However, it must be noted that these explanations are used by scholars not as mutually exclusive categories but as overlapping and interrelated ones. So one scholar may have offered multiple explanations for the structure of the book. The five explanations are represented here as follows:

(1) Rearrangement theory assumes that the material in the book of Micah was originally coherent but was confused during the process of transmission. This is posited by Halévy who sought to rearrange the material in a logically coherent way. P. Haupt also argues that the material must be rearranged in order to be coherent; and he proposes to rearrange the material chronologically to achieve that coherence (3.9-10; 3.2-3).

(2) Disconnected pericope theory contends that the book consists of pericopes from various eras brought together without concern for coherence. This perspective is represented by J. Smith who argues, for example, that chs. 6–7 as a unit lacks coherence.

(3) Compilation theory argues that independent oracles were compiled over time to form the present book of Micah.

(4) Literary development theory sees the incoherence of the book of Micah as the result of literary growth. According to this view, in various eras of the material was redacted for the purpose of resignifying it to the particular community.

(5) Chronological order theory says that the book is ordered chronologically and not logically. Therefore each of the main sections represents a different time period. Aspects of this view are present in both or all the other theories.

53. Willis, 'Structure, Setting', pp. 116-17. He critiques these proposals on several grounds: (a) The division results in a loss of symmetry with the division between chs. 2 and 3; (b) it ignores the 'And I said' in 3.1; (c) the division between chs. 3 and 4 destroys the full effectiveness of the contrast between 3.9-12 and 4.1-4.

54. Willis, 'Structure, Setting', p. 123.

the liturgical elements of the book (that is, 2.12-13; 4.5; 5.8; 6.9b; 7.7-20). It is, therefore, the intentionality of the redactor that is reflected in the structure of the extant form.[55]

According to Willis the A-B-A pattern shows an alternation between doom and hope in each section. The pattern is as follows: A, 1.2–2.13—doom (1.2–2.11) and hope (2.12-13); B, chs. 3–5—doom (ch. 3) and hope and doom in seven pericopes which make up chs. 4–5 (4.1-5, 6-8, 9-10, 11-13; 4.14–5.5, 6-8, 9-14); A, chs. 6–7—doom (6.1–7.6) and hope (7.7-20).[56] He then argues that the book exhibits 'horizontal' coherence—that is, the features shared by the similar units within the sections. As to chs. 1–2 and 6–7, these two units begin with a summons to hear and consist of the following sub-units: lawsuit (1.2-7; 6.1-8), in which Yahweh is depicted as bringing a suit against Israel; and lament (1.8-16; 7.1-6). In these two sections, the courtroom is the imagery created. These two sections also end with a hope section (2.12-13; 7.7-20).[57]

Concerning chs. 3–5, he further proposes that the unit is also symmetrical in that it consists of doom and hope. Chapter 3 consists of three units: vv. 1-4, 5-8 and 9-12, with its concluding unit juxtaposed to 4.1-4. This juxtaposition of 3.9-12 and 4.1-4 is intended to illustrate the contrast of their content in much the same way that contrast between doom and hope are exhibited in the unit formed by chs. 4–5. The latter unit, that is, chs. 4–5, consists of seven pericopes each exhibiting this contrast between doom and hope unified by the repetition of common themes.[58]

The horizontal coherence of the doom section is seen in their common beginning, that is, the summons to hear (1.2; 3.1; 6.1). Willis also cites other parallels in support of the proposal that the extant arrangement of the book is intentional, namely: the principle of *jus talionis* (3.3-4, 9-12); the extreme nature of the punishment (2.3-5; 3.12); the use of sin vocabulary (e.g. פֶּשַׁע, 1.5; 3.8; 6.7); the tracing of external sin to internal corruption (2.1, 2; 3.2, 9; 7.3); and focus on the capital (1.5; 3.9; 6.9).[59]

With regard to the horizontal coherence of the hope sections, Willis states that God as the God who saves is the central figure in these

---

55. Willis, 'Structure, Setting', p. 124.
56. Willis, 'Micah 3–5'.
57. Willis, 'Structure, Setting', p. 137.
58. Willis, 'Micah 3–5'.
59. Willis, 'Structure, Setting', pp. 140-42, 156.

sections where the punishments envisioned in the doom sections are viewed as necessary to the promises.[60] Sections I and III each consists of one pericope (2.12-13; 7.7-20) while section II consists of the seven pericopes of chs. 4–5. To counter any argument concerning the invalidity of the observation due to dissymmetry of the proposed structure, Willis states that '[t]he dissymmetry is greatly diminished when one realizes that the seven pericopes…are parallel and essentially repeat the same sequence of thought seven times'.[61] The difference in length— short hope in sections I and III and long hope in section II—is also present in the doom sections.

Concerning 'vertical' coherence he argues that there is a logical progression of thought in each section. Chapter 1 indicates the judgment that is to come on Samaria and Jerusalem. The specific reasons for the judgment are given in 2.1-11 and ch. 3. Likewise, a progression is seen between 6.1-8 (lawsuit), 6.9-16 (reproach and the expected announcement of judgment) between 7.1-7 (lament) and 7.8-20 (hope). This progression is signaled by the use of catchwords, contrasts and similarities.[62]

Willis concludes this study by proposing that the final redaction of the book happened between 597–538 BCE. [63]

T. Lescow (1972). Lescow believes the book of Micah to be liturgical. He further assumes that Micah is a prophet of doom and that the oracles of hope and salvation are all late—exilic or postexilic. His first article[64] aims at a reconstruction of the composition history of chs. 1–5. Accordingly, he argues that these chapters consist of chs. 1–3 to which various speeches were added until the completion of chs. 4–5 in the fourth century BCE. The finalization of chs. 1–5 coincided with the Samaritan schism; and 1.6-7 may have been added on this occasion as a liturgical expression of anti-Samaritan sentiments.

Lescow's second article[65] deals with chs. 6–7 with the aim of tracing

---

60. Willis, 'Structure, Setting', p. 192. Willis designates ABA as sections I, II and III respectively.

61. Willis, 'Structure, Setting', pp. 190-92.

62. Willis, 'Structure, Setting', pp. 248-49, 289-90.

63. Willis, 'Structure, Setting', pp. 299-300.

64. Lescow, 'Micha 1–5', pp. 46-85.

65. Lescow, 'Micha 6–7', pp. 182-212; cf. *idem, Micha 6, 6-8. Studien zu Sprache, Form und Auslegung* (Stuttgart: Calwer Verlag, 1966).

the compositional history of the text. He concludes that this development took place from around the seventh century BCE down to the fifth century BCE. Chapters 6–7 were also added to chs. 1–5 about the time of the Samaritan schism.

While Lescow does not speak in terms of coherence, his proposal of the unifying liturgical function and redactional intentionality indicates his awareness of issues of coherence—namely, that texts are generated and controlled by an underlying conceptuality which itself is the product of a larger conceptual framework.[66]

L. Allen (1976). Allen proposes that while the apparent disparity of the materials in the book of Micah suggests futility of the task of identifying in it a literary structure, closer observation reveals a deliberate and artistic arrangement of the book. This artistry, however, is often missed as suggested by the various proposals for the structure of the book and the debates over where the major divisions of the book are to be made. Allen follows Willis in suggesting an A-B-A pattern of the book: A, 1.2–2.13; B, 3.1–5.15; A, 6.1–7.20. He reviews the discussion concerning chs. 4–5 and concludes that, including 3.1-12, the unit is concentric with 5.1-6 as its focal point. He proposes the following structure: A, 3.1–4.5; B, 4.6-8; C (1), 4.9-10; C (2), 4.11-13; C (3), 5.1-6; B', 5.7-9; A', 5.10-15. The first and the last sections form the frame of the unit.[67]

Notably, for Allen, the decisive criteria for the structure are style, content and common historical context; and the coherence of the material is evidenced in the artistry of the redactional product.

J.L. Mays (1976). A significant advancement was made by Mays who makes explicit his awareness of the existence of a conceptuality of the book which is served by its diverse elements.[68] He articulates a threefold task of his commentary: to identify the sayings and their historical contexts; to trace the compositional history of the book; and 'to seek to do justice to the present form of the book as the final stage in the shaping of a prophetic witness to YHWH'.[69] The final task involves answering the question of the extent to which the book can be read with

66. For further discussion of intentionality and conceptuality see Chapter 2 below.

67. Allen, *The Books*, pp. 257-60.

68. Mays, *Micah*.

69. Mays, *Micah*, p. 2.

unity—under its title—as a prophecy. While Mays does not define the coherence which is present, he nonetheless demonstrates his awareness that it is more than the identification of the structure of the book. As seen in his detailed discussion of structural matters throughout his commentary, Mays does not minimize the importance of the structure of the book.

According to Mays, the final form of the book is the result of post-exilic redactional efforts to create a theological unity. Chapters 1–3 are Mican and come from the late eighth century BCE. The final form of the book was not reached until after the rebuilding of the Temple some time after 515 BCE.[70]

Mays proposes that the book is composed of two main units—namely, chs. 1–5 and 6–7—each of which is introduced by a summons to hear and arranged to depict God's unfolding revelation to the world. As to their differences, the first addresses a universal audience and is marked by an *inclusio* focused on the people/nations (1.2; 5.15). This unit consists of 1.3–3.12 and 4.1–5.15. In 1.3–3.12 the judgment of Israel is the focal point; while in 4.1–5.15 the focus is Yahweh's future work. Three motifs mark the structure: concern with the people/nation (4.1-3, 5, 11, 13; 5.15), Zion (4.2, 7, 8, 10, 11, 13), and the remnant (4.7; 5.7, 8). The unit consisting of chs. 4–5 further consists of 4.1-5; 4.8–5.4; 5.5-9; 5.10-15. Together the first part of the book shows that the judgment of Israel has a purpose in Yahweh's plans for the future.

The second part of the book is marked off by a depiction of a trial scene in which Yahweh addresses the covenant people. The two sections of this unit are 6.2–7.6 and 7.8-20. Mays acknowledges the difficulty of the placement of 7.7; and he further denies that the organizational principle is an alternation between the prophecies of doom and salvation since there is only one section of each in the main parts of the book.[71]

---

70. Mays, *Micah*, pp. 21-22; *idem*, 'The Theological Purpose of the Book of Micah', in H. Donner *et al.* (eds.), *Beiträge zur Alttestamentlichen Theologie* (Festschrift W. Zimmerli; Göttingen: Vandenhoeck & Ruprecht, 1977), pp. 276-87.

71. Other publications during this period include: Wilhelm Rudolph, 'Zu Micha 1, 10-16', in Josef Schreiner (ed.), *Wort, Lied und Gottesspruch* (Festschrift Joseph Zeigler; FzB, 2; Wurzburg: Echter Verlag; Stuttgart: Katholoisches Bibelwerk, 1972); *idem*, *Micha, Habakuk, Zephanja* (KAT, 13.3; Gütersloh: Gütersloher Verlagshaus, 1975).

c. *1980–1990*

H.W. Wolff (1982 and 1990). Wolff's[72] presentation of the composition of the book is based on his redactional analysis of the book. There are several presuppositions that underlie Wolff's analysis. First is the pre-supposition of authorship. Wolff argues that the book consists of both authentic (chs. 1–3) and inauthentic (chs. 4–7) materials. Second, he argues for the orality of the authentic material. Third, the later materials arose to answer questions raised by Micah's message and left unanswered by previous redactors. Wolff identifies these later additions by criteria including: the absence of judgment and accusation; and the presupposition of the execution of judgment.[73] On the basis of these criteria, he argues that chs. 1–3 were later expanded by redactors seeking to contemporize the message.

Regarding chs. 1–3, Wolff argues that the unit consists of six interpolations added to clarify the significance of the material for the exilic community. These interpolations include: (a) expanding the view of guilt to include cultic (1.5, 7) and military guilt (1.13-14); (b) a liturgical element (1.3); (c) literary transmission elements (1.1; 3.8); (d) oracles of salvation (2.12-13); (e) the addition of 1.2, that is, the mention of the nations which subsequently forged a link with 5.14; and (f) temporal transitions 2.3a, 4c, to link this unit to a neo-Babylonian era.[74]

According to Wolff, the book exhibits a four-part structure: 1–3; 4–5; 6.1–7.7; 7.8-20. Concerning chs. 4–5 he proposes that there are three units: 4.1-8; 4.9-5.5 (עתה[ו]) and 5.6-14 (והיה). These are all marked by temporal transitions meant to contemporize 3.12.[75]

Concerning Mic. 6.1-7.7 he proposes that this unit is basically liturgical and is followed by 7.8-20 (divided into vv. 8-10, 14-17, 18-20, with vv. 11-13 forming a bracket). Micah 6.2-8 is of postexilic origin showing no connection to chs. 4–5 but picking up some themes from chs. 1–3. By contrast, 6.9-16 in its indictment and announcement of disaster has a closer connection with the judgment prophecies in chs. 1–3. Micah 7.1-7 is a lament over the injustices of the land and focuses on the leaders as those responsible for the injustices. The unit 7.8-20

72. Wolff, *Micah*, pp. 17-26, 86. This was originally published in German (see bibliography) in 1982 and for this reason is included in this section.
73. Wolff, *Micah*, pp. 14-17.
74. Wolff, *Micah*, pp. 18-19.
75. Wolff, *Micah*, p. 20.

consists of three psalms: vv. 8-10, 14-17, 18-20 and a bracket vv. 11-13, all distinguished on the basis of style.[76]

With regard to the redactional history of the book, Wolff draws several conclusions. (a) The book itself grew from three sketches of scenes in which Micah proclaimed his saying: 1.6, 7b-13a, 14-16 (the first sketch); 2.1-3, 6-11 (the second); and 3.1-12 (the third). (b) There are deuteronomistic interpolations and changes found in chs. 1–3. (c) The materials in chs. 4–5 were accumulated from the early postexilic time. (d) The final redaction was to prepare chs. 1–3, 4–5 and 6.2–7.7 for liturgical use; and for this reason 7.8-20 was also added.[77]

For Wolff, the resulting structure of the book is a purposeful effort aimed at shaping the book for liturgical use. As to the identification of any conceptual basis for the structure, Wolff does not devote time to this endeavor. The fact that in this discussion of the message of Micah he treats only chs. 1–3 is indicative of his view of the unity of the whole. His detailed analysis of the redactional process, while insightful with respect to the way in which a particular unit may fit into its context, is highly conjectural at various points, especially in his certainty of the redactional levels of sub-units (e.g. 1.7b-13a; 2.3a, 4c). Thus, according to Wolff's arguments, to the extent that the book exhibits coherence that coherence is the result of the redactional rather than authorial intention of the book.

D. Hagstrom (1982 and 1988). Hagstrom[78] formulates his study as a response to Willis's work. He is concerned with what he terms 'literary coherence' and employs the literary critical method towards his aim of discerning the extent to which the book of Micah is coherent. His thesis is thus formulated:

> The book of Micah in its final form is so shaped as to render the book a unified, coherent whole; that is, the individual units of Micah are so shaped, structured, and linked as to make it possible to read the book as a unit.[79]

He uses 'unity' and coherence interchangeable and defines coherence as follows:

76.   Wolff, *Micah*, pp. 18-19, 20.
77.   Wolff, *Micah*, pp. 18-19, 20.
78.   Hagstrom, *The Coherence*. This work is considered here because it is a publication of the 1982 dissertation bearing the same title.
79.   Hagstrom, *The Coherence*, p. 1.

> A literary work displays coherence or unity when it is capable of being construed as a unit. A literary discourse is capable of being construed as a unit when there are features within the text that hold it together, that make it cohere, that provide keys as to how it might be construed.[80]

Hagstrom classifies these literary keys as consonance—those that are alike or refer to each other—and dissonance—those that underscore an adversative relationship between aspects, thus demonstating his awareness of types of coherence. One such type is that displayed by a collection such as the book of Psalms. However, in this type of coherence it is not evident how the whole is to be interpreted. Hagstrom denies that this is the type of coherence exhibited by the book of Micah, and therefore clarifies his aim saying that:

> My question is not simply 'Is the book of Micah coherent?', but rather 'What kind of coherence does the book of Micah display?' and, in particular, 'Does the book of Micah display a certain significant type of coherence which renders it capable of meaningful construal as a unit?'[81]

Hagstrom readily admits that the composite nature of the book of Micah renders it a prime specimen for consideration of this question of coherence and holds far-reaching implications for other texts of similar compositional nature. He believes that the coherence of the book is literary in as much as it is literature and employs literary features. In light of this focus on literary indicators, he critiques others (such as Willis) for looking at concepts. Instead he proposes that 'concepts' are too general and not verifiable by literary features but have to do with intentionality.[82] What are verifiably narrow are themes and motifs.[83]

After a critique of the various proposals of structure, Hagstrom, like Mays, his teacher, proposes a two-part structure of the final form of the book: chs. 1–5 and 6–7. In this proposal, the summons to hear in 1.2 and 6.1 are decisive to the macro-structure of the final form. The other occurrences (3.1, 9; 6.9), according to Hagstrom, are indicative of breaks but not of the macro-structural level. In 1.2 and 6.1 the summons depict a

---

80. Hagstrom, *The Coherence*, p. 3.
81. Hagstrom, *The Coherence*, p. 4.
82. Hagstrom, *The Coherence*, p. 9.
83. Note that Hagstrom makes no distinction between cohesion and coherence, and at points seems to deny the existence of coherence in arguing that concepts are too abstract to be verifiable. See Chapter 3 below for my discussion of the relationship of cohesion and coherence.

court setting in which Yahweh the plaintiff accuses Israel. In 3.1 and
6.9 there is no trial vocabulary. These occurrences are indicative of
intensifications of focus from the general to the specific accusation. In
this argument, Hagstrom parts company with Willis for whom the summons are significant to the macro-structure of the book.[84]

For Hagstrom, the two parts of the book of Micah begin with a summons to hear and bring into focus a trial setting in which Yahweh
accuses Israel of sin. Each section is sub-divided by a second summons
(3.1; 6.9) that serves both as continuation of the legal dispute introduced by the immediately preceding summons (1.2; 6.1-2), and as a
transition to achieve a more narrow focus. According to this analysis,
each part of the book ends with a hope for salvation. Hagstrom's analysis also displays other features shared by the two parts of the book,
including: (a) vocabulary and (b) common motifs. (a) Vocabulary: both
sections speak of God as אלהים and יהוה (1.2; 6.8), both speak of the
people with vocabulary designating nation and people of God—יעקב
(3.1, 9); ישראל (1.5; 3.1, 9); יהודה (5.1); עם (3.3 of the prophet and 6.3,
5 of God). (b) Common motifs: only those motifs are identified for
which vocabulary is explicitly present. In his attempt to identify only
'explicit' motifs the 'concepts' around which he builds his argument—
that is, judgment and salvation—are side-stepped. Nonetheless he is
careful to note those indicated by literary features. Yet while the form
of ch. 3, for example, illustrates the concept of judgment, Hagstrom's
reluctance to note 'generalities' leads him to ignore this indicator. He
identifies the following as motifs: (i) contrast between רע and טוב (3.2;
6.8); (ii) Israel in relation to the nations (1.2; 5.14; 4.3-5); (iii) emphasis
on the motif of 'to walk' (הלך); (iv) the concern for justice.[85]

Hagstrom's detailed analysis of the units proceeds with his attention
to the vocabulary, motifs of each unit, and the similarities to the immediately juxtaposed units. Finally, he undertakes consideration of the literary features shared in and across the major units. The result is two
units which he argues function together theologically.[86]

The sharing of the features and connections within a unit he terms as
'linear analysis'. His conclusion is that the coherence is demonstrated
on different levels in different ways. He denies that coherence is harmonization of dissonance. Instead, he proposes that coherence functions on

84.   Hagstrom, *The Coherence*, p. 23.
85.   Hagstrom, *The Coherence*, pp. 45-46.
86.   Hagstrom, *The Coherence*, p. 124.

a variety of levels and encompasses a variety of different phenomena, for example, grammatical and syntactical conventions; logical connectives; the structure of composition (on various levels); thematic development; recurrence of motifs; and other stylistic and rhetorical features. He notes that:

> while linear continuity is one important component of the coherence of the book of Micah, such continuity does not continue unbroken throughout the whole book. Coherence is maintained, nevertheless, by other literary characteristics which provide links which operate over some distance of text—rather than in a linear fashion.[87]

Hagstrom acknowledges that the book carries a theological message that is discernible through its parts and their interrelationship. He further acknowledges the limitation of his study in that it does not give attention to discerning this underlying message.[88] In this respect, Hagstrom is aware of conceptuality, though he does not use this term. What he alludes to as an underlying message is analogous to what is defined in this study as the 'conceptuality' of the text (see Chapter 2 below).

D.R. Hillers (1984). Hillers proposes that the critical approaches to the book of Micah, and particularly the redactional approach, have not given enough significance to the element of chance in the formation of the book. The book, he states, displays editorial elements that show signs that efforts were made to contemporize the message of the book. However, the redactional approaches of Wolff and Lescow are discarded in favor of a 'unifying explanatory approach'.[89] Micah is associated with a movement of revitalization. This association, according to Hillers, accounts for the message of the entire book.

Hillers admits to following the divisions made by other scholars but denies that there is any discernible structure to the book.[90] For him the unity is not in the literary integrity of the text but in its conceptual significance for its audience. Accordingly, Micah the person is seen as 'new age' prophet whose message is addressed to an audience suffering economic, spiritual and political devastation (see chs. 2–3). As a unit chs. 4–5 announces the inauguration a the 'new age of Messianic rule'.

87. Hagstrom, *The Coherence*, p. 127.
88. Hagstrom, *The Coherence*, p. 130.
89. Delbert R. Hillers, *Micah: Commentary on the Book of the Prophet Micah* (Hermeneia; Philadelphia: Fortress Press, 1984), pp. 1-4.
90. Hillers, *Micah*, p. 8.

In this part of the book there are at least five elements that parallel the movements of revitalization: the cleansing of foreign influences (5.10-15), the millennial theme, the reversal of social classes (4.6-7), the peaceful ruler (5.1-5), and emphasis on the new age as seen depicted in Micah.[91]

Hillers regards coherence as the significance of the text for its audience but minimizes the structure as an essential component in discerning that conceptual significance.

L.M. Luker (1985). Luker's[92] dissertation explores the question of whether the doom–hope scheme constitutes the redactional criterion that resulted in the final from of the book. He argues that the oracles of the book were intentionally redacted into a unified whole. This unity is achieved through the use of three traditions: the divine warrior, the lamentation and the personification of the city. These are indicated by wordplay and thematic features that permeate the book and contribute to its 'cohesiveness'. Thus, according to Luker, ch. 1 is united around the theophany while chs. 2 and 3 exhibit conceptual continuity centered on the theme of judgment.[93] The connection with chs. 4.1–5.3 is achieved through the use of wordplay, namely, the head of the mountains, mountain of the Lord (4.1-7//3.9-12). The following section, 5.4-15, is marked off by its use of והיה as compared to עתה in the previous section. The summons to hear in 6.1 renews the theme of 1.2; and by means of wordplay a conceptual continuity is formed between chs. 5 and 6.[94]

Luker concludes that the hope–doom scheme does not explain the redaction of the book:

> No collection is entirely autonomous and boundaries are sometimes vague, but seven are probably discernible, none of which is separate or is defined on the basis of 'doom' and 'hope'.[95]

He presupposes an understanding of the conceptuality of the final form as the determinant of the significance of the doom–hope scheme. However, he does not make explicit what that conceptuality is or how it is to be discerned.

91.   Hillers, *Micah*, p. 6.
92.   Luker, 'Doom and Hope'.
93.   Luker, 'Doom and Hope', pp. 166-70.
94.   Luker, 'Doom and Hope', pp. 185-88.
95.   Luker, 'Doom and Hope', pp. 224.

K.H. Cuffey (1987). Cuffey's[96] work is a comprehensive examination of the various proposals hithertofore presented on the coherence of the book of Micah and is the best attempt to define 'coherence'. In articulating his task, Cuffey presents his definition of coherence as follows:

> Coherence refers to the connectedness of a work. Any features which connect individual parts with each other, or all the parts into a whole, contribute to coherence in a work of literature.[97]

Fundamental to his argument is that there are different types of coherence in one work. A prophetic book in particular, may exhibit more than one of these types of coherence.[98]

Cuffey identifies four types of coherence. First, coherence of internal linkage is indicated by: recurrent features of style (e.g. genre, metaphor, address), and transitions and connections that clarify the interrelationship of the sections and their relationship to the whole.[99] More specifically, the transitions and connections may be explicit directions,[100] similarity with respect to meaning and structure,[101] and dissimilarity of structure or meaning.

Second, coherence of structural linkage refers to the coherence resulting from the arrangement of the parts. The basic idea is that such arrangements are themselves indicators of the way that the parts are to be construed in the whole. Furthermore, the meaning of the parts is resignified in light of the larger context, such that their meaning varies depending on their larger context. Cuffey's use of classical literary theory is again seen in his proposal that there are several types of arrangements of the material including: chronological, spatial, logical, natural, association and climatic.[102]

---

96. Cuffey, 'Coherence of Micah', p. 130.
97. Cuffey, 'Coherence of Micah', p. 130.
98. Cuffey, 'Coherence of Micah', pp. 153-54.
99. Cuffey, 'Coherence of Micah', pp. 130-31.
100. Cuffey, 'Coherence of Micah', pp. 130-31. He further classifies these as additive (and, also, furthermore), opposing (but, yet, rather, instead), temporal (then, next, now, later), and causal (for, so, therefore).
101. Cuffey, 'Coherence of Micah', pp 132-33, the repetition of words, verbal roots, subject, patterns of structure, personal and demonstrative pronouns since they presuppose an antecedent; repetition of structure through parallelism; the use of questions.
102. Cuffey, 'Coherence of Micah', pp 136-41, gives examples of this type of

Third, coherence of perspective is the common assumption that underlies a work, running throughout its parts. This may take the form of a shared historical context, the outlook of the author/redactor. The perspective, however, may have to be reconstructed from the text if there are no explicit references, as for example in the citation of a historical situation (cf. the book of Nahum).[103]

Fourth, coherence of theme is, for Cuffey, the most important type of coherence. This type is the sharing of a common theme or meaning by all parts of the whole. Such coherence is indicated by the links formed by the continuous content. The extent to which this is continued is the extent of the coherence of theme. So if this occurs in part of the book but not in the others, the coherence of theme is that of the part rather than the whole.

> To find coherence of theme, then, we look for a principle that creates oneness for a literary text, and then evaluate how the different component parts of the piece are integrated around that principle... Even if such a unifying theme originated with a later editor, it would still serve nicely to inform us of his concerns.[104]

Cuffey further argues that the connections and structural coherence do not necessarily indicate a thematic coherence.[105] However, the coherence of theme is the most significant because it is directly related to the purpose of the work as the expression of the intended message. The coherence of theme is then strengthened by the other types of coherence.[106]

While this may not have been his intention in the articulation of his argument, the importance of Cuffey's argument is that it allows for recognition of the values of various understandings of the coherence of the prophetic books, a recognition that does not have to have homogeneity of method and results to find value. From the perspective of his discussion of the types of coherence one can see value in the works that analyze one or the other 'types of coherence'.

coherence including Isa. 40–55; cf. Claus Westermann, *Isaiah 40–66: A Commentary* (trans. D.G. Stalker; OTL; Philadelphia: Westminster Press, 1969).

103. Cuffey, 'Coherence of Micah', pp. 142-44.

104. Cuffey, 'Coherence of Micah', pp. 145-46; he cites as an example Jonah and Habakkuk, noting that even Hab. 3 exhibits this coherence of theme, namely, God's word in spite of the apparent non-involvement of God.

105. Cuffey, 'Coherence of Micah', pp. 153, 156.

106. Cuffey, 'Coherence of Micah', pp. 154, 156.

Another of Cuffey's contributions to the research on the coherence of
the book of Micah is his recognition of the nature of coherence. He
argues that coherence occurs on various levels. This is not a new argument, but paired with his delineation of the types of coherence he provides the framework for understanding how it is possible. Thus, he
notes that there may be coherence on the level of the sentence linked by
transitions and recurrent literary features and not on the level of the
smaller units. He further recognizes that coherence is relative in several
way, including degree, criteria and contextual concerns. So while one
may talk of the coherence of a work, it is to be assumed that there is a
degree of coherence but not a perfect coherence. It is also relative in the
sense that the criteria for it may vary from time to time and certainly
from the time of the text to the present. For this reason and that a sub-
jective element may skew one's perspective with respect to the degree
of coherence, Cuffey issues a caveat that the exegesis be tightly controlled by the text and not by an outside scheme into which the parts of
the text are placed.[107]

(Again the arguments are logical, but it is the fact that hithertofore
they have not been articulated that increases their value. One can see in
the work of J.P. Smith, for example, that he does not deny coherence of
all parts of the book of Micah. He sees coherence in chs. 4–5. Willis
and Hagstrom clearly are aware that there is a principle of coherence
present in each part of the book. However, neither of these authors
articulated the nature of the coherence beyond their observation of the
structural and thematic elements.[108])

Finally, Cuffey's proposal concerning the coherence of the book of
Micah is that it 'has a well-crafted and intentional coherence in its final
form' organized around the four passages regarding the promises to the
remnant.[109] This coherence of theme is supported by the coherence of
structure and internal linkage and possibly a coherence of perspective
that underlies the whole. He argues that the structure of the book is
organized around the theme of the remnant 'to communicate a specific
theological theme, that God is the one who punishes yet restores what
sinfulness has corrupted'.[110] An understanding of their significance
allows a clearer understanding of the sections and their interrelation-

107. Cuffey, 'Coherence of Micah', pp. 147-50.
108. See above for discussion of the works of Willis and Hagstrom.
109. Cuffey, 'Coherence of Micah', p. 245.
110. Cuffey, 'Coherence of Micah', p. 300.

ship.[111] Thus he proposes an A-B-B-A pattern: A, 1.2–2.13; B, 3.1–4.8; B, 4.9–5.14; A, 6.1–7.20, each of these units consisting of oracles of doom concerned with the results of human sins (1.2–2.11; 3.1-12; 4.9–14; 6.1–7.6) and oracles of hope concerned with the remnant and the offering of a divine resolution to problems resulting from human sin.[112] He argues that his proposal best accounts for all the data and provides the most natural and simple way of explaining chs. 3–5.[113]

There is much plausibility in Cuffey's argument concerning the role of the remnant in the structure of the book and in particular 1.2–2.13, 3.1-12, and 6.1–7.6. However, the significance of the remnant in 7.18 is over-emphasized. He argues against the two-fold division of the text on the basis that while all the parts of chs. 1–5 are related to the central theme they treat different aspects of the theme. He further argues against the use of the summons to hear as indicators of major division, on the grounds that the summons in 1.2 and 6.1 are no more indicative of major divisions than those in 3.1, 9, and 6.9.

G. Stansell (1988). Stansell's[114] work makes at least two significant contributions to critical research on the book of Micah: (a) it calls attention to the particular use of traditions, themes and motifs in the book, and (b) it attempts to clarify the subject of its focus—that is, traditions as distinct from themes and motifs. While the latter is not the focus of the work, his brief treatment clarifies the focus of his work and the usefulness of its results.

Stansell's form- and tradition-historical comparison of the prophecies of Micah and Isaiah, while demonstrating sensitivity to Micah's distinctive use of traditions and themes vis-à-vis Isaiah's, does not intend any reconstruction of the overall conceptuality of the book of Micah. Based on Stade's and Mays' arguments and criteria for authenticity, Stansell asserts that chs. 1–3 as a unit is 'a critically assured minimum' and thus limits his analysis of the book of Micah to these chapters and in the case of Isaiah to chs. 1–39.[115]

So the argument for the particularity of Micah's use of the traditions is confined to the internal message of chs. 1–3 as a unit. For Stansell,

111. Cuffey, 'Coherence of Micah', p. 245.
112. Cuffey, 'Coherence of Micah', pp. 247-48, 304-305.
113. Cuffey, 'Coherence of Micah', p. 325.
114. Stansell, *Micah and Isaiah*.
115. Stansell, *Micah and Isaiah*, p. 7.

the understanding of the traditions in this unit seems to be unaffected by the juxtaposition to the other parts of the book of Micah. One may deduce from his analysis that he assumes that the particularity of the use is its diachronic aspect.

Stansell builds his method on the foundation laid by Old Testament scholarship that demonstrated 'that Israelite prophets were rooted deeply in the ancient traditions of their people, and that their message were informed by their use, adaptation and reinterpretation of tradition'.[116] He notes, however, that any comparison must deal with the issue of the roots of the traditions of Micah and Isaiah.[117]

In discussing Yahweh's punishing Zion, Stansell uses Isa. 5.14, 17 and 32.9-14. He argues that 5.14 was probably preceded in the original by a verse crying 'woe'; 5.15-16 are later additions separating 5.14 and 5.17 that belong together. This passage is most likely a threat of doom on the nobility of the city (5.14) and the city itself (5.17).[118] Concerning Isa. 32.9-14, Stansell believes them to be Isaiah's last words—32.9 didactic opening formula and 32.11-13 summons to lament. He sees Jerusalem as the focus of the passage and not the nation or the land. The imagery in this particular passage vis-à-vis the others (Isa. 1.21-23; 14.32; 28.16; 31.4-5) is that the capital city will be totally destroyed.[119]

As to the parallels with Mic. 1.8, 16 and 3.9-12, he argues that in Micah and in Isa. 32.11 the dirge announces and anticipates the disaster.[120] The texts share the same form and vocabulary; they both speak of the abandonment of the city—that is, Micah of exile and Isaiah of imminent abandonment of the palace— and total destruction of the city. Notably, though Isaiah avoids calling the city Zion or Jerusalem (Isa. 1.2-4; 29.1-7), Micah makes this reference explicit. Thus Stansell argues that:

> In Isa. 32.9f. we have, then, a significant analogy to Mic. 3.9f. It should not, finally, escape notice that elements or motifs of the Zion tradition are totally absent from Isaiah's word of destruction on Jerusalem, indicative of a change in his perspective.[121]

116. Stansell, *Micah and Isaiah*, p. 5.
117. Stansell, *Micah and Isaiah*, p. 5.
118. Stansell, *Micah and Isaiah*, p. 61.
119. Stansell, *Micah and Isaiah*, p. 62.
120. Stansell, *Micah and Isaiah*, p. 62.
121. Stansell, *Micah and Isaiah*, p. 63. Also note Stansell's discussion of the social critique in Chapter 4 of his book. Within this analysis the attention to the

Stansell seems to have represented the particularity of certain aspects of the book including the use of certain themes. It is in this respect that Stansell departs from others in his acknowledgment of the distinctions among themes, traditions, motifs, and so on, and the particularity of their use in various contexts—in this case Micah and Isaiah. Thus he states:

> it is obvious that a comparison of traditions does not exhaust all the possibilities of such a comparative study. There are also broader topics which we may simply designate as 'themes' and within those themes, smaller 'motifs' which could afford further critical access to a comparison and contrast to Micah with Isaiah. To briefly illustrate what is meant by the terms 'tradition', 'theme', and 'motif', we may with respect to Micah point to the presence of the theophany *tradition* (1.2f.), the *theme* of social critique (e.g., 3.1f.), or the recurrent *motif* 'my people' (2.8, 9; 3.2, 5).[122]

Stansell's contribution to the question of the coherence of the book is his awareness of the various uses of traditions as resignified within their various contexts.[123]

C.S. Shaw (1993). Shaw's[124] analysis focuses on the authorial intentionality of the text. Thus Shaw proposes a three stage process of analysis including determining the units, identifying their 'rhetorical situation', and finally exploring the material to determine how the sub-units work together towards a unified purpose.[125] Shaw presupposes that it is possible to accurately reconstruct the 'rhetorical situation'. His two assumptions as he identifies them are: (a) the prophets did not speak in short sayings but in lengthy discourses; (b) what scholars have usually identified as independent sayings are building blocks of the larger discourse.[126] He further presupposes that the individual units of the book of Micah are distinct speeches addressed to particular situations for

distinctive use of עמי further illustrates Stansell's argument for the distinctive use of the same traditions and motifs by different authors. He concludes that while Micah does not refer to 'my people' as the 'poor', Isaiah designates the poor as a part of 'my people' (p. 110).

122. Stansell, *Micah and Isaiah*, p. 6.

123. Another study published in the 1980s is Ralph L. Smith, *Micah–Malachi* (WBC, 32; Waco, TX: Word Books, 1984).

124. Shaw, *The Speeches of Micah*.

125. Shaw, *The Speeches of Micah*, p. 23.

126. Shaw, *The Speeches of Micah*, pp. 19-20.

particular purposes: 1.2-16; 2.1-13; 3.1–4.8; 4.9–5.14; 6.1–7.7; 7.8-20. These units are delineated based on their theme, rhetorical situation and date.[127]

According to this approach, the coherence lies within the individual speeches and not necessarily in their unification. Thus, Shaw's analysis focuses on the individual units and only cursorily makes mention of the possibility of a coherence of the book.[128] For Shaw, the coherence of the speeches is indicated by their authorial intention.

Conclusion

The review of previous research identifies the scholars' views on the sources of coherence and the criteria for discerning coherence. This information is presented in Table 1 below. The review also indicates the existence of trends in research on the book of Micah over the last two centuries of scholarship. The movement is from searching for authentic materials, to efforts aimed at reconstructing the composition history of the book, to views of the unity of the text units, and now questions concerning the nature and extent of the coherence of the book.

Those scholars identified above depict at least three presuppositions concerning the coherence of the book. The first presupposition concerns the coherence and origin of the material. This has to do with how to deal with the composite nature of the text. Fundamental to this presupposition is the superiority of the original. Secondary materials are inferior and as such less significant. This delimitation of the relative significance of the material is then carried over into all analysis of the text with a larger degree of attention to identifying the date of the materials. Fragmentation of the text in this way accounted for the proposed coherence within parts of the book and disallowed for coherence of the final and composite form.

In the course of time this attention to the 'original' text manifested itself in the analysis of the compositional history of the text. The very acknowledgment of a compositional history was built on the presupposition that the juxtaposition of materials derived from different origins results in the incoherence of the whole formed by these materials. With this presupposition it is hardly surprising that research focusing on the

---

127. Shaw, *The Speeches of Micah*, pp. 222-23.
128. Shaw, *The Speeches of Micah*, p. 225.

compositional history tends to perceive an overall incoherence of the book.

The second presupposition of the previous studies is an understanding of the conceptuality of the whole. This presupposed understanding is often paired with the absence of full-scale analysis of the text's conceptuality. Therefore, in past studies there is a significant gap between their assertions concerning the unifying element of the coherence and their presentation of the literary indicators of the coherence.

Finally, with the exception of a few scholars, an understanding of coherence is also assumed. This assumption results in the confusion about the nature of the task and most immediately about the nature and discernibility of coherence. These are the limitations as outlined above that the present study seeks to address in the following chapters—namely, clarifying what is meant by coherence (Chapter 2); demonstrating through structural analysis (Chapter 3) and a full-scale analysis of the text (Chapters 4–5) the various conceptual levels in the text; and suggesting through a discussion of the concepts and their possible conceptual framework the conceptuality of the book (Chapter 6).

The following table shows the opinions of the various scholars concerning the source of coherence and criteria for discerning it. The asterisk and shading indicate that a particular scholar regards this aspect as important to the existence and discerning of coherence. For example, Ewald believes that the author is the source of the coherence, and that the criteria for it are the shared historical context of the various materials and a logical progression within the text. A scholar's adherence to certain beliefs about coherence does not mean that the scholar believes that the book of Micah is coherent. Thus, upon applying their criteria, Haupt, Halévy, Smith and Lindblom conclude that the extant form of the book is incoherent.

Table 1. *Coherence in the History of Research on the Book of Micah*

	Sources of Coherence		Criteria for Discerning Coherence		
Scholars	*Author*	*Redactor*	*Historical Context*	*Theme*	*Logical Progression*
Ewald (1876)	*		*		*
Stade (1881+1883)	*		*		*
Halévy (1904+1905)	*				*
Haupt (1910+1911)	*		*		
Smith (1911)	*		*		*
Lindblom (1929)	*				
Weiser (1961+1963)		*			*
Renaud (1964+1977)		*		*	
Willis (1966)		*	*	*	*
Lescow (1972)		*	*		
Allen (1976)		*	*	*	*
Mays (1976)		*	*	*	*
Wolff (1982+1990)	*	*	*	*	*
Hagstrom (1982+1988)		*		*	*
Hillers (1984)		*	*	*	
Luker (1985)		*		*	
Cuffey (1987)		*	*	*	*
Stansell (1988)		*		*	
Shaw (1993)	*		*	*	
Jacobs (1997)	*	*		*	*

Chapter 2

METHODOLOGICAL CONCERNS

Delineation of the Present Task

1. *Perspectives on the Task*

The task of discerning the coherence of the book of Micah has been variously attempted. As to those works that deal specifically with the question of coherence, Willis,[1] Hagstrom[2] and Cuffey[3] are indispensable as points of departure for this study. Willis's attempt is noteworthy because of its departure from earlier studies on the book of Micah. He attempts to discern the coherence of the book by means of its literary features. He thus proposes that there are essentially two types of coherence—horizontal and vertical. In this proposal he recognizes that coherence has just as much to do with conceptual continuity within a unit as between the units of a literary work. He further recognizes that coherence is likewise a function of the conceptual aspects of the text. His limitation, however, also has to do with the latter recognition. For while he sees the conceptual aspects as being to some extent significant, he nonetheless subsumes the consideration of the conceptual aspects under the literary features. As a result, he does not attempt to discern how these conceptual aspects are to be regarded with reference to the 'conceptuality of the text'. Furthermore, his detailed study does not provide a clear definition of coherence and only implicitly refers to the criteria for discerning coherence.[4]

Hagstrom attempts to improve on Willis's work. This attempt, however, falls prey to some of Willis's limitations. Hagstrom's definition of coherence is at best ambiguous. Coherence, he proposes, is present in a

1. Willis, 'Structure, Setting'.
2. Hagstrom, *The Coherence*.
3. Cuffey, 'Coherence of Micah'.
4. Willis, 'Structure, Setting'.

work when there are features that bind it together and indicate how it may be construed.[5] Both in this definition and his detailed analysis of the literary features as indicators of the interrelationship of these units, Hagstrom minimizes the role of the conceptuality of the text in discerning the interrelationship of the units. His concern is that talk about issues such as concepts is an abstraction from the text and not verifiable by literary evidence.[6] For Hagstrom coherence is literary and has more to do with the text's integrity (cohesion) than with any other aspect of the text. This proposal is countered in the present study where it is proposed that coherence is fundamentally conceptual and has to do with the conceptuality of the text. Conceptuality generates the other discernible aspects of coherence including the evidence of its literary integrity (cohesion).[7]

To date, Cuffey's work is the most recent and insightful of these studies. He defines coherence as the connectedness of a literary work served by any feature that contributes to it.[8] There are various types of coherence including: coherence of internal linkage, structural linkage, perspective and theme. Of these four, he identifies coherence of theme to be the most important, because it is more closely related to the purpose of the work than any other.[9] His effort to discern the unifying theme leads him to the conclusion that it is the remnant of Israel. Cuffey is the first to admit that one of the limitations of his study is the absence of a full-scale analysis of the text as the basis for his conclusions. He simply does not demonstrate how 'the remnant', compared to other conceptual elements, is the unifying element of whole book.

All three of these scholars left unfinished the task of defining coherence with respect to the distinctive nature of the book, and the task of discerning its conceptuality in light of its coherence. Notably, others have analyzed the book with the particular intent of discerning its redac-

5. Hagstrom, *The Coherence.*

6. Hagstrom's view fits into the modern discussion on literary terms. In this discussion the indiscernibility of concept is its apparent synonymy with content, thought and authorial intention. Cf. R. Brown, 'Theme', in Irena R. Makaryk (ed.), *Encyclopedia of Contemporary Literary Theory: Approaches, Scholars, Terms* (Toronto: University of Toronto Press, 1993), pp. 642-46.

7. See Chapter 3 below for a discussion of cohesion and coherence.

8. Cuffey, 'Coherence of Micah', p. 130.

9. Brown, 'Theme'.

tional processes[10] and rhetorical situations.[11] None of these, however, are sufficient for the present study; nor is analysis focused only on literary features a sufficient basis for a discussion of conceptual coherence.

2. *Present Perspective on the Task*

a. *The question and crucial definitions*

The main question which this study addresses is: To what extent does the book of Micah exhibit conceptual coherence? Fundamental to this question is the presupposition that texts are inherently conceptual. Coherence then is an extension of conceptuality rather than an addition to it. Furthermore, intentionality is essential to texts in so far as they exist to say 'something'—they have intention. The acknowledgment of the intentionality of texts is basic to the proposal that texts are products of their community.[12] It further presupposes that intentionality is in some way reflected in discernible features of the text, namely, structure, conceptuality and vocabulary. This intentionality employs from its conceptual framework elements that actualize its object—the 'something that is said'. As such the selected and crafted entity constituted by the selected elements is a part—a manifestation—of the larger sum of the conceptual framework, that is, the ideology out of which these elements and their resultant entity arose—texts. Nonetheless, the texts themselves are not necessarily intended to comment on that ideology for the sake of doing so.[13] That conceptual framework is at once incidental and essential to the text.

That which controlled the selection and crafting of the text—the specific manifestation of the conceptual framework—is what is referred to in this study as conceptuality. It is the guiding principle in whose

10. Wolff, *Micah*.

11. Shaw, *The Speeches of Micah*.

12. Cf. James A. Sanders, *Torah and Canon* (Philadelphia: Fortress Press, 1972); *idem*, 'Text and Canon: Concepts and Methods', *JBL* 98 (1979), pp. 5-29.

13. Note that 'intentionality' is used here to refer to both authorial and redactional intention. Intentionality is the means by which the conceptuality of the whole is achieved. At the same time, the intentionality is necessary to achieving a particular conceptuality. Certainly, a conceptuality may be achieved with little intention. However, the more specific the conceptuality, the more intention is required to achieve it. To the extent that a work evidences a compositional history, the redactional intentionality may be important to understanding the coherence of that work.

service the text is employed. It is the overarching idea that accounts for what is said.

In modern literature, the ideology of the author and intent of the work are expressed by a thesis. So while it may be suggested that such a 'thesis' is analogous to conceptuality in as much as it is generative of the literary work,[14] it must be further noted that the thesis itself is generated by its conceptual framework. It demonstrates itself by means of concepts, structures, and so on. As there may be many theses in a single work—each paragraph and chapter having one but all complementing and contributing to the overarching thesis—such is the case with conceptuality. There may be various conceptualities in a text like the book of Micah seen in different structural levels and units. By means of their distinctive structures, concepts, and so on, all conceptualities exhibit the coherence essential to them. It is the coherence that facilitates the discernibility of the conceptuality. The challenge then is to discern the conceptualities and their interrelationship within the whole. This interrelationship of the various conceptualities toward an overarching conceptuality is what is called here 'conceptual coherence'. Therefore, it is the factor of discernibility that is the source of the challenges confronting this study rather than the determination of whether or not coherence exists.

b. *Delineation of aspects/terms*

Theme. The theme of a literary work is generally defined as 'the subject of thought, writing, composition'.[15] It has also been defined as 'the semantic dimensions of a work dispersed by and through its formal elements'.[16] However, the definition of theme is a debated matter in modern literary theory. With regard to biblical studies the term is no less problematic. Theme and concept are often used interchangeably. Likewise, theme is used of a variety of different entities. Thus, M. Noth seems to use theme to refer to the basic content of confessional state-

14. Karl Beckson and Authur Ganz, *Literary Terms: A Dictionary* (New York: Farrar, Straus & Giroux, 1975), p. 255, give a definition of thesis: 'a proposition to be maintained especially one laid down for formal defense or proof'. The theme according to this definition is the central idea—the thesis.

15. *Oxford American Dictionary* (New York: Oxford University Press, 1980), p. 711.

16. Brown, 'Theme', p. 643.

ments about Israel's history. These themes, he states, were joined together over time to form the Pentateuchal tradition. However, there is not a
single unifying theme in the Pentateuch but at least five, namely, guidance out of Egypt, guidance into the arable land, promise to the Patri-
archs, guidance in the wilderness and revelation at Sinai.[17]

Narrative literature is Clines's focus in defining theme. He gives five
ways of formulating a definition of theme: (a) 'The theme of a narrative
work may first be regarded as a conceptualization of its plot... If plot
can correctly be defined as "a narrative of events the emphasis falling
on causality", theme may be regarded as plot with the emphasis on con-
ceptualized plot'.[18] An example of a theme is: 'How power corrupts'. (b)
The theme is the central or dominant idea of a literary work. It is the
abstract concept which is made concrete through literary means.[19] (c)
The articulation of the theme gives the rationale for the existence of the
work and its particular content and structure. (d) The statement of the
theme serves as evidence for the coherence of the work. (e) Theme is
distinct from motif, topos and narrative pattern in that it concerns a
larger unit of material than the other terms.[20] For Clines, there can be
only one theme in a literary work. 'When different, divergent, or con-
tradictory themes emerge other than the theme the critic has first identified, one has to adapt one's statement of the theme to take account of
them.'[21] He further argues that it is not necessary to posit the presence
of the authorial intentionality of the theme in order to identify the
theme of a work.[22]

On the basis of these formulations, it seems that what Clines refers to
as theme is what I have defined here as conceptuality. The theme is one
aspect of conceptuality. It is different from conceptuality in that it is not
generative of the text but is a generated aspect of the text that exhibits

17. Martin Noth, *A History of Pentateuchal Traditions* (trans. B.W. Anderson;
Scholars Press Reprints and Translations Series; Atlanta: Scholars Press, 1981),
pp. 46-62.

18. David J.A. Clines, *The Theme of the Pentateuch* (JSOTSup, 10; Sheffield:
JSOT Press, 1978), pp. 17-18; Clines cites D.L. Petersen, 'A Thrice-Told Tale:
Genre, Theme, and Motif', *BR* 18 (1973), pp. 30-43; G.W. Coats, 'Conquest Tra-
ditions in the Wilderness Theme', *JBL* 95 (1976), pp. 177-90.

19. Clines, *Theme of the Pentateuch*, p. 18, citing W.F. Thrall and A. Hibberd,
A Handbook of Literature (New York: Odyssey, 1960), p. 486.

20. Clines, *Theme of the Pentateuch*, pp. 18-19.

21. Clines, *Theme of the Pentateuch*, p. 20.

22. Clines, *Theme of the Pentateuch*, p. 21.

the conceptuality. A theme such as God's response to sin, consists of ideas/concepts, for example, judgment, hope, forgiveness.

Conceptuality is not used to refer to conceptual aspects such as justice and sin. It is used here to refer to that which accounts for the existence of the text. For the sake of consistency with the formulations in this study, the term conceptuality will be used to refer to the generative principle responsible for the content, structure and logical progression of the text.[23] Knierim, in his focus on the relationship of text and concept, sees conceptuality as lying beneath the surface of the text, that is, not necessarily 'explicit but operative underneath the text as its coherent design'.[24]

Coherence. Broadly defined, to be coherent is to be 'connected logically; not rambling in speech or in reasoning'.[25] Coherence is the conceptual interrelationship of the parts of a work. This interrelationship is constituted by the conceptuality of the work and is discerned in the text's structure and the other literary and substantive features that together define the text's literary and conceptual integrity.

Conceptual coherence is the product of its constitutive units such that the units lend to and are constitutive of the whole. The coherence of the constitutive units as units, however, does not necessarily mean the coherence of the whole constituted by those units. This challenges the presupposition of those who have argued for the incoherence of the book of Micah on the grounds that it consists of various inconsistencies.[26] My basic argument is that conceptual coherence is discernible at various levels of the book's structure.

Concerning the issue of the levels of coherence, while the coherence of the constitutive units does not mean the coherence of the whole, the

23. Rolf P. Knierim, *The Task of Old Testament Theology: Method and Cases* (Grand Rapids: Eerdmans, 1995), pp. 61-62.

24. Knierim, *Task of Old Testament Theology*, p. 291, cf. pp. 270-71; *idem, Text and Concept in Leviticus 1.1-9: A Case in Exegetical Method* (Forschungen zum Alten Testament, 2; Tübingen: J.C.B. Mohr, 1992), p. 3.

25. *Oxford American Dictionary*, p. 121. Cf. Jeremy Hawthorn, *A Glossary of Contemporary Literary Theory* (New York: Edward Arnold, 1992), p. 35. He believes that 'coherence involves the imposition of some form of unity upon disparate elements'.

26. Thus, for example, Smith, *Micah, Zephaniah*, argues that the book as a whole lacks unity. He, however, does not discount the unity of chs. 4–5, albeit on the basis of literary style, and divergent content from ch. 3.

question remains as to whether or not there can be coherence of the whole apart from the coherence of the constitutive units. For example, ch. 3 is coherent; but do chs. 3 and 4 produce a coherent unit? If so, is the unit they constitute coherent in the same way as ch. 3? How is coherence of the whole dependent on the coherence of the individual units? Willis would argue that the coherence of the whole is dependent or at least mirrored in that of the constitutive elements.[27]

In light of the apparent disunity or divergence within the text, a further question arises regarding the nature of coherence. The divergence in the text may be the result of deliberate organization of the text by using older materials, creating links between these texts and adding new materials.[28] All these redactional activities are deliberate within a particular setting/context. This deliberate redaction of the text results in the juxtaposition of apparently—and in some case originally—unrelated materials—that is, materials that would otherwise be validly deemed unrelated but whose juxtaposition in the whole challenges their separateness. In essence, then, the coherence of each distinct unit is indispensable but the coherence of the whole is implausible apart from the conceptuality served by the various units.

The proper realm of the coherence, then, is not of the individual units but the conceptuality of the whole, that is, the larger purpose for which these elements were brought together. Perhaps, this statement may lead some to believe that coherence and its clues are incidental. This is not necessarily the case. Because we are dealing with a text and all texts are subject by their very nature to incidentals, a measure of the incidental is not to be entirely discounted.

The incidental nature of any aspect is not synonymous with minimal importance. The clues and coherence are to some extent the result of the redactor's effort to signal a coherence which otherwise would be missed. To this realm of the conceptuality then belongs the conceptual framework. This is not simply the textual indicators, as vital as they are to the identification of the conceptuality of the text. Indicators are indispensable for discerning conceptuality but are not the sum total of it. Is the conceptuality of one text, then, the same as that of other texts or any other generalizable thought? Does the conceptuality of any given

27. Willis, 'Structure, Setting'.

28. Simon DeVries, *From Old Revelation to New* (Grand Rapids: Eerdmans, 1995). His fundamental argument is that redactional activity on the text is deliberate and not merely an accidental grouping together of materials.

whole have particularity? By what criteria are these particularities determined? Though it is not the sole indicator, the structure may in fact be the primary indicator of the particularity of the text's conceptuality.

Types of coherence. Most recently, the question of the coherence of the book of Micah has been centered on the types of coherence that the book exhibits. Fundamentally, this question grows out of the presupposition that there are several types of coherence observable in a literary work. This awareness of the multiplicity of coherence is evident in the works of Willis, Hagstrom and Cuffey.[29]

As in any instance where a plurality of phenomena is identified, there is the risk of confusion concerning the nature of the plurality and consequently the phenomena themselves. If a phenomenon itself has not been clearly defined, the potential exists that what is being identified as a plurality of phenomena may in fact be a plurality of perspectives on a single phenomenon. Furthermore, the lack of a clear definition or any definition at all may lead to the classifications of essential aspects of the phenomenon as distinctive phenomena.

I propose that what Cuffey[30] sees as types of coherence, are essential aspects of a single albeit complex phenomenon. Thus, internal and structural linkages are textual indicators of the coherence. Furthermore, the 'coherence of perspective' is the conceptual framework that gives actualization to the text. Finally, the 'coherence of theme' is what is defined in this study as the conceptuality of the text. All these are indispensable aspects of the conceptual coherence of a text.

Structure, genre and coherence. Is structure itself a type of coherence or is it an essential aspect of a type of coherence? In agreement with Hawthorn, it is proposed that:

> [t]he idea of structure carries with it a suggestion of necessary internal coherence, suggesting that just as the rule of grammar and syntax impose coherence on disparate parts of speech, so the linguistic paradigm implies that a comparable coherence can be found in non-linguistic structures.[31]

Structure and genre are not the focus of the text—that is, the text is not in existence for the sake of the structure or genre; but the existence of structure and genre is owed to the preservation of the conceptuality of the text. The structure is another means of actualizing the conceptuality.

29. See Chapter 1 above for discussion.
30. Cuffey, 'Coherence of Micah'.
31. Hawthorn, *Glossary*, p. 35.

This is done by bringing some order to the elements of the conceptuality. Furthermore, genre by itself is not indicative of a particular concept. A genre may be adapted to present many concepts. There are some genres associated with some concepts, for example, the judgment speech with the concepts of sin, judgment, punishment; but narratives, for example, do not presuppose a particular concept. The concept of a text is more than the individual genres or structural elements.

Proposed Method

The method of concept-critical analysis is being employed to address the question of the extent of the conceptual coherence of the book of Micah. The method is used here because of the perceived limitations of previous methods to address the issues particular to the discerning of conceptual coherence. Granted, the perceived limitations of any method are measured by the task to which that method is applied. Thus I do not discount the value of other methods nor discard them.

Concept-critical analysis as employed here, is a method that complements form criticism[32]—analyzing the concepts in the delimited text units—and literary criticism—in seeking to discern the literary integrity of the text.[33] The method seeks primarily to reconstruct the conceptuality of the extant text in light of its literary integrity.

32. Cf. James Muilenburg, 'Form Criticism and Beyond', *JBL* 88 (1969), pp. 1-18.

33. Knierim, 'Criticism of Literary Features, Form, Tradition, and Redaction', in Douglas A. Knight and Gene Tucker (eds.), *The Hebrew Bible and its Modern Interpreters* (Chico, CA: Scholars Press, 1995), pp. 123-53 (138-39). With regard to the place of structural analysis in exegesis he proposes that 'as the analysis of a text's integrity, the step belongs to literary criticism. As the analysis of a genre exemplar, it belongs to form criticism.' See *idem*, 'Old Testament Form Criticism Reconsidered', *Int* 27 (1973), pp. 435-68. Cf. M. Sweeney, *Isaiah 1–39: With an Introduction to Prophetic Literature* (FOTL, 16; Grand Rapids: Eerdmans, 1996), pp. 10-11. Sweeney discusses 'form-criticism and prophetic literature' and especially the challenges posed by the composite nature of the extant text. See Sweeney, 'Formation and Form in Prophetic Literature', in J.L. Mays, D.L. Petersen and Kent H. Richards (eds.), *Old Testament Interpretation: Past, Present, and Future* (Festschrift Gene Tucker; Nashville: Abingdon Press, 1995), pp. 113-26. He advocates that the prophetic books be interpreted in their entirety. Using the book of Amos as his example, he demonstrates the three steps for interpreting prophetic books: defining the major textual blocks; determining the genre of the book; and establishing the social and historical setting of the book.

1. *Presuppositions*
This method has several presuppositions that shape its formulation and its objectives.

a. *Concerning the text*

Texts as multi-conceptual entities. Texts are multi-conceptual entities. Thus to identify a concept in a text does not mean that one has identified the conceptuality of the text unit. As in other literary compositions, a governing concept is supported by other concepts; but the supportive concepts are not themselves the controlling/governing concept uniting all the others.

Diverse origins of concepts. Concepts come into the text at various points in the transmission process—for example, oral tradition, the author's use and resignification of tradition, the redactional process(es). The focus of concept-critical analysis is the extant text. However, it recognizes the process(es) in the production of the extant text. In this respect, this method is cognizant of the fact that concepts are signaled by semantic indicators which are themselves products of their historical realities and yet to some extent particular to the conceptuality of their present context.

Generic terminology and concept. The presence or absence of generic terminology in a text unit is not the single determinant of the presence or absence of a particular concept. That is to say that the presence of terminologies—in whatever quantity—may or may not be an indicator of their predominance in a text unit or corpus. For example, the semantic field of the concept of justice— משפט and צדק—may be present, but the concept of justice may be secondary to another concept whose semantic field may or may not be present in the text unit. Likewise, the absence of semantic indicators does not mean the absence of the concept or its influence in the conceptuality of the text and hence its coherence. Concept-critical analysis, therefore, calls for examination of those features characteristic of a concept when the typical semantic indicators are present. It also calls for the examination of the features characteristic of the concept even where the particular semantic indicators are absent. Furthermore, it requires scrutiny of the particularity of the semantic indicators when present, for they may function with various nuances and towards different and possibly opposing ideologies. (See Chapter 6 below for further discussion.)

For now the example of the concept of the poor will suffice. As found in the book of Proverbs the poor are regarded in various ways. Even there the different conceptualities signaled by the proverbs are to be assessed. Thus רשׁ is used of those who are despised by others (Prov. 14.20). Other instances of explicit semantic indicators include דל in Prov. 22.22, which states that the poor are not to be oppressed because they are poor (my paraphrase). Furthermore, such oppression is regarded as an insult to God (Prov. 14.31). In the prophets the concept is typically signaled by עני and אביון. Here the poor are depicted as being of special interest to God and are not to be oppressed but helped.[34]

b. *Concerning the method*
The method of concept-critical analysis is built on the results of other methods, in particular form criticism and literary criticism. It is, therefore, intrinsic to these methods rather than a replacement of them. The concept-critical method is also inter-disciplinary in so far as it employs the results, methods and insights from disciplines such as sociology and anthropology as necessitated by a fuller understanding of the conceptualities of texts.

2. *Objectives*
The objectives of the concept-critical method are thus formulated: (a) To identify the form of the extant text by means of structural analysis and both literary and conceptual indicators/signals. (b) To discern the various concepts within the whole in light of the distinctive units and their conceptualities. (c) To discern through exposition of the text its particular conceptualities, by looking contextually and intertextually at their typical characteristics—via the semantic field and etymology— and infratextually at their particular characteristics and functions.[35] (d) To discern the conceptuality of the text distinguishing between the governing concept and the supporting concepts.

---

34. Peter D. Miscall, 'The Concept of the Poor in the Old Testament' (unpublished PhD dissertation, Harvard University, 1972), pp. 30-31. Cf. קסם 'divination' in the Dtr perspective vs. קסם in Mic. 3.

35. Knierim, *Text and Concept*, p. 3, where he mentions infratextual; intratextual (pericope-immanent), contextual (the literary work as a whole); intertextual (separate literary works); and supratextual (the world-view of the concepts).

The governing concept is what is termed here the conceptual coherence. It should, however, be noted that in the cases where a particular semantic field is the focus of analysis—rather than a text unit—the same objectives apply to each unit where the semantic field is represented. The goal of the method would then be to identify from among the various occurrences of the terms the common denominator that unifies the particularity of the occurrences. Even then, concept-critical analysis recognizes the probability of diametrically opposed uses of a concept; therefore, the method reserves judgment that there is always a readily identifiable coherence to be found in any given semantic field and/or text unit. Consequently, an analysis of the text must be undertaken as an essential part in discerning its coherence. Such analysis is the focus of Chapters 3–6 of this study.

Part II

ANALYSIS OF THE TEXT

Chapter 3

STRUCTURE AND COHERENCE

Introduction

The structure of the book of Micah is essential to an analysis its coherence. Therefore, the structure may not be assumed on any basis, especially when its discernibility is obscured by the composite nature of the
text—for example, diversity of genres and generic elements, various
types of transitions and apparently competing concepts. Such is the case
with the book of Micah, with respect to both its macro- and micro-
structure. The nature of the text itself poses significant challenges to
discerning its structure. These challenges are constituted in the fact that
the text engenders ambivalence in the interpretation of the function and
significance of its structural and conceptual aspects. The interpretation
of this ambivalence is evident in the many proposals concerning the
structure of the book of Micah. A brief survey of scholars—as presented in Table 2 below—shows that there are at least eight such proposals of the macro-structure, ranging from six to two major divisions:
(a) six-fold division, 1.2-16; 2.1-13; 3.1–4.8; 4.9–5.14; 6.1–7.7; 7.8-
20;[1] (b) four-fold division, 1–3; 4–5; 6.1–7.7; 7.8-20;[2] (c) three-fold
division, 1–3; 4–5; 6–7;[3] (d) three-fold division, 1–2, 3–5, 6–7;[4] (e)
two-fold division, 1–5; 6–7.[5]

1. Shaw, *The Speeches of Micah*.
2. O. Procksch, *Die kleinen prophetischen Schriften vor dem Exil* (Stuttgart:
Verlag der Vereinsbuchhandlung, 1910); Wolff, *Micah*, pp. 17-26, 86. Another proposal, namely, 1–2; 3.1–4.8; 4.9–5.14; 6.1–7.20, is offered by Cuffey, 'Coherence
of Micah'. Yet another proposal, namely, 1; 2–3; 4–5; 6–7, is offered by Orelli, *The
Twelve Minor Prophets*, pp. 190-222.
3. Smith, *Micah, Zephaniah*; George L. Robinson, *The Twelve Minor Prophets*
(New York: George H. Doran, 1926), p. 97; Theodor H. Gaster, 'Micah', in Isaac
Landman (ed.), *The Universal Jewish Encyclopedia*, VII (New York: Ktav, 1969),
p. 528; S. Goldman, 'Micah', in A. Cohen (ed.), *The Twelve Prophets* (Bourne-

Each proposal assumes an understanding of the coherence of the text and the role of the distinctive features in producing and signaling that coherence. Yet the trend is to focus on literary features, often to the exclusion of conceptual elements, or else to measure the significance of the conceptual elements by the presence of typical literary and generic features associated with them. Consequently, in the absence of such typical features, or in the presence of less salient features, important conceptual elements are missed or misinterpreted. Potentially problematic is the tendency to assume the structure on the basis of the relative distinctiveness of literary and generic features and/or on the basis of preconceptions about the text's conceptuality. Furthermore, this problem is not erased by the best and most conscientious efforts. Especially in light of the potential problems, structural analysis must nonetheless be attempted.

For this reason, this chapter aims at understanding the structure of the book of Micah with respect to its literary and conceptual elements. Yet while the structural analysis presented here is part of the larger task of discerning the coherence of the book of Micah, this analysis is neither an accessory to nor the totality of that task. In the sense that its particularity is dependent on the distinctiveness of both cohesion and coherence, structure at every level (to varying degrees) is a function of both cohesion and coherence. Even so, the nature of its relationship to cohesion and coherence is characterized more by its inextricability than by its contiguity. Structure—a function of coherence which is itself conceptual—is an exhibitor of the conceptual organization of the literary work. Structure does not define, but is defined by coherence. By the

mouth: Soncino, 1948), p. 153; I. Willi-Plein, *Vorformen der Schriftexegese innerhalb des Alten Testaments* (BZAW, 123; New York: W. de Gruyter, 1971); Bruce K. Waltke, 'Micah', in Thomas E. McComiskey (ed.), *The Minor Prophets: An Exegetical and Expository Commentary* (2 vols.; Grand Rapids: Baker Books, 1993), II, p. 594.

4.   C.F. Keil and F. Delitzsch, *The Twelve Minor Prophets* (trans. J. Martin; 2 vols.; Edinburgh: T. & T. Clark, 1885), I, pp. 422; S.R. Driver, *An Introduction to the Literature of the Old Testament* (New York: Meridian Library, 1956), p. 326; Willis, 'Structure, Setting', pp. 122-24; Allen, *The Books*, pp. 260-61; Renaud, *La Formation*.

5.   Ewald, *Commentary on the Prophets*; F.C. Burkitt, 'Micah 6 and 7 a Northern Prophecy', *JBL* 45 (1926), pp. 159-61; Lescow, 'Micha 1–5'; *idem*, 'Micha 6–7'; Mays, *Micah*, pp. 23-25; Hagstrom, *The Coherence*; another proposal, namely, 1–3; 4–7 is offered by Haupt, 'Critical Notes'.

same token, structure is exhibited by cohesion such that the grammatical and syntactical aspects of the text are indispensable to the analysis of structure.[6]

As seen in Chapter 1 above, the diverse opinions regarding the macro-structure of the book of Micah is such that there is no discernible correlation between the method used in discerning the structure and the proposed structure. What appears to be indicative of a scholar's proposal of the structure of the book of Micah—and any text—is the author's understanding of the 'conceptuality' of the text, as well as the understanding of the interrelationships of literary and other conceptual features. As such, Table 2 is to be read in light of these observations as well as the discussion of the scholars already presented.

Table 2. *Macro-Structures Proposed for the Book of Micah*

Macro-Structural Divisions	*Scholar (Date)*
Six-fold	
1.2-16; 2.1-13; 3.1–4.8; 4.9–5.14; 6.1–7.7; 7.8-20	Shaw (1993)
Four-fold	
(a) 1; 2–3; 4–5; 6–7	von Orelli (1897)
(b) 1–2; 3.1–4.8; 4.9–5.14; 6.1–7.20	Cuffey (1987)
(c) 1–3; 4–5; 6.1–7.7; 7.8-20	Procksch (1910)
	Wolff (1982+1990)
Three-fold	
(a) 1–3; 4–5; 6–7	Marti (1904)
	Smith (1911)
	Willi-Plein (1971)
	Waltke (1993)
(b) 1–2; 3–5; 6–7	Keil (1885)
	Willis (1966)
	Allen (1976)
Two-fold	
(a) 1–5; 6–7	Ewald (1867)
	Lescow (1972)
	Mays (1976)
	Hagstrom (1988)
(c) 1–3; 4–7	Haupt (1910+1911)

6.   Knierim, *Text and Concept*, p. 3; *idem*, 'Conceptual Aspects in Exodus 25.1-9', in *idem*, *The Task of Old Testament Theology*, pp. 391-92.

Macro-Structure

1. *Proposal*

Whether one starts with the macro- or micro-structure, the legitimacy of the reconstruction of the structure demands that the analysis of each structural level (that is, macro- and micro-level) be done in conjunction with and not independent of consultation with the other. That the macro-structure of the final form of the book of Micah is most likely the product of redactional efforts, is reason enough to consider both the distinctiveness of the structure at both levels as well as the typical generic elements and concepts that constitute these levels.[7] This is not to imply that the structure at all levels is the product of redactional activity/effort. Certainly, there may be aspects of the micro-structure that were not altered by the redactors. However, to the extent that such redactional activity took place as a deliberate shaping of the material, even the oldest portions of the material may have to be reconsidered as having been resignified in light of the conceptuality of the whole in which they are presently situated.[8] It is for this reason, among others, that the structure may not be assumed—neither on the basis of presuppositions about the function and significance of various aspects of the text (for example, generic features, concepts), nor on the basis of their interrelationships.

---

7.   There are several aspects that facilitate the observation that the macro-structure is mostly the result of redactional efforts. These include: the superscription (1.1), ויאמר (3.1), and the reference to Babylon in 4.10bα. Mays, *Micah*, p. 3, argues that the discernible pattern in the material is the result of deliberate effort to use all the parts to say something. He dates this final effort to the fifth century BCE. There is little consensus as to the redactional process that results in the final form. Wolff, *Micah*; Renaud, *La Formation*; Lescow 'Micha 1–5'; *idem*, 'Micha 6–7'; Willi-Plein, *Vorformen der Schriftexegese*, pp. 70-114. This study acknowledges the importance of identifying the redactional elements and sees the potential value of this identification as part of the larger effort of discerning conceptuality and coherence of the final form. However, the reconstruction of the redactional process lies outside the scope of this study. Remarks about the redactional elements will therefore be limited and included only as necessitated by the larger task of discerning the conceptual coherence of the book.

8.   Cf. James Nogalski, *Literary Precursors to the Book of the Twelve* (BZAW, 217; New York: W. de Gruyter, 1993). See Knierim, *Text and Concept*, p. 6, for a discussion of reconceptualization and recontextualization.

The coherence of the macro-structure presupposes both an understanding and incorporation of the distinct aspects of the micro-structure.
However, it does not assume the existence of the same degree of
coherence at all levels of either the macro- or micro-structure. On the
macro-structural level, indicators of coherence may include the interrelationship of structural elements, namely, generic features, formulas,
transitional phrases and thought progression.[9] The appearance, frequency, particularity or typicality of the generic features, as well as the
interrelationship of these elements, are functions of the text's conceptuality and therefore of its coherence. Nonetheless, the coherence is
not dictated by the mere appearance, frequency, or even the typicality
of the generic features.

The appearance and frequency of various features and indicators
have contributed to multivalency in the interpretation of their function
and significance. In the book of Micah, the indicators include: the
'summons to hear' formula (שמעו־נא/שמעו, 1.2; 3.1, 9; 6.1-2, 9); language and generic features of the dispute (1.2-7; 6.1-8) and the judgment speeches (2.1-11; 3.1-12; 6.9-16); woe oracles and lament (1.8;
2.1-5; 7.1-6); oracles of hope (2.12-13; 4–5; 7.7-20); and various types
of transitional formulas/phrases, for example, ואמר (3.1aα); והיה באחרית
הימים (4.1aα); ביום ההוא (4.6); והיה ביום ההוא (5.9). The interrelationship of these indicators in conjunction with the thought progression in
the book of Micah exhibit distinctive clues to understanding of the
macro-structure. Therefore, it is a vital part of the task of structural
analysis that these interrelationships be understood. The importance of
this task lies in the fact that the text itself does not specify the nature of
the interrelationships but suggests it via the indicators.[10] Thus, the
following proposal of the macro-structure is accompanied by some
observations regarding the cohesion of the various units. These observations are based on an understanding of the grammatical and syntactical features and the interrelationship of the structural and conceptual
elements of the book of Micah.

9.   Cf. Cuffey, 'Coherence of Micah', for a discussion of what he calls the
various types of coherence.
10.   Knierim, 'Conceptual Aspects in Exodus 25:1-9', p. 389.

Macro-structure[11]

Yahweh's Disputes With Israel Concerning Israel's Fate

2. *Delimitation of the Text*

a. *Formulas and transition phrases*

Chapters 1–5 and 6–7. The repetition of a given formula within a text is itself not indicative of the significance of that formula to the macro-structure. With respect to the summonses to hear in the book of Micah —שִׁמְעוּ/שִׁמְעוּ־נָא, 1.2; 3.1, 9; 6.1-2, 9—it must be considered whether or not all instances of the formula function as indicators of a macro-structural unit. This task entails two aspects: discerning the relationship of the summonses to hear to other generic and conceptual features, and then discerning the place of the unit in the book of Micah, that is, the units created by the conceptuality and signaled by the relationship of the various indicators and by their distinctive function.

At this point, the following statement is given as a disclaimer, lest it appears that essential aspects of the book of Micah are being minimized to incidental accessories. The identification of aspects of the text as

---

11. See Appendix for author's translation. Note that the versifications are based on the MT. All other scriptural quotations are from the NRSV unless otherwise indicated.

indicators in no way lessens their grammatical, syntactical, conceptual, generic, or formulaic nature, but rather recognizes their functional and literary nature as essentially constitutive of the book's conceptuality.

While possibly indicative of divisions, the occurrences of the summonses may not all be indicative of major divisions. The interpretation of the relationship of the summonses the units they mark off and the place of the units in the macro-structure are areas of ambivalence in the reconstruction of the macro-structure. Thus, for example, Willis notes that the summonses in 1.2, 3.1 and 6.1 are indicators of major divisions in his ABA pattern (A, 1–2; B, 3–5; A, 6–7); but he accounts for its occurrence in 3.9 only as a summary of 3.1-4, 5-8. This is consistent with his proposal that ch. 3 consists of three small units (namely, 3.1-4, 5-8, 9-12).[12] While there may be three units as identified by Willis, the absence of the summons in 3.5 along with its presence in the two adjacent units are not clearly accounted for by this interpretation of the relationship of the summons to the other aspects of the text—that is, 3.1-12.

Allen, who generally follows Willis's proposal of macro-structure, notes the similarities of the summonses in 1.2 and 6.1: that they mark off units whose language is from the legal setting, and whose contents are similar—that is, both contain Yahweh's accusation against his people and end with a hope section. On the same basis, Allen argues that the occurrence in 3.1 constitutes a major division; while on the basis of its genre (judgment speech) and the presence of the accusation against Israel, a legal setting is attributed to 3.1-12. Yet while these aspects are also present in 3.9 and 6.9, these occurrences are considered to be secondary—that is, not indicative of a major division.[13]

Much like Willis and Allen, Hagstrom notes that the attribution of the summons in 3.9 as secondary is defensible. He argues this on the grounds that 3.9 is resumptive and is a marker that signals the climax of the unit—that is, 3.1-12. However, he does not hold the opinion that the summons in 6.9 is secondary.[14] Herein lies the significance of his analysis. He seeks to discern the distinctive uses of the summonses and to further discern how the interrelationship of the various units are signaled by these summonses. Toward this end, he observes that while the theophany in 1.2 is lacking in 6.1 both summonses share some similarities: both lack introduction, have addressees, refer to legal witnesses,

12. Willis, 'Structure, Setting', pp. 274-75.
13. Allen, *The Books*, pp. 257-58.
14. Hagstrom, *The Coherence*, pp. 23-25.

and contain an accusation. Both instances are modified by a narrow-
ing of focus achieved by the repetition of the summonses in 3.1 and
9; 6.9.[15]

Following Hagstrom's line of thought concerning the distinctive
functions of the summons, it is argued here that perhaps the issue of 3.9
is better explained as an indicator of the second unit in ch. 3—the first,
3.1-8, the second, 3.9-12—more so than as resumptive of 3.1 or climatic of 3.1-4 and 5-8. The basis for this argument includes several
observations: the lack of the summons in 3.5 as well as the shared focus
of 3.1-4 and 3.5-8 (the leaders) vis-à-vis that of 3.9 (the city of Jerusalem). The summonses in 3.1, 9 and 6.9 are understood here as means of
focusing attention on a particular group or aspect of the whole. As such,
the larger focus signaled at the outset of the unit is retained. Thus, the
context of 3.1, 9 is still universal to the extent that all peoples are
summoned—שמעו עמים כלם (1.2)—that is, while attention is focused
on Israel's leaders and Jerusalem as part of that universal scope of
Yahweh's activities. This is not a refocus of attention which may suggest change or a periodic absence of the focus. Rather, it is a tightening
of the focus achieved by the magnification of a particular sub-group of
the larger group that is already indicated at the beginning of the unit,
that is, שמעו עמים כלם (1.2). Furthermore, while their addressees are
essentially the same and their immediately juxtaposed units are both
judgment speeches, these two summonses (3.1, 9) focus on different
aspects of the leaders' responsibility. It is this difference of focus,
together with the summonses, that sets the units apart from each other.

Likewise, the summons in 6.9 represents a tightening of the focus
and is a part of an introduction to a judgment speech. Israel is the larger
focus and in 6.9 the 'city' becomes the focal point. Israel as the people
of God is no less the focus as indicated by the conclusion in 7.20 where
the language of the 'covenant relationship' is present.

In spite of its relative dominance as a structural indicator, by itself
the summons (שמעו־נא/שמעו) may not be as decisive to the macro-structure as its interrelationship with other aspects of the book of Micah. The
decisiveness of this aspect—and any aspect for that matter—is due not
merely to its occurrence, frequency, salience, or typicality, but to its
relationship with other aspects.

15. Hagstrom, *The Coherence*, pp. 25-26.

In this brief consideration of the summonses, some groupings are already apparent. These groupings are based on the perceived relationship of the summonses with their immediately adjacent units. The immediately adjacent units to 1.2 and 6.2 are disputes, while judgment speeches are introduced by 3.1, 9 and 6.9. The focus of 1.2 and 6.2 is broad when compared to that of the units they precede.

Therefore, in considering the significance of the summons to hear to the macro-structure, it is observed that its relationship with the language and typical generic features of the 'dispute'—signaled by the '*rîb* pattern'—may be significant to the macro-structure. Yet in light of the preponderance of proposals on the subject[16] and the lack of consensus on the nature of the form, an attempt to clarify what is meant here by *rîb* is fundamental to this analysis.

Bovati notes that the *rîb* has three parts: (a) the beginning, which consists of the accusation; (b) the development, in which one or two aspects are present (the accused confess guilt or protest innocence); and (c) the conclusion, wherein there is either some form of reconciliation or declaration of war.[17] Willis contends that *rîb*—lawsuit—consists of a summons (1.2; 6.1-2), an accusation (1.5; 6.3) in the form of rhetorical

---

16. Herbert B. Huffmon, 'The Covenant Lawsuit in the Prophets', *JBL* 78 (1959), pp. 285-95; J. Harvey, 'Le "rîb-pattern": requisitoire prophétique sur la rapture de l'alliance', *Bib* 43 (1962), pp. 172-96; James Limburg, 'The Root ריב and the Prophetic Lawsuit Speeches', *JBL* 88 (1969), pp. 291-304; George W. Ramsey, 'Speech-Forms in Hebrew Law and Prophetic Oracles', *JBL* 96 (1977), pp. 45-58; K. Nielsen, *Yahweh as Prosecutor and Judge* (JSOTSup, 9; Sheffield: JSOT Press, 1978); Michael de Roche 'Yahweh's Rîb Against Israel: A Reassessment of the So-Called "Prophetic Lawsuit" in the Re-Exilic Prophets', *JBL* 102 (1983), pp. 563-74; D.R. Daniels, 'Is there a "Prophetic Lawsuit" Genre?', *ZAW* 99 (1987), pp. 339-60. Most recently the work of Pietro Bovati, *Re-Establishing Justice: Legal Terms, Concepts and Procedures in the Hebrew Bible* (trans. M. Smith; JSOTSup, 105; Sheffield: JSOT Press, 1994), pp. 23, 42-43, attempts to clarify the nature of the *rîb* noting the distinctive vocabulary, forms, and stages of the *rîb*. Cf. Sweeney, *Isaiah 1–39*, pp. 541-42. He refers to the 'trial genres' of which the trial speech—identified by the *rîb* pattern—is a form usually consisting of: a call to attention, appeal for legal proceeding, rhetorical questions, and announcement of judgment or in some cases an instruction. For further consideration of the form see: G.W. Anderson, 'A Study of Micah 6.1-8', *SJT* 4 (1951), pp. 191-97; A. Deissler, 'Micha 6, 1-8: Der Rechtsstreit Jahwes mit Israel um das rechte Bundesverhältnis', *TTZ* 68 (1959), pp. 229-34.

17. Bovati, *Re-Establishing Justice*, pp. 32-33; cf. Sweeney, *Isaiah 1–39*, pp. 541-42.

questions, and an indictment or declaration of sin (1.6-7; 6.4-5). He observes that while 6.1-8 in its lack of an announcement of judgment appears to be unlike 1.2-7,[18] that is, the announcement is not missing.[19] The apparent departure from the typical generic form of the lawsuit is explained by Willis as a difference in *Sitz im Leben*—cultic (6.1-8) vs. legal (1.2-7). Willis further reasons that 'just as the prophet is about to announce the divine punishment, when he is about to remind Israel of certain mighty acts of Yahweh in the framework of Davidic tradition, his hearers interrupt him'.[20] Accordingly, he reasons that 6.9 resumes the summons, and that the anticipated announcement of judgment comes in 6.13-15. This continuation, according to Willis, is also marked by the contrast of Israel's behavior (6.9-12) with Yahweh's requirement (6.8).[21]

This brief mention of the dispute already indicates that like the appearance of the summons to hear, its distinctiveness in the present context needs to be examined. While all points of the current discussion about the dispute will not be reiterated here, it is necessary to indicate the perspective of the present writer. In following Shaw[22] and Bovati,[23] it is here argued that 1.2 and 6.1-2 indicate a dispute or controversy. Essential to the dispute is its bilateral nature, where one party is displeased with another and voices the discontent in the form of an accusation. The legitimacy of the dispute is constituted by the relationship between the parties involved.[24] Likewise, any resolution of the dispute also comes out of this relationship and the parties' recognition and/or acceptance of the relationship and its conditions. In 1.2-7 the summons signals the parameters as being universal in scope—that is, in the sense that the summons is issued to all peoples. All peoples are subject to

18. Willis, 'Structure, Setting', p. 262. Harvey, 'Le "*rîb*-pattern"', pp. 178, 188, who contends that this lack of announcement of salvation is due to the special nature of the *rîb*, that is, that the omission indicatives that it is an ultimatum issued to subordinates by the suzerain.

19. Smith, *Micah, Zephaniah*, p. 122, assumes that the announcement of judgment is lost.

20. Willis, 'Structure, Setting', p. 262, points to 2.6-7 as another case of interruption.

21. Willis, 'Structure, Setting', p. 264; cf. Shaw, *Speeches of Micah*, p. 182.

22. Shaw, *Speeches of Micah*, p. 182; cf. de Roche, 'Yahweh's *Rîb* Against Israel', pp. 563-74.

23. Bovati, *Re-Establishing Justice*, p. 34.

24. Bovati, *Re-Establishing Justice*, p. 34.

God's witness against them. Furthermore, the theophany establishes the universal scope of God's appearance in human history, thus noting God as God of all peoples and the earth. Placed within this framework, the dispute homes in on Samaria's and Jerusalem's fates, fates influenced by their deeds (1.5). The articulation of the announcement connects the judgment with the accusation in such a way as to suggest the justification of the punishment. This portrayal of the justification, in this instance as in others, is a form of acknowledging the legitimacy of Yahweh's dispute with the accused concerning their fate.

It is not being argued that all the elements of the macro-structure conform to the typical structure of the 'dispute'. The argument is that the dispute sets off the major parts of the whole and provides the framework for understanding the content of the parts. Conceptually, this framework presumes the displeasure of Yahweh with the accused and the confrontation of the accused concerning their deeds. Each of the major parts consists of the dispute proper (1.2-7; 6.1-8), judgment speech(es) (3.1-12; 6.9-16), the lament (1.8-16; 2.1-5; 7.1-7), and hope oracle(s) (2.12-13; 4.1-5; 7.7-20). While the units do not mirror each other's order and form, the thought progression in each raises questions concerning the fate of the accused and offers responses to those questions. Notably, the relative symmetry of the two units may be a supportive argument for the two-fold division; however, the presence or absence of such symmetry is not necessary to the macro-structure.

Conceptually, the dispute is constituted by observations concerning the dynamics of deeds and consequences which are constitutive of the nature and extent of the existence of the accused. The observations are first signaled by the implicit comparison of Samaria and Jerusalem (1.8-9) and then by the pairing of the concepts of judgment and hope.

Table 3. *Generic Features Shared by the Units in the Macro-Structure*

Features	Location	
Summons to hear	1.2	6.1-2
Dispute	1.2-7	6.1-8
Lament	1.8-16	7.1-6
Woe oracle	2.1-5	7.1-6
Judgment Speech	3.1-12	6.9-16
Oracle of Hope	2.12-13; 4.1-5.14	7.7-20

Chapters 1–3 and 4–5. The connection between chs. 1–3 and 4–5 is not signaled by a summons. Instead, it is signaled by the temporal transition

formula וְהָיָה בְּאַחֲרִית הַיָּמִים. In this instance, the formula introduces a time in the remote future which, in the perspective of the text, is still a matter of hope. According to DeVries, the formula has a variety of 'patterns of time relationships', indicating a sequence from one event to another'.[25] Among these is the sequence from 'an implied present to a remote future' as in the case of Mic. 4.1-4//Isa. 2.2-4. The implied present is the state of judgment initiated by the announcement of judgment in 3.12.

Syntactically, וְהָיָה marks the transition from the implied present to the future announced by the temporal transition formula. Its function is adversative, reflecting the contrast between the preceding and the following, that is, the present and the future. This introductory transition formula is paired with a focus on Zion—on both sides of the division (3.12 and 4.1-5). However, the Zion tradition is presented from different perspectives—the announcement of judgment on the presumed indestructible Zion (3.11-12), and the future exaltation of Zion (4.1-5).[26] It has been argued by some scholars (e.g. Willis), that the nature of the difference between the two passages disallows for a break between them. Therefore, on the basis of his commitment to find the symmetry of all major units, Willis proposes that 3.9–4.5 constitutes a single unit with two sub-units: 3.9-12 (doom) and 4.1-5 (hope).[27]

While I am in agreement with Willis's observation of the contrasting perspectives between 3.9-12 and 4.1-5, I would argue further that the break between chs 3 and 4 is not a major division. It is a sub-division of the unit constituted by chs. 1–5. However, the division between chs. 3 and 4 is supported in large measure by the presence of the temporal transition formula between the two units. As to why a division on the same level is not made between 2.11 and 2.12-13, it is proposed that 2.12-13 is indicative of a 'semi-climax'.[28] That is to say that the major focus of the unit formed by chs. 1–5 is the fate of Israel the nation, of which Jerusalem/Zion is the center. Both 1.5, 1.6-7 indicate this focus: the

25. DeVries, *From Old Revelation to New*, pp. 89-93, he discusses the various uses of the formula including the non-formulaic uses as 'time identifiers' rather than transitions. Cf. *idem, Yesterday, Today, and Tomorrow* (Grand Rapids: Eerdmans, 1975).

26. Ben C. Ollenburger, *Zion the City of the Great King: A Theological Symbol of the Jerusalem Cult* (JSOTSup, 41; Sheffield: JSOT Press, 1987).

27. Willis, 'Structure, Setting'.

28. Cf. Hagstrom, *The Coherence*, p. 85.

exile in 1.16 (and possibly 2.4) is cast within this framework. As such the oracle in 2.12-13 presupposes exile in its announcement of the restoration of the remnant. Chapter 2.12-13 is a completion of a second-ary element—though no less significant—and may be the first signal of hope concerning the fates of Jacob and Israel. The announcement in 3.12 and its close parallel to 1.6-7 further indicate the nature of the connection between the two chapters as well as the concern about Jeru-salem's future, that is, as compared to Samaria.

Chapters 4–5 as a unit then addresses the issue of Jerusalem's fate beyond the implied present disaster. In this way, the emphasis is on Zion, not as the exclusive providence of Israel's existence, but as the particular locale of Yahweh's reign in human history—and within this emphasis, the future of the nations (cf. 1.2). The characteristic feature of the reign is peace. The establishment of that reign entails restoration of the remnant (4.6-7)—signaled by the combination of the temporal transition formula (ביום ההוא) and divine utterance formula (נאם־יהוה) —and the purification of the nation (5.9-14)—signaled by the combina-tion of the temporal transition formula (והיה ביום ההוא) and the divine utterance formula (נאם־יהוה). The actualization of this reign proceeds by means of resolutions to the adverse situations of the present (4.8–5.8). Each situation is introduced by a transition formula: for example, ועתה, עתה, ואתה.

The interrelationships described thus far are represented in Figure 1. This figure shows some elements of the interrelationship between the units (□) containing the verses cited. The following interrelationships will be discussed below.

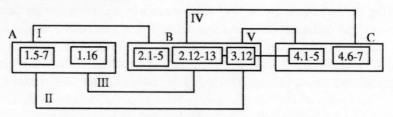

Figure 1. *The Interrelationship of Units in Chapters 1–5.*

The elements of Figure 1 are to be understood as follows:[29]

---

29. The designations A B C I II III IV V are not intended to represent the macro- or micro-structural designations. Instead, these are used in this instance only to identify the elements under discussion.

A   Chapter 1. The first chapter of Micah introduces the concern
     about the fates of Samaria and Jerusalem in light of their ways
     and Yahweh's displeasure with those ways (sins and crimes).

B   Chapters 2 and 3. This unit expands on the reason for Yah-
     weh's displeasure and contains announcements of judgment
     on Israel.

C   Chapters 4 and 5. As a unit it addresses the issue of Israel's
     existence beyond the state of judgment through its announce-
     ment of promise concerning the future.

I   1.5-7 and 2.1-5. The continuity is most readily indicated by
     the presence and function of the 'sin' vocabulary—חטאות, פשע
     (1.5); רע, און (2.1-5). As to their relationship, the occurrences
     in 1.5 are a part of a general statement which is expanded and
     specified in 2.1-2.

II   1.5-7 and 3.1-12. With regard to continuity, 3.1-12 makes
     explicit what is signaled in 1.5-7 in a general way. Both regard
     the sins of Israel; however, a further relationship is observable
     between the announcement of judgment in 1.6 and 3.12.
     Notably, while the language and imagery of the judgment is
     similar, 1.6 is concerned with Samaria, 3.12 is concerned with
     Jerusalem, ציון שדה (1.6); ושמתי שמרון לעי השדה למטעי כרם
     תחרש וירושלם עיין תהיה (3.12).

III 1.16 and 2.12-13. The reality of exile is mentioned in 1.16 and
     presupposed in 2.12-13. In the latter, the gathering of the
     remnant suggests a previous state of dispersion. In neither case
     is the agent of the exile mentioned.

IV   2.12-13 and 4.6-7. These units share a concern for the remnant
     (שארית). While the state of dispersion is presupposed in 2.12-
     13, it is mentioned in 4.6-7. In the latter case, the agent who
     disperses also creates the remnant—namely, Yahweh.

V   3.12 and 4.1-5. Though they represent different aspects of the
     existence of Jerusalem/Zion, both focus on Jerusalem/Zion.

b. *Conceptual continuity*

Elements of the continuity within chs. 1–5 are shown in Figure 1. These
are directly and indirectly indicated in various ways, including shared
vocabulary and concepts, generic features, grammar, and syntax. Furthermore, the continuity is more than the juxtaposition of units. As
such, continuity may be exhibited by units that are separated in the overall structure by intervening units. These intervening units may expand,

complement and/or conclude the preceding unit while introducing and anticipating other units. That an immediate juxtaposition is not necessary to continuity, is essential to its conceptual nature.

The first dispute, introduced by the dispute proper (1.2-5), is set within the universal scope of Yahweh's activity. Samaria and Jerusalem are parts of this scope. They become the focus as the reason for Yahweh's intervention (1.3-4). This focus is continued and modified in ch. 2 which specifies the sins (חטאות, 1.5) of Israel and begins to answer the question concerning Israel's fate as influenced by its sins, that is, the question implied by 1.5-7.

The first attention to the specifics of Israel's sin concerns the land and the oppression of the people by those with power (2.1-5). The continuity within this unit is signaled by לכן, a device used here and elsewhere to depict the just nature of the judgment. In this way, a correspondence of the sin and the judgment is indicated.[30] Yet the announcement of the judgment is met with some opposition (2.6-11). In its present context, 2.12-13 as a unit is an announcement of promise which addresses the fate of Israel. Its perspective is that there is hope, insofar as the existence of Israel will not be terminated by the judgment, but will be preserved through a remnant. This concept of Israel's hope as signified by the remnant is again addressed in 4.6-7 and 5.6-8.

The conceptual continuity extends on through ch. 3 in the further specification of the sins of Israel (1.5). The announcement of Zion's destruction in 3.12, like 2.12-13, addresses the issue of Israel's fate and specifically the temporal extent of this fate in relation to Yahweh's reign (chs. 4–5). The argument is that conceptual continuity is a factor of the units' coherence. The conceptuality of chs. 1–5 is Israel's fate in light of Israel's sin and Yahweh's response to the sin (see Chapter 4 of this study).

The focus of the second part of the book of Micah (chs. 6–7) is on a different aspect—the particular relationship of Israel and Yahweh. This is made more explicit in the nature of this dispute (6.3-5) regarding Yahweh's requirement (6.8). Micah 6.8 performs double duty by looking back to earlier parts—'you plot evil' (2.2); 'is it not for you to know justice?' (3.1)—and forward to the judgment on the 'city' (6.9-16) because of the sin of those who engaged in deceitful economic practices. Here, as in chs. 1–5, the correspondence between sin and judgment

---

30. See Chapters 4, 5 and 6 of this study for further discussion.

is noted (6.9-16; 7.9). From the text's perspective, hope is again born out of Yahweh's character and not the presumption of the innocence of the accused or Yahweh repentance for judgment—just or unjust. The language of the text, seen mainly in the attention to 'sin' and Yahweh's response to it, links the two parts of the book, each part bringing into focus judgment and hope constituted by Yahweh's response to sin. Thus, to the questions concerning whether or not the fate of Israel is sealed by the sin–judgment dynamics, the text suggests that while the sin–judgment dynamics are constitutive elements in that fate, these dynamics are not its sole determinant.

Addendum: *On 'Fate'*

It is necessary to clarify the use of the term 'fate' in this discussion. It is used to indicate the nature of existence as influenced and shaped by humans and God. This nature includes the extent and quality of that existence. Furthermore, 'fate' is essentially a dynamic process. The term is not used here with the exclusively deterministic nuance commonly associated with it. Rather its dynamic nature is that which is being observed. As a basis for the observation, it is further noted that the dynamics are shaped qualitatively and quantitatively by the relative influence of those involved in the process. However, those involved do not all have the same degree of influence on the process at every point in the process. Their relative influence is defined both by their role and their capacity to influence realities. It is this aspect that potentially questions the extent to which parties of unequal capacity can be equally involved in influencing the dynamic process of their existence. Nonetheless, the outcome of the process is not determined by any single participant or observer. Nor is the outcome a static unalterable reality. What constitutes an outcome at one point in the process is a part or a beginning of another aspect of the process. As such, one reality may have different significance in the process although its essence is unchanged. As I define it, what is essential to 'fate' is the possibility for change in the process. 'Fate' by this definition is then a dynamic reality. Furthermore, the influence on the process is not limited to intentional efforts to influence that process since change itself is not contingent upon intention. What is contingent is the nature of the change such that one always influences the process. Since to be in the process itself influences it consciously or unconsciously, deliberately or inadvertently, the dynamics of the process of existence are perpetually influenced.

Fate, by its very nature, facilitates hope insofar as the possibility for change is essential to hope.

Micro-Structure

1. *Proposal*

This proposal is about the structural analysis of the text (see Chapter 3 above for further details). It represents the conceptual flow of the book of Micah by expanding each of the macro-structural levels. The goal of this part of the study is to demonstrate the various levels at which the text exhibits coherence. Each of these levels is constituted by a unit in the text, for example, I.A. (second level) is represented by 1.2-16 (text unit). The proposal made about the macro-structure above in this chapter also holds true of the micro-structure, namely, that the units of the structure are interdependent and to be understood as a part of a larger conceptual framework which accounts for their distinctive uses and place in the hierarchical structure. The system of hierarchical headings is as follows: I.A.1.a.1)a)(1)(a)α.aa. While each segment of the discussion is marked by the indication of the level of the text in the hierarchy (e.g. I.A.1.a.), the reader is strongly encouraged to keep Chapter 3 as reference while reading through Chapters 4 and 5.

Yahweh's Disputes with Israel Concerning Israel's Fate
Superscription	1.1
I. First Dispute	1.2–5.14
A. Introduction	1.2-16
1. Dispute proper—the sins of Samaria and Jerusalem	1.2-7
a. Introduction	1.2-4
1) Summons to hear (שמעו)	1.2
2) Theophany report	1.3-4
b. Accusation—reason for the divine intervention (כי)	1.5
c. Announcement of judgment (on Samaria)	1.6-7
2. Response to the announcement of judgment	1.8-16
a. Introduction—prophet's lament	1.8-9
1) Declaration of intent to lament (...אספדה ואילילה)	1.8
2) Statement of the reason for the lament (כי)	1.9
b. Expansion of the lament	1.10-16
1) Admonition to the nations	1.10-15
2) Conclusion—call to lament	1.16
B. Concerning Israel's Fate	2.1–5.14
1. Present: Israel's sin and impending judgment	2.1–3.12
a. Oppression regarding the land	2.1-13
1) Woe oracle (הוי)	2.1-11

2. *Observations Concerning the Nature and Limits of the Units*

One of the goals of these observations is to identify the distinctiveness of the various units and how they function together. The observations examine the genres of the units, their vocabulary and conceptuality. Another goal of the observations is to justify the limits of the units in preparation for Chapters 4–6 of this study. See above under the heading *Macro-Structure* for the method involved in justifying the units.

a. *1.1: Superscription*

The superscription introduces the content of the book as the word of Yahweh. Through its mention of the kings—מלכי יחזקיה אחז יותם יהודה—it locates this prophetic activity in the pre-exilic period. It also establishes the focus of the book—Samaria and Jerusalem—אשר־חזה על־שמרון וירושלם.

b. *1.2–5.14*

This unit consists of two main sections: 1.2–3.12 and 4.1–5.14. The first indicator of a new unit is the summons to hear in 1.2. This introduces the unit of 1.3–5.14 which is further sub-divided into 1.3–3.12 and chs. 4–5.

1.2-16. The unit functions as an introduction to chs. 2–5 in several ways. First, it establishes the basis for the immediate intervention of God as the פשע of Jacob and חטאות of the house of Israel. The general statement regarding the reason for the intervention (v. 5) is paired with the announcement of judgment against Samaria in vv. 6-7. Second, in its use of the vocabulary for sin (פשע and חטא), it signals the concern that is mirrored in chs. 2–3. Third, the universal framework is carried through to chs. 4–5 where the nations, as a part of God's plan in history, are brought into focus. Finally, the introduction of the lament in 1.8 and the reason (1.9), raise the question concerning the fate of

Jerusalem as compared to that of Samaria against whom judgment had been announced (1.6-7). A hint about that fate is in 1.16. Chapters 2–3 and 4–5 are then responses to the question underlying 1.8-9.

Micah 1.2 is a summons constituted by distinctive elements, namely, the summons to hear formula (שמעו), the identification of the addressees (עמים כלם הקשיבי ארץ ומלאה, v. 2a), and in this case, a statement of the reason for the summons (ויהי אדני יהוה בכם לעד, v. 2b), as well as an appositive to the subject (אדני יהוה) named in the purpose clause (אדני מהיכל קדשו, v. 2bβ).

The purpose clause כי הנה indicates the connection of the unit, vv. 3-4, to the preceding (v. 2). Verses 3-4 present a theophany report indicating Yahweh's departure from 'his place' (v. 3a—יהוה יצא ממקומו), Yahweh's destination and activity (וירד ודרך על־במותי־ארץ, v. 3b), and the effects of the intervention (v. 4). The effects are first described (ונמסו ההרים תחתיו, v. 4aα; והעמקים יתבקעו, v. 4aβ)—then followed by similes that further describe the effects (כדונג מפני האש, v. 4bα; כמים מגרים במורד, v. 4bβ). The immediate reason for the present intervention is signaled by the phrase כל־זאת (v. 5aα) whose logical antecedent is vv. 3-4.

The connection of v. 5 and vv. 6-7 is not indicated by a connective particle such as לכן (cf. 2.3, 5; 3.6, 12; 6.13 [וגם]). However, its logical connection is signaled by the conjunction (ו), which in this instance carries with it the meaning of לכן. The judgment on Samaria is announced in vv. 6-7 and expanded via the lament in vv. 8-16 (על־זאת אספדה). Possibly, על־זאת presupposes the judgment in vv. 6-7. This proposal supports those who attribute an anaphoric meaning to the phrase (cf. Jer. 2.12; 4.8; Amos 7.3, 6; 8.8).[31] The anaphoric meaning then sees the referent of על־זאת as vv. 6-7 rather than the content of v. 9. The כי-clause in v. 9 may be an expansion of the statement in v. 8, thus pro-

---

31. Cf. Wolff, *Micah*, pp. 47-48; Hillers, *Micah*, p. 22, who divides the unit into: 2–7; 8–9; 10–16. See also Richard Lux, 'An Exegetical Study of Micah 1.8-16' (unpublished PhD dissertation, University of Notre Dame, 1976), p. 78, who proposes 1.1, 2-4, 5-7, 8-16 with vv. 8-9 serving as an introduction to vv. 10-16. Mays, *Micah*, p. 50, proposes that v. 8 is not a conclusion to the preceding verses but an introduction to the lament section (vv. 10-16). His argument is centered on whether or not the judgment is presumed to have happened. However, whether or not the judgment has happened, the perspective of v. 8 is that the prophet will lament either at the prospect of the destruction or at the reality of it. The reason is the destruction—imminent or actual.

viding further reason for the lament. The lament is expanded in vv. 10-
15 and culminates in the call to mourn concerning the impending
exile (v. 16).

2.1–3.12. The continuity between of chs. 1 and 2 is not made apparent
by a transitional formula (cf. 3.1). Instead, an apparent modification of
focus is indicated in the address to specific groups (חשבי־און ופעלי רע)
in contrast to the general audience summoned in 1.2 (עמים כלם הקשיבי
ארץ ומלאה) and the nations mentioned in 1.5-9 (בית ישראל and יעקב).
Thus the focus is continually sharpened.

2.1-5. This unit is a woe oracle concerning those who plan and execute
evil (הוי חשבי־און). Here additional information is made explicit regarding the nature of the sins referred to in 1.5. The woe oracle conveys the
accusation in the form of the participial phrases (חשבי־און ופעלי רע).
The announcement of judgment introduced by the לכן of 2.3 uses the
same language as the accusation. In this way, the connection between
the sin and the judgment is also made evident. Verse 4 uses the temporal formula ביום ההוא to indicate temporal relationships between the
components of the judgment. The formula ביום ההוא usually occurs in
instances where 'a new event expands or modifies the event of the
material to which it is attached'.[32] The two events or time periods are
'roughly synchronous with each other'.[33] As such, the time frame introduced by v. 4 would mostly likely be that introduced by the announcement of judgment in v. 3.[34] The לכן in v. 5 indicates a logical and
syntactical dependence of this verse on the preceding vis-à-vis the
following (that is, vv. 6-11).

2.6-11. The command at the beginning of v. 6 (אל־תטפו) signals a
switch from the 3rd person account of the announcement of judgment

---

32. DeVries, *From Old Revelation to New*, p. 52.
33. DeVries, *From Old Revelation to New*, p. 52.
34. DeVries, *From Old Revelation to New*, pp. 52-55. He discusses the various
uses of ביום ההוא. He notes, for example, that among the various uses are the non-
formulaic futuristic uses as simple time-designatives (Exod. 8.18 [Eng. v. 22]; Deut.
31.17; 1 Kgs 13.3; 22.25//2 Chron. 18.24; Isa. 3.7; 5.30; 19.21, and so on). These
he proposes, 'appears in the secondary rather than primary position within syntactical structure' (p. 39). Another indicator of a simple time-designative is the absence
of a prophetic utterance formula נאם־יהוה and/or the presence of a futuristic והיה
preceding ביום ההוא. Cf. *idem*, *Yesterday, Today, and Tomorrow*.

to a 2nd person response of the announcement. Likewise, vv. 6-11 display a conversational mode in contrast to the declarative mode of the previous and following units. Its form is typical of the disputation, consisting of the opposing perspectives of the prophet on the one hand and the opponents to the prophetic announcement on the other.[35] This disputation speech represents the opponents' perspective (vv. 6-7) and the prophets' perspective and counter argument in vv. 8-11. The characterization of the misdeeds using the language of oppression and imagery of dispossession shared by the accusation in 2.1-2, shows continuity between the units.

2.12-13. A break occurs in vv. 12-13 as indicated by the switch from the 3rd person account in v. 11 to the 1st person address in v. 12. The change in subject matter between vv. 6-11 and vv. 12-13 as well as a change in speaker are also indicative of the new unit. In its use of Jacob and Israel it is connected to ch. 1 (1.5). The use of אָסֹף אֶאֱסֹף with קַבֵּץ אֲקַבֵּץ suggests gathering as the dominant imagery more so than removal or destruction (cf. Zeph. 1.2 where אָסֹף is associated with other words denoting destruction). The reference to the remnant (שְׁאֵרִית) as those whom Yahweh will gather (קַבֵּץ אֲקַבֵּץ)[36] presupposes a state of dispersion, for example, the exile mentioned in 1.16. In its concern with the gathering of the remnant, it anticipates 4.6-7 and in a more general way 5.6-8. The coherence of this unit is its concern with the remnant. The indicators do not readily suggest how this unit may be construed in relation to the preceding and the following units.

There is little question about the coherence of 2.12-13, but a debate persists concerning the coherence of the unit of which this is a part. The basic problem is that vv. 12-13, interpreted as an oracle of hope, seems to interrupt the focus on judgment achieved in 2.1-11 and 3.1-12. In response to the problem, several suggestions have been offered including Willis's proposal to make a major division after 2.13. With that proposal, 2.12-13 is taken as the hope section to the previous unit

---

35. A. Graffy, *A Prophet Confronts his People* (AnBib, 104; Rome: Biblical Institute Press, 1984); cf. D.F. Murray, 'The Rhetoric of Disputation: Re-Examination of a Prophetic Genre', *JSOT* 38 (1987), pp. 95-121.

36. C.L. Feinberg 'אסף', in *TWOT*, I, pp. 60-61. Note Zeph. 1.2, 3 and Jer. 8.13 concerning the use of אָסֹף אָסֵף. What is the significance of the use and the implication for the interpretation of this text? Is this a text about exile, restoration, or both? See discussion in Chapter 4 of this study.

1.2–2.11.[37] Others have opted to transpose the passage to the section of hope in chs. 4–5, and specifically between 4.6-7 and 4.8-14.[38]

3.1-12. The specification of the sins of Israel is continued in ch. 3. The connection to ch. 2 is indicated by its conceptual continuity and the presence of the verbal clause ויאמר, which is most often attributed to a redactor. Willis proposes that it is a transitional element intended by the redactor to create a new arrangement of the units. His division between chs. 2 and 3 is based in part on this observation.[39]

The present writer proposes that ויאמר in this final form presupposes a prior discussion to which it is responding. The closest such discussion is the disputation speech in 2.6-11. The contrast is therefore set up between this falsehood (cf. 2.6-7) and the message of the prophet as presented in ch. 3. Yet ch. 3 is more than a response to the opponents. It is also the further specification of the reason for Yahweh's case against Israel, for which Yahweh has descended to argue.

Most scholars present a three-fold division of the ch. 3 on the basis of the three judgment speeches and their introductory formulas: שמעו־נא (vv. 1, 9) and כה אמר יהוה (v. 5). Thus they propose the divisions of ch. 3 to be vv. 1-4, 5-8 and 9-12.[40] While the textual signals are clear, they must be weighed in light of the conceptual signals, and further consideration must be given to the relationship of the units marked off by these signals. The question has to do with the extent to which a delimited unit has conceptual dissonance or consonance[41] with the other unit.

---

37. Willis, 'Structure, Setting'.

38. Renaud, *Structure*, pp. 20-25; *idem*, *La Formation*, pp. 404-408.

39. Willis, 'A Note on ויאמר', pp. 50-54.

40. Cheyne, *Micah*; Wolff, *Micah*; Mays, *Micah*; Hillers, *Micah*; *idem*, 'Micah', in *ABD*, IV, pp. 807-810; Smith, *Micah, Zephaniah*; Keil and Delitzsch, *The Twelve Minor Prophets*; Hagstrom, *The Coherence*; Allen, *The Books*; Procksch, *Die kleinen prophetischen Schriften*; Willis, 'Structure, Setting'; James Wolfendale, *A Homiletic Commentary on the Minor Prophets* (The Preacher's Complete Homiletic Commentary on the Old Testament, 20; New York: Funk & Wagnalis); René Vuilleumier, 'Michée', in C.-A. Keller (ed.), *Michée, Nahoum, Habacuc, Sophonie* (CAT; Neuchâtel: Delachaux & Niestlé, 1971), pp. 1-92; cf. Ewald, *Commentary on the Prophets*, pp. 302-304, 306, who places 3.1-4 with 2.11-12 so that the divisions are 2.11–3.4, 3.5-8; 3.9-12; Waltke, 'Micah', 3.1-4, 5-7, 8, 9-12.

41. Hagstrom, *The Coherence*, p. 3, adheres to the three-fold division despite his concern about the coherence of the text unit.

There are three occurrences of the formulas that indicate divisions in the text: the 'summons to hear' (שִׁמְעוּ־נָא) in vv. 1 and 9 and the messenger formula (כֹּה אָמַר יְהוָה) in v 5. Notably, vv. 1 and 9 are addressed to groups identified by almost identical designations. This fact is to be taken into consideration in order to assess whether or not vv. 1-4, 5-8 and 9-12 are units on the same level of the structure of the text.[42] A conclusion about this matter, however, cannot be made solely on the basis of the textual signals/indicators. A conclusion must be reached in conjunction with the conceptual indicators.

The present writer proposes that a two-fold division of ch. 3 be considered, that is, vv. 1-8 and vv. 9-12. The basis of such consideration is first the generic features and second the conceptual signals. Each summons marks off a unit which exhibits the typical form of a judgment speech.[43] However, the generic features do not by themselves signal the relationship of the units they introduce. The similarity of introductions in vv. 1 and 9 as compared to that in v. 5 is to be considered, but it is not the main criterion in assessing the relationship of the units. The basis of the two-fold division is largely conceptual and specifically concerned with the nature and scope of the judgment of each delimited unit. The units vv. 1-4 and 5-8 exhibit a correspondence of sin and judgment in which the focus is the leaders. The judgment portions of each of the units are focused on the leaders and shows an instrumental correspondence[44] between sin and judgment—that is, the means of the sin is the means of the judgment. (This will be discussed in further detail in Chapter 4 of this study.) Here it will suffice to say that in the unit consisting of vv. 9-12 the correspondence of sin and judgment is different from that in the two preceding units. In vv. 1-4 and 5-8 the leaders are judged because of their sin, while in vv. 9-12 the entire city

42. Wolff, *Micah*, p. 93, recognizes the similarity of the formulations in arguing for the congruity of the text. However, he does not consider the possibility of them being indicators of main divisions, that is, vv. 1-8, vv. 9-12. Yet he observes that the judgments in v. 4 and v. 6 are similar and together are different from that in v. 12.

43. Introduction + Accusation + Announcement of judgment; cf. Claus Westermann, *Basic Forms of Prophetic Speech* (trans. H.C. White; Louisville, KY: Westminster/John Knox Press, 1991), pp. 142-43.

44. Patrick D. Miller, *Sin and Judgment in the Prophets: A Stylistic and Theological Analysis* (SBLMS, 27; Chico, CA: Scholars Press, 1982), p. 109. He sees 3.1-4 as exhibiting talionic correspondence.

is the focus of the judgment although the leaders are the focus of the accusation.

3.1αβ-8. This unit consists of vv. 1-4 and vv. 5-8. Verses 1-4 may be further sub-divided into three units: v. 1aβ, vv. 1b-3 and v. 4. This subdivision exhibits the typical form of a judgment speech: the introduction (v. 1aβ) in this case is in the form of the 'summons to hear'. The accusation (vv. 1b-3) incorporates the rhetorical question (v. 1b) followed immediately by the relative participle, then continued by the finite verb in the 3rd person. The unity of this sub-unit is indicated by its use of the metaphor of cannibalism to depict the violent and oppressive practices of the leaders. Verse 4, the announcement of judgment, is introduced by the temporal transitional formula, אז, indicating the conceptual and syntactical connection of the v. 4 and vv. 1aβ-3.[45] The coherence of the unit is the concern with judgment as a consequence of sin.

Verses 5-8 form a judgment speech and are sub-divided into four parts as seen above. In contrast to vv. 1-4, the unit is introduced by the messenger formula כה אמר יהוה. Typically a quotation of the message would be expected (e.g. 2.3-5), but in this instance the message is deferred.[46] The messenger formula is followed by the accusation in the form of participial phrases functioning in apposition to the addressees named in v. 5aα. This description/accusation is similar to that in vv. 1-4 where the description also functions as accusation (cf. 2.1). Verses 6-7, the announcement of judgment, are introduced by לכן (cf. vv. 6–7 and

45. See Hagstrom, *The Coherence*, pp. 31-34, who sub-divides the unit into vv. 1a-2a, vv. 3a-e, 2bc (in light of the transposition of 2b+c) and v. 4a-d on the basis of the switch from 2nd to 3rd person between v. 2a and v. 3a, and the adverbial particle אז as indication of transition to v. 4a; Wolff, *Micah*, p. 971, sub-divides vv. 2a, 2b-3, 4; Allen, *The Books*, pp. 304-305, sub-divides vv. 1b-2a, 2b-3, 4; see Westermann, *Basic Forms*, p. 174 for the layout of the structure. Concerning the use of אז as a futuristic transition, see DeVries, *From Old Revelation to New*, p. 36. He notes that the use indicates a transition from the 'present to an approximate future'.

46. Hillers, *Micah*, p. 44, notes an argument that there is most likely a missing element the inclusion of which would restore to the text a smoother and more logical connection between the messenger formula and the following accusation. He therefore reconstructs הוי thus reading כה אמר יהוה הוי על... on the assumption of a haplography יהוה הוי (cf. Jer. 50.27; Ezek. 13.3). Cf. Hagstrom, *The Coherence*, p. 34; Allen, *The Books*, pp. 81-82; Lescow, 'Micha 1–5', pp. 48-49 who views the phrase as redactional; Willis, 'Structure and Setting', p. 274.

v. 12; vis-à-vis v. 4). This announcement employs parallel expressions with the dominant theme of the hiddenness of Yahweh. Verse 7 expands the announcement of the judgment. Unlike the expansion in v. 4bβ which gives the reason for the judgment, v. 7 presents the result of the judgment. The result itself is expressed by two verbs used in parallel expressions (v. 7a) to depict humiliation and consternation. These are followed by a further development of the expansion consisting of a description of the action demonstrative of the feeling of shame (v. 7aβ). The final expansion of the announcement of judgment is introduced by a ‏כי‎-clause, and takes the form of a reason for the judgment and its results. This sub-unit picks up the language and concept of the with-holding of revelation seen in v. 4aβ.[47]

Verse 8 in is present place in the text is an expansion of the judgment speech in vv. 5-7. Mostly, the question of the place of v. 8 in ch. 3 has at its root the question of its nature—for instance, the autobiographical note typical of a report of a 'call',[48] or the remains of a disputation speech. In this study, it is regarded as disputational in function. The presence of the adverbial particle ‏ואולם‎ links v. 8 syntactically to the preceding unit (vv. 5-7).[49] Conceptually, it continues the discussion about the prophets by presenting, in 1st person account, a strong anti-thetical statement about Micah the prophet as compared to the prophets addressed in v. 5 (cf. 2.6-11).

Thus, in both its vocabulary and theme v. 8 functions as a link be-tween vv. 5-7 and vv. 9-12. The terms ‏פשע‎ and ‏חטא‎ echo back to 1.5, 13—the articulation of the purpose for the impending judgment upon Israel. Conceptually, the judgments in vv. 1-4 and vv. 5-8 are closely related. In these two sub-units, the judgment is aimed at the destruction of that which sanctioned the leaders as leaders—namely, revelation from Yahweh. The source of their authorization will be destroyed resulting in

47. Notably, the text does not use the vocabulary typical of the concept of revelation: ‏גלה‎, ‏רצה‎ and ‏ידע‎. However, the concept is implicit in its depiction of the impending judgment. See Knierim, 'Revelation in the Old Testament', in *idem*, *Task of Old Testament Theology*, pp. 139-49, for discussion of the concept in relation to its semantic indicators.

48. Waltke, 'Micah', pp. 661-68, argues that 3.8 is an autobiographical note similar to Amos 7.14-15. Cf. Mays, *Micah*, pp. 84-85, in contrast to Wolff, *Micah*, who sees no allusion to 'call' here.

49. Hagstrom, *The Coherence*, p. 35.

the destruction of their role and identity in the community. In contrast to this, the judgment in vv. 9-12 is aimed at the city—Jerusalem (cf. 6.9-16). In this instance, the destruction of the city is the destruction of the false security of the leaders. This clearly suggests collective retribution for the sins of a few. The judgment is presented as a consequence of sin; however, the judgment has a wider focus than the sin it is intended to punish. Therein lies the point of dissonance between vv. 1-8 and vv. 9-12.

3.9-12. This sub-unit is introduced by a 'summons to hear' (שמעו־נא, v. 9a; cf. v. 1aβ). The sub-unit vv. 9b-11 constitutes the accusation expressed in general terms (v. 9b) and expanded in vv. 10-11. The leaders are characterized by their violation of משפט—presented in synthetically parallel expressions of the action (v. 10)—and the center of their actions —Jerusalem (cf. 1.5). Verse 11 itself has two components unified by reference to the leaders as violators of justice. Verse 11a depicts the violation by groups (ראשים, כהנים and נביאים). It is unified by its vocabulary used to refer to the acts of performing their various functions for personal compensation, namely, שחד 'bribe', מחיר 'price' and כסף 'silver'. It is also unified by its triple use of the 3rd person feminine pronominal suffix to refer to Jerusalem. So in both v. 10 and v. 11a, Jerusalem is at the center of the accusation. Verse 11b deals with the misconception of the leaders that predisposed them to practice the perversion of justice without concern about the adverse consequences of their practices. While there is no explicit mention of Jerusalem, by its allusion to the Zion tradition, the citation of the belief of the leaders brings into focus Jerusalem—the dwelling place of Yahweh.

Verse 12 is the announcement of judgment introduced by לכן (cf. v. 6). This is immediately followed by the reason for the judgment—it comes about because of the leaders accused in vv. 9-11. Thus, once again, the sin–judgment correspondence is illustrated in the form of the text. This correspondence is further indicated in the conceptual dependence of v. 12 (the judgment) on vv. 9-11 (the accusation). The second sub-division of this sub-unit consists of v. 12aβ-b. It is unified by its parallel articulations of the impending destruction of Zion/Jerusalem.

4.1–5.14. The unit formed by 4.1–5.14 is signaled both textually in its use of vocabulary and conceptually in its concern with the future. Textually, like ואמר in 3.1, והיה indicates a new unit while presupposing a preceding discussion.[50] It articulates a promise that itself presupposes the actualization of circumstances opposite to it. Such circumstances may be found in ch. 3. The unit is characterized by its use of temporal indicators as elements of demarcation between its major units and as indicators of the temporal relationship between the circumstances it depicts. The first of these temporal indicators occurs in 4.1, 'in the latter days' (והיה באחרית הימים).[51] This unit consists of two sub-units: 4.1-5 and 4.6–5.14. The latter is further sub-divided into: 4.6-7; 4.8–5.8; 5.9-14.

4.1-5. The first sub-unit, 4.1-5, concerns the establishment of Yahweh's future reign in Zion. It is marked off by the phrase והיה באחרית הימים. This is followed by an announcement of promise in 4.1aβ-4. This announcement ends with its own concluding formula (כי־פי יהוה צבאות דבר) thus authenticating the promise and the possibility of its actualization. The כי־clause in v. 5 indicates a logical continuity between 4.1-4 and this verse. It also signals the conclusion of the unit and offers a rationale for the preceding. Its 1st person address is distinct from the unit it concludes. Its concluding formula (לעולם ועד) sets it apart from the following unit.

4.6-7. That 4.6-7 begins another unit is indicted first by the temporal transition formula (ביום ההוא) plus oracular formula (נאם־יהוה)[52] and the modification in focus from Zion (vv. 1-5) to the restoration of a remnant in Zion (vv. 6-7). The connection with 4.1-5 is that Zion is the place to which the remnant will be restored; and the reign of Yahweh will include the remnant. This continuity with the preceding is further indicated by the formula ביום ההוא. The antecedent may be the 'latter days' of 4.1 (באחרית הימים). As such, the circumstances in 4.6-7 are not

---

50. DeVries, *From Old Revelation to New*, pp. 60-63, והיה as one of the signals that the following transition is a futuristic transition.

51. DeVries, *From Old Revelation to New*, pp. 60-63, 90, 118. As to the other occurrences of the waw-consecutive perfect with the temporal phrase ביום ההוא, he cites the following: Isa. 1.18, 21, 23; 10.20; 11.10, 11; 17.4; 22.20; 23.15; Jer. 4.9; 30.8; Ezek. 38.10, 18; Hos. 1.5; 2.18 (Eng. v. 16), 23 (Eng. v. 21).

52. DeVries, *From Old Revelation to New*, p. 63. DeVries cites the introductory uses of the formula in Jer. 4.9; 30.8; Hos. 2.18 (Eng, v. 21); Amos. 8.9; Mic. 5.9 (Eng. v. 10); Zeph. 1.10.

ascribed to a time later than those of 4.1-5 but to the same time frame.[53]
Whether one would chronologically and sequentially precede the other
is not at issue. The temporal formula is used in this instance to focus on
a different aspect of one time frame in much the same way as the summons are used to focus on different aspects of a groups.

4.8–5.8. The unit is introduced by v. 8 (ואתה), identifying the persons
who are the focus of the following units. This is followed by 4.9-14 and
5.1-8. Verses 4.9-14 consist of three units introduced by the temporal
transition formula עתה.[54] Each depicts the present distress and reality to
be overcome toward the actualization of the promised 'ideal' reign of
Yahweh. Verses 9-10 provide the general statement that is further expanded in 4.11-13 and 4.14. By means of rhetorical questions and the
use of עתה, vv. 9-10 as a unit depicts the distress of the present. Using
the language of childbirth, the present is characterized by the distress of
the impending captivity (v. 10). Verses 11-13 speak of the subjection of
Zion by its enemies who in turn will be subjected by Zion. Finally, in
v. 14 the city is besieged and its ruler humiliated.

It is not necessary to find a chiastic pattern in order to make sense of
the units and their interrelationship.[55] Noteworthy is the fact that the
'now' (עתה) of 4.9-14 is not the same time as the 'latter days' (באחרית
הימים) of 4.1 nor the time frame of ch 3. The 'now' (עתה) of this section
lies between the time of ch 3 and the time of the actualization of that
which is promised in 4.1-4.

Micah 5.1-8 concerns the resolution to the present distress created by
the lack of effective leadership (5.1-3; cf. 4.9-10, 14), the advancement
of powerful nations (5.4-5; cf. 4.11-13), and the exile (5.6-8; cf. 4.10).
Verses 5.1-3 pick up on the questions of 4.9 regarding the absence of a
king and the apparently powerless ruler depicted in 4.14. The unit is
marked off by the ואתה (cf. 4.8) and the personification of the city, as
well as its focus on the origin and deeds of the new ruler. The לכן in 5.2
connects the promise to the distress of the present by qualifying the

53. DeVries, *From Old Revelation to New*, pp. 56-63, regarding the temporal
relationship indicated by the use of this futuristic transition formula—נאם־יהוה
ביום ההוא. Notably, one of the indicators that it is more than a simple time-designative is the presence of the prophetic utterance formula—נאם־יהוה.

54. DeVries, *From Old Revelation to New*, pp. 23-24.

55. Renaud, *Structure*; *idem, La Formation*; Willis, 'Structure, Setting'. See
Chapters 1 and 4 of this study for further information on their views.

distress as a factor considered in the promise. This is followed in 5.3 by the characterization of the reign of that ruler.

5.4-5 as a unit addresses the issue of the enemies of Zion (cf. 4.11-13), in this case Assyria. The nation will deal with this external force by conquering it. In 5.6 והיה presupposes preceding circumstances—the remnant in exile (cf. 4.9-10). Is this the same time frame as 4.6? Determining the time frame is a little more complex at this juncture; however, it may be suggested that 5.6-8 speaks of a time frame other than that of 4.1 and 4.6. This proposal is made on the basis of the contrasting situations. In 4.6 the remnant will be gathered to Zion. However, in 5.6-8 there is no mention of the return of the remnant to Zion. Instead, the concern is to give the remnant victory over its captors while it is living in exile. That this is a reference to a time frame other than that of 4.6 is further suggested in the proposal that 4.8–5.8 constitute a unit whose focus is the preparatory steps toward the actualization of the plans articulated in the units—that is, those signaled by the temporal transition formulas (4.1-5, 6-8; 5.9-14).

5.9-14. What is the presumed time frame of this unit? The temporal indicator (ביום ההוא; cf. 4.1 and esp. 4.6) may point to the immediately preceding unit, 5.6-8. This would suggest that during the exile the elements that displease God will be removed from among the people. However, it may also point back to the time frame introduced in 4.1 and continued on in 4.6-8. In this case 5.9 is an extension of the plan to establish Yahweh's reign in Zion. The oracular formula (נאם־יהוה) serves as a means of authenticating the promise as Yahweh's, and is comparable to the function of the phrase in 4.4b—כי־פי יהוה צבאות דבר.[56]

c. *6.1–7.20*
The second part of the book of Micah begins with the summons to hear and extends to 7.20. The first sub-unit is 6.1-8, a dispute and the introduction to the unit. As an introduction to the unit 6.1-8 provides the larger basis for the judgment and for understanding Yahweh's response to Israel's sin. This is followed by 6.9-16, a judgment speech, the woe

---

56. DeVries, *From Old Revelation to New*, p. 63; 'We may be certain that in each instance the redactor in question intended to draw special attention to the prediction and to identify it with the sign of emphatic authority.'

oracle (7.1-6)—which reflects the response to the judgment—and oracles of hope (7.7-20). See Chapter 5 below.

6.1-8. Chapter 6 is viewed by most as the beginning of a new unit marked off from ch. 5 by a 'summons to hear' (שׁמעו־נא; cf. 1.2; 3.1, 9). As seen in the different ways of dividing the book,[57] there are questions about the place of ch. 6 in relation to the rest of the book. Most agree that part or all of it belongs to a unit with ch. 7.

One of the main questions has been the relationship of vv. 1-5 and vv. 6-8. Most scholars sub-divide the unit into these two parts.[58] In some cases, this division is made in the recognition of two genres: covenant lawsuit (vv. 1-5)[59] and Torah liturgy (vv. 6-8).[60] In other cases, the unit vv. 1-8 is identified as a covenant lawsuit in which there are various components.[61]

The similarities of vv. 1-8 to the covenant lawsuit necessitate consideration of this genre as a part of understanding the composition of the present text since it has sometimes been sub-divided in view of the components of the covenant lawsuit. According to Ramsey, this genre consists of the following components: (a) summons to witnesses; (b) reference to historical benefits conferred by Yahweh upon Israel; (c) accusation against Israel's apostasy; (d) assertion of futility of appeal

57. See Table 2 above.
58. Wellhausen, *Einleitung*, pp. 146-47; Lindblom, *Micha literarisch untersucht*, pp. 99-100; Lescow, *Micha 6, 6-8*; A.R. Osborn, 'The Nature of True Religion: Micah 6.1-8', *BR* 17 (1932), pp. 74-78 (74); M. Bennett, *The Book of Micah* (Grand Rapids: Baker Book House, 1968), p. 57; Cheyne, *Micah*, p. 49; W.J. Deane, 'Micah', in H.D.M. Spence, *et. al.* (eds.), *The Pulpit Commentary* (New York: Funk & Wagnalis, 1950), p. 86; Goldman, 'Micah', p. 180; Keil and Delitzsch, *The Twelve Minor Prophets*; p. 492; Mays, *Micah*, pp. 128-29; Smith, *Micah, Zephaniah*, pp. 15, 118, 123; Waltke, 'Micah', p. 726; Allen, *The Books*, p. 364; Renaud, *La Formation*, p. 301; Vuilleumeir, 'Michée', pp. 70-73.
59. Limburg, 'The Root ריב', p. 291; Hillers, *Micah*, p. 77; Ramsey, 'Speech-Forms', pp. 45-48, sees complaint speech as a part of the covenant lawsuit whose purpose is restoration of the broken relationship; Huffmon, 'The Covenant Lawsuit', pp. 285-95; Westermann, *Basic Forms*, pp. 199-200; Allen, *The Books*, p. 363.
60. Renaud, *La Formation*, p. 301; Lescow, *Micha 6, 6-8*, denies that vv. 6-8 is a Torah liturgy and argues that it is a prophetic sermon.
61. Willis, 'Structure, Setting', pp. 259-61; Hillers, 'Micah', p. 808; Wolff, *Micah*, pp. 167-69, vv. 3-5 a speech of self-defense and vv. 6-8 an instructional dialogue are both part of a didactic sermon.

to other gods.[62] The announcement of judgment, typical of judgment speeches, is most often absent from the covenant lawsuit (cf. Isa. 1.2-3; Jer. 2.6-13; vis-à-vis Deut. 32 where it is present).[63] What is evident is that the text is an adaptation of genres, and its analysis is to take into account its particular adaptation of genres.

For reasons stated above, 6.1-8 is regarded here as a dispute. As such, several elements are identifiable. The structural analysis of 6.1-8 may thus be presented based on the following discussion of the textual and conceptual indicators. The beginning of the dispute, in this instance, consists of the summons followed by an accusation.[64] Verses 1-2 constitute the 'summons to hear'. In this instance, there are two summonses whose significance are debated.[65] The accusation in the form of rhetorical questions (v. 3) is a 1st person account signaled by the vocative עמי and by parallel expressions introduced with the particle מה. What follows is in essence an argument against the accused. This refutation of the claims (vv. 4-5) is introduced by כי, the first part of the refutation concerned with the Exodus and guidance traditions. The עמי in v. 5 functions in the same way as that in v. 3—as vocative. However, in v. 5 it introduces a unit, though this unit is not a unit on the same level as that introduced by v. 3. The עמי in v. 5 (declarative statement) continues the refutation of the charges against Yahweh, that is, those presupposed in the rhetorical questions of v. 3.

Verses 6-7 make up the response of the accused. The unit is introduced by the interrogative במה and is perhaps rhetorical in nature.[66] In

62. Ramsey, 'Speech-Forms', p. 45; Cf. Westermann, *Isaiah 40–66*, pp. 17-19, regarding the form of the *rîb*; Huffmon, 'The Covenant Lawsuit', pp. 285-95; Harvey, 'Le "*rîb*-pattern"', pp. 172-96; Limburg, 'The Root ריב', pp. 291-96; de Roche, 'Yahweh's Rîb Against Israel', pp. 563-66, 569-70; Daniels, 'Is there a "Prophetic Lawsuit" Genre?', pp. 339-45.

63. Cf. Willis, 'Structure, Setting', pp. 259, 264-66, who argues for the coherence of ch. 6 in view of the form of the covenant lawsuit; vv. 1-2, theophany; vv. 4-5, indictment; vv. 6-7, appeal to sacrifice; and vv. 13-15, announcement of judgment.

64. Cf. Bovati, *Re-Establishing Justice*, pp. 32-35, who identifies an accusation in the beginning of the dispute, followed by response of the accused, and concluded by reconciliation or declaration of war. Cf. Sweeney, *Isaiah 1–39*, pp. 541-42. He identifies at least four elements of the *rîb* pattern including: the call to attention, the appeal for legal proceeding, rhetorical question, announcement of judgment or an instruction.

65. Wolff, *Micah*; Hagstrom, *The Coherence*.

66. Westermann, *Isaiah 40–66*, pp. 17-19, this is a noticeable departure from

this instance, the questions indicate the misconception of the accused, that is, that underlying their charge that Yahweh has wearied them. Verses 6-7 as a unit function as the testimony of the accused against Yahweh—a response to the challenge of v. 3b, ענה בי. In the process of the dispute as presented by Bovati, vv. 6-7 may be construed as the protestation of the accused and reluctance to acknowledge the validity of the accusation.[67]

With its use of מה־טוב, v. 8 also seems to bring into focus the questions of v. 3 and v. 6. Furthermore, its use of אלהיך recalls עמי (vv. 3, 5), an indication the relationship of God and Israel. Its content is signaled by the phrase הגיד לך which presupposes a previous process to which it addresses itself. There is a switch to the declarative as compared to the interrogative mode of vv. 6-7.

6.9-16. This unit is marked off from 6.8 in form and content. It is a judgment speech with a narrative introduction (v. 9a). The summons to hear in v. 9 addresses the tribe and the city. By means of rhetorical questions (vv. 10-11) and a declarative statement in v. 12, the accusation is articulated against the city and specifically those who engage in deceitful economic practices. The announcement of judgment consists of v. 13 and is signaled by וגם at the beginning of the general statement of the judgment. Verses 14-16 form an expansion of the judgment, consisting of the resulting circumstances of the judgment (vv. 14-15) and the reiteration of the reason for the judgment (v. 16). This reiteration incorporates an accusation and a further statement of the reason for the desolation.

7.1-6. Chapter 7 has variously been treated as a dialogue involving several speakers. However, very little consensus exists about the identity of the speakers.[68] The chapter begins with a woe oracle in the 1st person (אללי לי). The speaker, using the collective 'I', is most likely addressed in the summons in 6.9—the tribe/assembly. Unlike the woe oracle in 2.1-5. which functions as a judgment speech, this woe oracle functions as a lament. As such it recalls the function of 1.8-16, as a response to

---

the pattern since an indictment is expected. See also Ramsey, 'Speech-Forms', p. 45.

67. Bovati, *Re-Establishing Justice.*

68. Cf. Hagstrom, *The Coherence*, pp. 96-102, for a discussion of the various proposals made by scholars.

the judgment which precedes it. For this reason 7.1-6 is seen as a part of the judgment.

7.7. The decisive change in mood is introduced by 7.7. A number scholars (including Mays) have argued that ואני is a waw-adversative and as such is never used to introduce a new unit.[69] However, its contrast with the lament in 7.1-6 suggests a new unit. The mood of confidence introduced in 7.7 is further expressed in the following section (7.8-20). Therefore, it is argued that 7.7 functions as an introduction to 7.8-20, and as such provides the general expression of confidence/hope. The section closes with an expression of hope constituted in looking to God for salvation.[70]

7.8-20. Verses 7.8-20 may be further divided into vv. 8-17 and vv. 18-20. The first sub-unit addresses historical realities of Israel's hope. The second sub-unit addresses the character of God as the basis of the hope and signals the covenant relationship as a part Israel's hope.

Verses 8-17 also may be sub-divided into vv. 8-10, 11-13 and 14-17. Verses 8-10 continue the 1st person of 7.1-9. There is a clear logical progression of thought in this unit centered on the confidence that God will deliver the speaker. This confidence is constituted in the fact that the desolation of the speaker will no longer be a catalyst for the enemies' taunt. The speaker's acknowledgment of sin and the fact that the present desolation may be the consequence of that sin (cf. 6.13, 16), is significant for understanding the connection between this unit and its larger context.

The use of the 2nd person pronouns in 7.11-13 and the attention to the wall, suggest that it is Yahweh's address to the city. The desolate city is assured that one day its wall will be rebuilt. The use of the temporal formula יום ההוא further qualifies the time frame in which the wall will be built as a time when other nations will come to the city.

The coherence of 7.14-15 and 7.16-17 as a unit is not evident. It seems that either Yahweh or the city is admonished to be a shepherd to the people. The language recalls 2.12-13 and may therefore suggest that the speaker is addressing Yahweh. It is argued here that the middle unit

69. Mays, *Micah*, p. 156; Hagstrom, *The Coherence*, pp. 97-99; Cuffey, 'Coherence of Micah', pp. 356-57.

70. Note that this verse has been placed with the following (7.8-20) as an introduction.

consists of vv. 11-15, the city's words addressed to Yahweh. This unit it further sub-divided into vv. 11-13, a response and affirmation, and vv. 8-10, an expression of hope. Verses 16-17 then return to the concern about the enemies as witnesses to both the desolation and deliverance of Israel by Yahweh. This unit (vv. 16-17) indicates the desired effects sought by the addressees in vv. 14-15. It also serves to conclude the first part of this unit by picking up the concern about the opinions of the nations, that is, those voiced in vv. 8-10. So the unit formed by vv. 8-17 begins and ends with reference to how the fate of Israel is perceived by others.

The conclusion of the unit—vv. 18-20—is a song of praise to Yahweh. This praise is expressed in the confidence that God will forgive Israel's sin. The first part consists of vv. 18-19a , the 3rd person expression of hope. It begins with a rhetorical question which is followed by two declarative statements (vv. 18b, 19a). The switch to the 2nd person indicates an address to God which expresses confidence in God's forgiveness.

Conclusion

The interrelationships of the units of the book of Micah have been discussed in light of the question of the coherence of the whole. It was noted that there are instances in which the coherence is not as evident as in other instances. It is also noted that the generic form alone is not the indicator of the relationship between various units. Furthermore, the coherence of the whole is a function of all its parts. Having discussed the boundaries of the units and offered initial suggestions as to their interrelationship and coherence, the unit-by-unit analysis in Chapters 4 and 5 intends to further discern the coherence of the whole.

Chapter 4

LEVELS OF COHERENCE: CHAPTERS 1–5

Introduction

There are different levels and spheres of conceptual coherence evidenced respectively by the structural levels and the compositional history. At the various stages of its history, the composition may exhibit a different conceptuality due to its adaptation to its historical context and the resignification of the text toward that adaptation.[1] The present study is not aimed at identifying the conceptuality of the text at the various stages of its composition history. Its aim is the conceptual coherence of the final form. There is no denying that to the extent that the text exhibits a discernible composition history, issues of conceptuality with regard to the different stages of the composition history may be addressed.

One of the main challenges of the present method—concept-critical analysis—is dealing with the fact that texts are composed of levels (structural) and spheres (composition history) of coherence. In Chapters 4 and 5 I seek to demonstrate that there are various levels of coherence indicated by the extant structure of the book of Micah. These levels are constituted by units that may themselves exhibit their own coherence. However, it is not necessarily the case that the same degree of coherence is discernible in each unit or the levels they constitute. The coherence of some units—as evident by their generic features and/or logical continuity—is more discernible than that of others (e.g. ch. 3 compared to chs. 2 and 4). Thus a unit or level may cohere around a particular concept that is neither readily discernible nor present in any or all of its constitutive sub-units—much less in its adjacent units. The

---

1.   Knierim, *Text and Concept*, p. 1 n. 1, where he defines reconceptualization and recontextualization.

coherence then of these units is not that they share a concept nor that they are juxtaposed.

Although it may be indicated textually, coherence is inherently substantive. Furthermore, the coherence of the levels is dependent on and contributive to the conceptuality of the whole. Yet neither the dependence nor the contribution nullifies the particular conceptuality of a structural unit or the level it comprises. The particular conceptuality may be resignified toward an overarching conceptuality.[2] For this reason, the more salient features of one unit or level—for example, shared vocabulary, genre and continuity of thought—may potentially distract from the discernibility of the coherence of the whole that also includes other units with less salient features. As such, there are potential dangers in seeking to discern coherence including: overlooking the significance of one unit in favor of another; relativizing the importance of one over against the other; or even reducing and harmonizing the less salient features to the conceptuality of units with more salient features.

All of these are inherent dangers of this type of analysis which further necessitate a full-scale analysis of the text's conceptuality—in this case the book of Micah.[3] Such analysis is noticeably absent from the studies to-date that have proposed to discern the coherence of the book of Micah. In keeping with their definitions of coherence and their presuppositions about the conceptuality of the whole,[4] scholars such as

2.   See Chapter 2 above for further discussion.

3.   At this point in the discussion it is necessary to state that the aim of this study is the conceptuality of the text as observed in the text and generative of the text. For the present approach, the meaning of the text does not begin to exist at the point of interpretation nor is it created by the reader as claimed by reader-response criticism. Cf. Jane P. Tompkins, (ed.), *Reader-Response Criticism: From Formalism to Post-Structuralism* (Baltimore: The Johns Hopkins University Press, 1980); Robert Detweiler (ed.), *Reader Response Approaches to Biblical and Secular Texts* (Semeia, 31; Atlanta: Scholars Press, 1985); J. Severino Croatto, *Biblical Hermeneutics: Towards a Theory of Reading as the Production of Meaning* (Maryknoll, NY: Orbis Books, 1987). Cf. J. Cheryl Exum and David J.A. Clines, *The New Literary Criticism and the Hebrew Bible* (JSOTSup, 143; Sheffield: JSOT Press, 1993), pp. 15-16. 'New literary criticism' has been broadly defined to include studies that view the extant texts as unified entities and/or to examine structure, theme, character, and so on.

4.   See Chapter 1 above for discussion of Willis, 'Structure, Setting'. His discussion is focused on identifying the symmetry of the text. Hagstrom, *The*

Willis and Hagstrom carry out an analysis of the literary features in order to identify clues of coherence. While these studies do not admit to limitations resulting from the absence of a full-scale analysis of the text, Cuffey admits that the absence of this analysis is a limitation of his study.[5]

What follows here is a unit-by-unit analysis of the book of Micah aimed at identifying the conceptual basis of the coherence of major units and the interrelationship of these units. The analysis is presented according to the micro-structure proposed above in Chapter 3 and is complemented by the observations already noted. The reasons for the delimitation of the units were also presented. In light of this, for some units in the discussion below (in Chapters 4–5) only a brief discussion is given. Some of the smaller units are omitted not because they are devalued in this analysis. Their presence in the micro-structure is intended to illustrate their role in the whole. So, elements like *nkl* which were already discussed in Chapter 3 are not given a new discussion in Chapters 4–5. The reader is advised to refer back to Chapter 3 for more details on the particularity of these units. In any case, the design of this study intends the reader to keep the micro-structure presented in Chapter 3 as a ready reference. The headings (e.g. I.A.1.) indicate the various levels and are also intended to signal where each unit is located in the overall structure of the book of Micah.

Superscription (1.1)

The superscription in 1.1 is typical of the redaction of prophetic books.[6] This superscription consists of two main parts: the primary designation,

Coherence, p. 38, recognizes the need for a unit-by-unit analysis in finding evidence of coherence and hence the contextual significance of the substantive aspects. However, he focuses on literary features and only secondarily on the substantive aspects. His discussion amounts to an overview of the complexity of the issues involved in addressing the coherence of the book. For example, in his discussion of Mic. 3 he divides the texts as follows: vv. 1-4, 5-8, 9-12. He argues that 3.9-12 is composed of three units distinguished by the differences in address. Concerning 3.12, he notes that the presence of the theme of Jerusalem's destruction is a distinguishing factor. However, no analysis of the units precedes or follows which would supply the basis of these conclusions.

    5.   Cuffey, 'Coherence of Micah'.

    6.   Cf. Isa. 1.1; Jer. 1.1-2; Hos. 1.1; Joel 1.1; Zeph. 1.1; Hag. 1.1; Zech. 1.1; Mal 1.1; Jonah 1.1. Nogalski, *Literary Precursors*, pp. 76-77; Gene. M. Tucker,

the subject (דבר־יהוה, 1.1aα$_1$), followed by its qualifiers (1.1aα$_2$-b). The first relative clause (אשר היה אל־מיכה המרשתי, 1.1aα$_2$-b) qualifies the subject by indicating the person to whom the 'word of the Yahweh' came. The next phrase (בימי יותם אחז יחזקיה מלכי יהודה, 1.1aβ) qualifies the first relative clause. It is a prepositional phrase that indicates the time frame of the specific 'word of the Yahweh'.

The second relative clause (אשר־חזה על־שמרון וירושלם, 1.1b) is usually categorized as a later addition (cf. Amos 1.1; Isa. 1.1), originating from a later redactor. It further qualifies the scope of the 'word received by the prophet' as specifically regarding Samaria and Jerusalem.[7] The focus on the cities, although it extends beyond the superscription, is dominated by attention to Jerusalem, for example, 1.2-7 (Samaria); chs. 3; 4–5; 6.9-16 (Jerusalem/Zion). The limited attention to Samaria has led some to the conclusion that 1.1b may have been added with or some time after 1.2-9.[8] The larger issue, however, is the extent to which the superscription represents the book as a whole and what it contributes to the discerning of the conceptual coherence of that whole.

I. *First Dispute (1.2–5.14)*

I.A. *Introduction (1.2-16)*

This unit introduces chs. 2–5 by identifying the main elements to be addressed in the following units. It indicates these elements in its vocabulary and the accusation against Samaria and Jerusalem. Through the lament, it also indicates the question concerning Jerusalem's fate as compared to that of Samaria.

Micah 1.2-16 has posed problems for scholars due to its composite nature. In spite of the discernibility of the various elements, their rela-

---

'Prophetic Superscriptions and the Growth of a Canon', in George W. Coats and Burke O. Long (eds.), *Canon and Authority: Essays in Old Testament Religion and Theology* (Philadelphia: Fortress Press, 1977), pp. 56-70 (62); S.M. Meier, *Speaking of Speaking: Marking Direct Discourse in the Hebrew Bible* (VTSup, 46; Leiden: E.J. Brill, 1992), pp. 314-15.

7. Nogalski, *Literary Precursors*, pp. 76-77, 126-28; cf. Mays, *Micah*, pp. 38-39; *idem*, *Amos* (OTL; Philadelphia: Westminster Press, 1969), pp. 18-20, whose discussion of Amos 1.1 has been used in the discussion of Micah because of their similarity; Hillers, *Micah*, pp. 14-15.

8. Nogalski, *Literary Precursors*, pp. 127-28. For a discussion of the textual difficulties in 1.2-9 see Hillers, *Micah*, p. 16; Lescow, 'Micha 1–5', pp. 54-61, 70, 82-84.

tionship and the extent of the unit to which they belong are not as evident in the extant form of the text. This is one instance in which the form of the unit itself facilitates questions of its own coherence. The sub-units themselves (namely, 1.2-7, 8-9, 10-16) exhibit coherence, but the extent of the unit of which they are constitutive is not readily discernible. It is proposed here that 1.2-16 consists of vv. 2-7 and vv. 8-16.

I.A.1. *Dispute proper (1.2-7)—the sins of Samaria and Jerusalem*
The dispute itself uses elements of the judgment speech, namely, the introduction (1.2-4), accusation (1.5) and the announcement of judgment (1.6-7).

I.A.1.a. *Introduction (1.2-4)*. The dispute is introduced by two elements: the summons to hear and the theophany report.
I.A.1.a.1) *Summons to hear (שצעו) (1.2)* Verse 2 begins with the summons to hear (שמעו) addressed to 'all the peoples' (עמים כלם). The naming of the addressees, עמים 'peoples' and ארץ 'earth', qualifies the scope of the address as the entirety of the earth's population, without exception.[9] In this context where it is present with the qualifier מלאה, ארץ 'earth' can hardly be seen as a metonymy for peoples. The summons is further qualified by the articulation of its purpose, namely, that Yahweh may be a witness against the peoples.[10] This is indicated by the phrase בכם לעד which usually denotes 'against' (e.g. Deut. 31.19, 26).[11] The earth in 1.2 does not function as a witness or an audience as in 6.2

---

9.   Cf. Wolff, *Micah*, p. 45-46; contrast Waltke, 'Micah', p. 617, who argues that עמים could refer to the covenant people and the ארץ to the land. The other option, namely, all the nations and the earth in the cosmological sense—does not fit the context as designated by the superscription. He favors a restrictive sense and argues that the addressees are the covenant people and their land.

10.   See Bruce Waltke and M. O'Connor, *An Introduction to Biblical Hebrew Syntax* (Winona Lake, IN: Eisenbrauns, 1990), §34.6 #1-2 for discussion of the purposive use of ויהי. For further information on the textual aspects of 1.2b see D. Barthélemy and J.T. Milik, *Qumran Cave 1* (DJD, 1; Oxford: Clarendon Press, 1955), pp. 77-80; see Waltke, 'Micah', p. 617, who argues in favor of the MT over against 1QpMic and Mur 88; Wolff, *Micah*, p. 46, sees ויהי as the work of a redactor.

11.   In Deut. 31.19 a song is indicated as a witness against Israel—למען תהיה-לי השירה הזאת לעד בבני ישראל—while in 31.26 the book of the law is the witness בך לעד. Cf. J.T. Willis, 'Some Suggestions on the Interpretation of Micah 1.2', *VT* 18 (1968), pp. 372-79. He lists other instances of the phrase בכם לעד, for example, Num 5.13; Josh. 24.22; Prov. 24.28.

(cf. Isa. 1.2; Deut. 31.28b). Similarly, the peoples do not serve as examples to Israel in order to prepare Israel to be receptive of Yahweh's judgment against her (cf. Amos 1.3–2.5).[12] To whatever extent this nuance is present (that is, one person or group serving as an example to another), it has much more to do with Samaria and Jerusalem than with the nations on the one hand vis-à-vis Samaria and Jerusalem on the other. The summons is also qualified by the indication of Yahweh's location—his holy temple (היכל קדשו). This may denote the place of judgment whether in the heavenly palace or the Jerusalem temple.[13] On the basis of vv. 3-4, it is most likely that the reference is to the heavenly palace.

I.A.1.a.2) *The theophany report (1.3-4).* The theophany report in 1.3-4 is introduced by the כי-clause כי הנה. This clause provides the link between v. 2 and vv. 3-4 and is possibly the motivation to respond to the summons.[14] The report depicts Yahweh's descent from a place located above the high places of the earth (v. 3),[15] indicating that the high places of the earth are not synonymous with Yahweh's place. The result of the descent is the destruction of various natural elements—ההרים and עמקים—in v. 4. However, this destruction is a residual effect of but not the purpose for Yahweh's intervention. The purpose is otherwise indicated (v. 5). Thus, while the superscription indicates the focus on Samaria and Jerusalem, the summons and theophany report incorporate a more extensive focus. The latter focus is universal in the sense that all of the peoples of the earth and the earth itself are objects against whom Yahweh is a witness.

I.A.1.b. *Accusation—reason for the divine intervention (כי) (1.5).* Verse 5 articulates both the reason for the theophany as well as the accusation against Jacob (Samaria) and Israel (Jerusalem). The reason is signaled by כל־זאת, indicating a connection with the preceding unit (that is, vv. 3-4). As discussed in Chapter 3 above, this particle is used to connect

---

12. Wolff, *Micah*, p. 46; *idem, Joel and Amos* (Hermeneia; Philadelphia: Fortress Press, 1977).

13. Mays, *Micah*, p. 40, interprets the occurrence of the phrase in 1.2 as analogous to this latter use and offers as support 4.1-4. Yet he contradicts himself by saying of v. 3 that Yahweh is coming to earth. If Yahweh is depicted as being in Jerusalem why then the depiction of Yahweh coming to earth?

14. Cf. Hagstrom, *The Coherence*, p. 46.

15. According to Wolff, *Micah*, p. 46, this is the typical style of a theophany report.

parts of an argument and usually has its antecedent in what precedes rather than in what follows.[16] In this instance, the rationale for the immediate intervention of Yahweh is expressed in the declarative statement in v. 5a and expanded by a question and answer schema in v. 5b.[17] As for the accusation, v. 5 indicates the basis for the announcement of judgment in vv. 6-7.

The intervention of Yahweh is therefore a purposeful response. It is not an initiated action, and is more than Yahweh's continual presence. Rather the intervention is compelled action (cf. Exod. 3.7-8)[18] coming out of the awareness of the crime (פשע) of Jacob and the sins (חטאות) of Israel, and necessarily out of the existence and nature of the crime and sins themselves as that which captivated the awareness.

Thus far in the progression of the book of Micah, no indication has been given as to the nature or specifics of what is referred to by the terms פשע and חטא.[19] The possibility exists that the terms are being

16. Cf. Renaud, *La Formation*, p. 30; Waltke, 'Micah', p. 619; Willis, 'Structure, Setting', p. 250; Smith, *Micah, Zephaniah*, p. 38.

17. S. DeVries, *1 and 2 Chronicles* (FOTL, 11; Grand Rapids: Eerdmans, 1989), p. 426, e.g., 2 Chron. 7.21-22. He defines it as a 'Literary device which projects a question and its answer as a means of describing a future state'. Cf. Burke O. Long, *1 Kings: With an Introduction to Historical Literature* (FOTL, 9; Grand Rapids: Eerdmans, 1984), p. 258, e.g., Jer 5.19; 22.8-9; 23.33; 1 Kgs 9.8-9; Ezek. 37.18-19.

18. In Exod. 3.7-8 the intervention is compelled by Yahweh's observation of the suffering of the people. Thus, the reason for the intervention is to deal with the suffering, and specifically by removing the people from the agent and place of their suffering. The nature of the intervention is therefore defined by the reason that compels the intervention.

19. Wolff, *Micah*, p. 56, argues that Samaria's (722 BCE) and Jerusalem's (587 BCE) catastrophes are the result of guilt. Accordingly, he observes that פשע is 'international criminal rebellion against the law (1 Kgs 12.19; Jer. 2.29)', and that חטאת is an objective error of one who loses the way and is confused (Judg. 20.16; Prov. 19.2). Regarding פשע, see R.P. Knierim, 'On the Contours of Old Testament and Biblical Hamartiology', in *idem*, *The Task of Old Testament Theology* (Grand Rapids: Eerdmans, 1995), p. 425. Knierim defines פשע as follows: '..."to commit a breach". [The term] points to the nature of an act itself within social and international relations (as in Amos 1–2). It is, therefore, also a legal word for crime.' *Idem, Die Hauptbegriffe für Sünde im Alten Testament* (Gütersloh: Gerd Mohn, 1965), pp. 113-15; *idem*, 'פשע', in *THAT*, II, pp. 488-95. Cf. Robert Koch, *Die Sünde im Alten Testament* (Bern: Peter Lang, 1992), pp. 27-28. He follows Knierim in interpreting פשע as crime; contrast L. Köhler, *Theologie des Alten Testaments*

used in synonymous parallelism. As such the crime of Jacob (פשע יעקב)
would be further expressed in parallelism with v. 5ab, sins of the house
of Israel (בחטאות בית ישראל). Note other uses of the parallelism in 3.8,
(בכורי פשעי//חטאת נפשי) 6.7 ;(ליעקב פשעת//לישראל חטאתו); 7.9ab, כי
חטאתי לו; 7.18aα₂, (ועבר על־פשע). Further information regarding the
nature of פשע and חטא is revealed only through further reading of the
book of Micah and specifically chs. 2, 3 and 6. However, there is general information that an intertextual examination may reveal. Such a
discussion is deferred until Chapter 6 of this work.

The text further specifies the פשע of Jacob as Samaria. However,
where one would expect the continuation of the parallel to be the חטא
of Israel is Jerusalem, one finds במות of יהודה is Jerusalem. Freedman
suggests that the correlation is such that the transgression is equated
with the high places—the high places themselves constituting the transgression.[20] It is here suggested that in v. 5a Jacob designates the Northern Kingdom, Israel, while Judah designates Jerusalem, the Southern
Kingdom. The synonymous parallelism in 3.1, 9, however, does not
share this distinction. It presupposes disaster or judgment and by this
means designates responsibility for the disaster.[21]

I.A.1.c. *Announcement of judgment (on Samaria) (1.6-7)*. Micah 1.6
begins the announcement of judgment without the use of לכן (cf. 6.13;
vis-à-vis 2.3; 3.4, 12); nonetheless, it indicates a correspondence between the accusation and the judgment. The announcement of judgment
consists of the judgment (1.6) and, in this instance, the expansion which
provides the specification of the conditions that will constitute the judgment (1.7). Notably, while the accusation includes both Samaria and
Jerusalem, the announcement of judgment is focused on Samaria, leaving open the announcement on Jerusalem (cf. chs. 2–3). The judgment
is that Samaria will be made into a heap, a place for planting a vineyard.

(Tübingen: J.C.B. Mohr, 1947), p. 158, according to whom the term denotes 'rebellion'; see HALAT, *s.v.*

20.   David N. Freedman, 'Discourse on Prophetic Discourse', in H.B. Huffmon
(ed.), *The Quest for the Kingdom of God: Studies in Honor of George E. Mendenhall* (Winona Lake, IN: Eisenbrauns, 1983), p. 147; Nogalski, *Literary Precursors*,
pp. 132-33. In his excursus on Samaria, he concludes that the occurrence in Micah
is peripheral and already 'presupposes a polemic against Samaria as the *starting
point* for a thorough going judgment against cultic abuses in Jerusalem'.

21.   Sweeney, *Isaiah 1–39*, pp. 5-36.

Verse 7 expands on v. 6 by specifying the aspects of the desolation—namely, the images and idols—thus depicting an idolatrous nation.[22] Through this depiction the פשׁע יעקב is associated with these aspects of idolatry.

The similarity to 3.12 is evident: 'Zion will be plowed like a field, Jerusalem will become a heap of ruins…and the mountain of the house a wooded height'. Notably, the destruction of both Samaria and Jerusalem focuses on cultic aspects: Samaria, the cultic implements; Jerusalem, the cultic center. In this respect, the two judgments are indicated as parallel acts of God.[23] It may also be said that פשׁע is associated with the cultic aspects.[24] Micah 3.12 may serve as the concluding section of judgment whose introduction is in 1.5.[25]

I.A.2. *Response to the announcement of judgment (1.8-16)*

I.A.2.a. *Introduction—prophet's lament (1.8-9)*. Micah 1.8, marked off by the phrase על־זאת, has had its measure of debate centered on whether it belongs with what precedes or what follows. Mays is among those who argue that it is unlikely that v. 8 is a conclusion to 1.2-7. It is instead

> a natural introduction to the lament proper (vv. 10-15) identifying the genre of the saying and its occasion. The mourning song can stand on its own; it is self-contained with respect to type and theme. Only the demonstrative 'this' at the beginning seems to point back; but it could as well point forward to the content (v. 9) in the way that 'hear this', the abbreviated summons to attention refers to the following 'word' (e.g., Micah 3.9; Amos 8.4; Hos. 5.1.[26]

Renaud's explanation is that v. 8 forms the introduction to the lament whose body consists of two strophes, vv. 9-10 and vv. 12-15. The conclusion occurs in v. 16. He bases his conclusion on the observation

22. Cf. Willis, 'Structure, Setting', p. 378.

23. Nogalski, *Literary Precursors*, pp. 135-36; cf. Mays, *Micah*, p. 47; Allen, *The Books*, p. 267; Waltke, 'Micah', pp. 620-21.

24. This association does not alter the nature of that which is labeled פשׁע. See note 19 above.

25. See Chapter 3 above for discussion. Cf. Willis, 'Structure, Setting', who while recognizing this correspondence between 1.6 and 3.12, denies that 3.12 is the end of the first section of the book. I agree with Willis on this point though not with his macro-structural representation.

26. Mays, *Micah*, pp. 50-51.

that v. 9 and v. 12 are similar, that is, they both begin with כי and mention the catastrophe approaching the gate of Jerusalem. He further observes that על־זאת may introduce a unit within the progression of an argument, but is not usually used to introduce a new argument.[27] This interpretation seems the most plausible because of its attention to the substantive as well as the textual aspects of the text.[28] The demonstrative זאת is typically used to point to an antecedent in a preceding unit. Here as elsewhere, it indicates one aspect of a continuity and not the beginning of its own argument. The antecedent of זאת is therefore to be found in the preceding verse—the judgment on Samaria.[29]

The change to the 1st person account signals a change in speaker from the preceding 3rd person account. The judgment is presupposed, and whether it exists in actuality or is only anticipated, the prophet sees it as a reason to lament. The strong language of mourning depicts the resolve to mourn. It is not a contemplation on the possibility of mourning. Verse 9 expands on the resolve by providing a reason, namely, the inevitability of the judgment.

The term ספד typically denotes mourning rites associated with death (e.g. Gen. 23.2; 50.10; 1 Sam. 25.1; 28.3; 2 Sam. 1.12). This nuance was adopted by the prophets in response to impending judgment—a response admonished to others (e.g. Isa. 32.11-15; Jer. 4.8; Joel 1.8, 13-14).[30] The other term ילל ('to howl, wail') is usually presented in parallel with זעק. The parallel with ספד indicates mourning in response to death and destruction (cf. Joel 1.5, 8, 11, 13).[31] 'In Old Testament prophetic texts which are form critically parallel to Mic. 1.8-16, the funerary metaphors in the dirge and laments over destruction always function as a proclamation of impending doom (Amos 5.2, 16-17; Isa. 3.25–4.1; 32.11-14; Jer. 9.16-21).'[32]

---

27.   Renaud, *La Formation*, pp. 36-37, 38-41; cf. Hagstrom, *The Coherence*, pp. 46f.; Waltke, 'Micah', p. 624.

28.   Contrast Willis, 'Structure, Setting', p. 251, who argues that 1.8-9 and 1.10-16 should not be separated.

29.   See Erhard Gerstenberger, *Psalms, Part 1: With an Introduction to Cultic Poetry* (FOTL, 14; Grand Rapids: Eerdmans, 1988), pp. 10-11, regarding the dirge and lament and the components of the call to weep and wail as in 2 Sam. 1.24, Lam. 2.18 and Isa. 14.31; Westermann, *Basic Forms*, pp. 202-203.

30.   R.D. Patterson, 'ספד', in *TWOT*, II, p. 630; cf. Wolff, *Micah*, p. 58.

31.   P.R. Gilchrist, 'ילל', in *TWOT*, I, pp. 868-69.

32.   Wolff, *Micah*, p. 49.

The prophet goes on to specify the symbolic act of the response—going barefoot and naked. While 'going barefoot' is usually a part of the mourning ritual (cf. 2 Sam. 15.30; Ezek. 24.17, 23), going about naked is usually symbolic of being taken prisoner (Amos 2.16).[33] These symbolic actions are paired in Isa. 20.2-4 where Isaiah is instructed to remove the loin cloth. There they symbolize impending captivity.

> At that time the Lord had spoken by Isaiah...saying, 'Go, and loose the sackcloth from your loins and take off your sandals from your feet', and he had done so, walking naked and barefoot—the Lord said, 'as my servant Isaiah has walked naked and barefoot for three years as a sign and a portent against Egypt and Ethiopia, so shall the king of Assyria lead away the Egyptians captives and the Ethiopians exiles, both the young and the old, naked and barefoot, with buttocks uncovered, to the shame of Egypt (Isa. 20.2-4).

So it may be that the symbolic actions are to signify the impending exile (1.16) of Jerusalem's inhabitants. The antecedent of the pronominal suffix (הָ) in v. 9 is believed to be Samaria. However, it is not only that Samaria's punishment will not be forgiven, suggesting Yahweh's resolve to punish (cf. Amos 1.3-4), but rather that the inevitability of the punishment is in the sins. They are incurable and furthermore the incurable wounds (מכות) have reached Judah. Verses 8-9 look back at Samaria's sin and imminent judgment and forward to Jerusalem's judgment. In the perspective of the speaker, the fate of Samaria is sealed. Whether this is the case for Jerusalem may be an open question as suggested by the imagery of it reaching the gate.[34]

I.A.2.b. *Expansion of the lament (1.10-16).* The relationship of vv. 8-9 to vv. 10-16 is not as clear as the coherence of either unit. There is a debate as to the content of vv. 10-16. This debate and the textual difficulties will not be reproduced here.[35] Rather, it is observed that the admonition in vv. 10-15 culminates in the call to mourn because of the

---

33. Wolff, *Micah*, p. 58.

34. Waltke, 'Micah', p. 625, presumes that there is a hint that 'a remnant will survive'.

35. Cf. Lux, 'Micah 1.8-16'; Waltke, 'Micah', pp. 625-33. Cf. Shaw, *Speeches of Micah*, pp. 55-56. The dirge functions as an accusation against the cities because of their disloyalty. In light of 1.6, Wolff, *Micah*, p. 53, puts the *terminus ad quem* at 722 BCE.

impending exile. This call to mourn looks back at the reason for the lament and forward to the judgments in chs. 2–3. Summarily, the connection between judgment and sin is already signaled in v. 5 and vv. 6-7. So in as much as Samaria's sin results in judgment, so Jerusalem's sin will result in judgment. What is left to be realized is the extent of that judgment.

The conceptual coherence of 1.2-16, then, is the fate of a nation that has sinned and against which Yahweh bears witness. All units, though exhibiting differences of genre and possibly diversion of content, are interrelated in focus—reason for judgment, judgment, response to judgment. In this way, 1.2-16 may function as an introduction to chs. 2–3 serving to clarify and justify the attention to Israel's sin and impending judgment. Chapters 2 and 3, as a unit, address the nature of Israel's sin first by addressing the oppressors in a general way (ch. 2), and next by addressing them by title and role (ch. 3). In both sections, there is a discernible correspondence between the sin and the announcement of judgment. Likewise, the terms for sin from 1.5 are repeated or implied in these two chapters.

I.B. *Concerning Israel's Fate (2.1–5.14)*
This is the first part of the book's focus on Israel's fate after it has introduced the question about Israel's fate as compared to Samaria's. It will address the question by looking first at Israel present and the situations there that are decisive to its future (2.1–3.12). It will then examine the future that ensues from the present and articulate promise concerning a future beyond the immediate horizon (4.1–5.14).

I.B.1. *Present: Israel's sin and impending judgment (2.1–3.12)*
Israel's sin and the ensuing judgment are indicated in the depiction of oppression (2.13) and the sins of Israel's leaders (3.1-12). In these instances the announcement of judgment shows a dependency on the sins by use of לכן (2.3; 3.6, 12) and אז (3.4).

I.B.1.a. *Oppression regarding the land (2.1-13).* From the perspective of this unit, Israel's oppressive practices are directly related to its loss of its land in the furutre. This unit presents the connection between the practices and the loss of the land in the form of a woe oracle (2.1-5) and its expansion (2.6-11) and a response to judgment (2.12-13).

I.B.1.a.1) *Woe oracle (הוֹי) (2.1-11)*. The woe oracle and its limited focus set off ch. 2 from the preceding as a distinct form.[36] While the focus of ch. 1 is universal—all peoples and the earth (1.2)—it increasingly narrows to יעקב and ישׂראל (1.5), to Samaria/Jacob שׁמרון (1.6-7), then to Judah/Jerusalem ירושׁלם/יהודה (1.9). The latter remains the focus in 1.13, 14, 15.

I.B.1.a.1)a) *Oracle proper (2.1-5)*. The oracle itself consists of an introduction (2.1a) and the judgment (2.1a-5). The oracle is then expanded (2.6-11).

I.B.1.a.1)a)(1) *Introduction (הוֹי) (2.1a)*. The הוֹי plus nouns (participial phrases) in 2.1a signal the woe oracle. This introduction is expanded with an appositive attached to the participial phrases (2.1b). In this instance, the noun forms (the addressees) also function to reveal the accusation. The accusation is expanded in 2.2 followed by the announcement of judgment in 2.3-5. According to Clifford, הוֹי has various uses including 'alas' (Jer 22.18; 34.5; Amos 5.16) and 'woe' (Isa. 29.15). The latter nuance is usually found in the context of an accusation.[37]

I.B.1.a.1)a)(2) *Judgment (2.1a-5)*. The judgment portion of this unit consists of the accusation (2.1a-2) and the announcement of judgment (2.3-5).

I.B.1.a.1)a)(2)(a) *Accusation—oppression (2.1a-2)*. In ch. 2, the narrowed focus is signaled by the participial phrases חשׁבי־און and ופעלי רע. The focus is not necessarily Jerusalem—no mention is made of Jerusalem, though presumably, those designated by these phrases are a part of Jerusalem.[38] Some argue for the unity of 2.1-13 as a rhetorical unit.[39] The unit is usually divided into 2.1-5, 6-11 and 12-13.[40]

36.   R.J. Clifford, 'The Use of Hôy in the Prophets', *CBQ* 28 (1966), pp. 458-64 (461); Waltke, 'Micah', p. 635.

37.   Clifford, 'The Use of Hôy', p. 461-62.

38.   Wolff, *Micah*, p. 74, sees this as being directed to the inhabitants of Moresheth. Contrast Mays, *Micah*, p. 62, who sees it directed as to Jerusalem.

39.   Shaw, *Speeches of Micah*, p. 71-72, argues that 2.1-11 is a unit and that 2.12-13 can be understood as a part of the prophet's speech.

40.   Allen, *Micah*, pp. 284-85; Wolff, *Micah*, p. 75, who further regards this unit (2.1-11) not as a rhetorical unit (*contra* Shaw), but as a unit that nonetheless originated in the same time and place. He believes this to be a sketch of a scene of which the prophet and his opponents are a part. In support of his argument, he refers to the quotation in 2.6-7a, that is, the perspective of the prophet's opponents. For discussion of the form and uses cf. Clifford, 'The Use of Hôy', pp. 458-64;

The designation of the addressees by deeds, however, is typical of this genre and is more specific than it may first appear. The image is of persons who do evil as deliberate acts of planning. They devote time to their deeds and are occupied with that planning. Thus their evil is not an unreflected ad hoc action. The term חשׁב ('to think, plan, devise'), is used of thinking in the sense of creating new ideas, not simply in comprehending (בין). It has the nuance of devising and plotting in reference to both humans and God (cf. Gen. 50.20). This is usually its nuance in qal and piel. To devise or plan evil is warned against in Zech. 7.10. There are several variations including: 'to make judgment' (qal and niphal, Isa. 53.4); 'to think' (Mal. 3.16); 'to invent' (only qal, cf. Exod. 31.4; 35.32, 35; 2 Chron. 26.15).[41] In this context (Mic. 2.1), the term seems to connote active planning in the sense of devising or scheming. This connotation comes through in 2.1b which indicates the execution of the plans.

The second term used to identify and accuse the addressees is פעל. Its direct object is רע, and it is qualified by the prepositional phrase על־משׁכבותם. The prepositional phrase itself may qualify both participial phrases (חשׁבי־און and פעלי רע) so that it is not just the latter part (פעלי רע) that happens in the beds but also the former (חשׁבי־און)—the plotting. When used of human actions, פעל usually refers to moral acts, positively (Ps. 15.2; Zeph. 2.3) or most often negatively (Prov. 30.20, 'wickedness'; Job 34.32, 'iniquity'; Isa. 44.15, 'idolatry'). The expression 'workers of iniquity' is said to have variations of meaning, including און as magical powers—thus the phrase meaning 'sorcery'. Others take it to mean harassment and gloating over their enemies as Israel's enemies do over Israel (Isa. 31.2; Hos. 6.8; Job 31.3; 34.8; Prov. 10.29; 21.15).[42] None of these seems to fit the present context.

The pairing of פעל with חשׁב seems to imply a further aspect of the devising and plotting (cf. Ps. 58.3).[43] That to which the plotting and blueprinting is dedicated is termed און and רע respectively. The term און

E. Gerstenberger, 'The Woe-Oracles of the Prophets', *JBL* 81 (1962), pp. 249-63; Westermann, *Basic Forms*, pp. 190-94; Sweeney, *Isaiah 1–39*; Mays, *Micah*, p. 62.

41.   Leon J. Wood, 'חשׁב', in *TWOT*, I, pp. 329-30.

42.   V.P. Hamilton, 'פעל', in *TWOT*, II, pp. 729-30; G.H. Livingston 'און', in *TWOT*, I, pp. 23-24; Knierim, 'Hamartiology', p. 426.

43.   Cf. Renaud, *La Formation*, p. 66, who suggests the synonymity of the two acts.

('wickedness, iniquity') has various nuances including 'trouble, sorrow'
(Gen. 35.18), 'deception' (Prov. 17.4; Isa. 32.6; Ezek. 11.2; Hos. 12.12),
'idolatry' (Isa. 66.3), and 'iniquity' in the phrase 'workers of iniquity'
(Job 31.3; 34.8; Prov. 10.29). The word is mostly taken to mean the
planning of deception.[44] Its meaning may be discerned from it frequent
pairing with טוב 'good' (Mic. 3.2; 1 Kgs 3.9; 2 Sam. 14.17; Isa. 7.15;
Amos 5). און may denote behaviors that are contrary to the will of God
(Isa. 31.2; Zeph. 1.12; cf. Num. 22.34; Prov. 24.18), including, rejection of God (Isa. 1.4; 9.17) and abuse of others (Num. 16.15; Ps. 22.17;
Exod. 5.22-23). Also, in some instances, there is the idea that those who
practice 'evil' lack understanding of what they do (Jer. 4.22; Prov.
24.8). In the context of ch. 2, the accused are portrayed as fully cognizant of their actions. Their evil is deliberately planned.

God, while sometimes the subject of evil (Mic. 2.3; 4.6; Ps. 44.3; Jer.
25.29) is presented as justifiable. God is against evil and therefore responds to it with judgment or graciously admonishes repentance (Amos
5.14-15; Zech. 1.4).[45]

The qualifier 'upon their beds' further indicates that this plotting of
evil is done at a time when one should be resting. It is not an instance of
a lazy person remaining in bed while there is work to be done. If anything, the persons depicted do not sacrifice work but sacrifice their rest
for the sake of their work. Verse 2b clearly supports this reasoning by
qualifying the nature of the addressees—that is, their potential to execute their plot. First the phrase, באור הבקר, presents contrast to the
immediately preceding prepositional phrase, further suggesting noctur-
nal rather than diurnal activities.

The plans are not fantasies. The ones plotting evil in this instance
have the power to execute it—כי יש־לאל ידם (cf. Gen. 31.29). Note the
expression in the following texts.

> ...it shall not be in the power of your hand to prevent it (ואין לאל ידך)
> (Deut. 28.32).

> Do not withhold good from those to whom it is due when it is in your
> power to do it (בהיות לאל ידך לעשות) (Prov. 3.27).

> ...some of our daughters have already been enslaved; but it is not in our
> power to help it, for other men have our fields and our vineyards' (ואין
> לאל ידנו) (Neh. 5.5).

44. Livingston 'און', pp. 23-24.
45. G.H. Livingston, 'רע', in *TWOT*, II, pp. 854-56.

As such the designation and qualification sharpen the focus on those with some measure of power over others. This could be a power of access to the means by which to execute the plans, as well as the power that is to some extent without restraint or without insurmountable restraint. So while the accused are not labeled by title as in ch. 3, their position is indicated as one of power. The legitimacy of that power—that is, its source—is not in question. The question is how that power is used.

The woe oracle depicts a dedication that would be adored were it not for the direction of the dedication. So the woe is for those dedicated to evil, while in ch. 3 the judgment is against those who lack dedication to do good but are dedicated to evil. In this way, ch. 2 anticipates the theme of abuse of power and the skewed nature of the dedication.

How the power is used is indicated in the accusation in 2.2. The accusation depicts a breaking of at least two commandments. First, they covet (חמד) fields and houses. To covet itself does not require power. Anyone can covet. Second, coveting has resulted in robbery (גזל, cf. Exod. 20.15).[46] גזל has the meaning not only of stealing but of force-fully seizing another's belongings. This is the same term used in 3.2 to depict the abuses of the leaders; however, in 3.2 its objects are skin and flesh. The violence of the act which the verb is used to convey is further seen in passages such as Job 24.9, Gen. 21.25 and Eccl. 5.8.

In the present context, those in power seize the fields and take away the houses of others. Clearly, this is not a situation of power and power-lessness but a matter of degree of power and wealth.[47] Those who had fields and houses are not necessarily powerless. They are usually male adult citizens rather than marginalized strangers, widows or orphans. Mic. 2.2b adds that they oppress a גבר and his house. As distinct from אדם, איש and אנוש, גבר denotes 'a male at his height of power and strength'.[48] This is also a person who has the rights of citizenship. Furthermore, this גבר has an inheritance, namely, that which is one's right and to be had permanently.[49]

---

46. E.B. Smick, 'גזל', in *TWOT*, I, pp. 157-58.

47. Some scholars argue that the oppressors are officials; e.g., Mays, *Micah*. Hillers, *Micah*, p. 33, argues that they are rich Judeans. Shaw, *Speeches of Micah*, p. 79, sees them as those who had power.

48. J.N. Oswalt, 'גבר', in *TWOT*, I, pp. 148-49; cf. J. Schupphaus, 'גזל', in *TDOT*, I, pp. 456-58; Wolff, *Micah*, p. 78.

49. L.J. Coppes, 'נחל', in *TWOT*, II, pp. 569-70.

The conceptual framework underlying this text is the right to possess the land.[50] The seizing of the property would leave the גבר and his family without land and without shelter. Thus, by weakening the landowners and oppressing them, landowners become powerless and susceptible to further oppression.

I.B.1.a.1)a)(2)(b) *Announcement of judgment (2.3-5)*. Punishment for these abuses—in essence the abuse of power used to disenfranchise those who can take care of themselves—is introduced by לכן and the oracular formula. Also present in the announcement of judgment is a correspondence between the evil of the oppressors and their punishment signaled in the repetition of the words חשב...רעה. As they have devised evil, so Yahweh is devising evil against them. Notably, the focus goes beyond the oppressors.[51] The scope of the judgment seems to include everyone—the oppressors and oppressed—inasmuch as they are part of the group referred to by המשפחה הזאת. There is no precedence for attributing to this term a restrictive meaning of crowd or group. Furthermore, the announcement of judgment qualifies the impending judgment as inescapable.

Verse 4 expands the general announcement by further specifying what will happen with respect to persons and property. Persons will be humiliated and bemoaned as if they were dead. As the oppressed were reduced to a state of debasement, so the whole 'family' will be reduced. The taunt will be not only that the 'family' is ruined, but also that it is ruined by God. Its very possessions, its ancient right, are taken away. As Yahweh divided the land among his people, entrusting it to them to their stewardship, so Yahweh the possessor of the land redistributes the land. The devastation is summarized in 2.5 which serves both as expansion of judgment and as conclusion to the woe oracle.

I.B.1.a.1)b) *Expansion of the oracle—disputation (2.6-11)*. This section has been categorized as disputation (cf. Isa. 28.23-29).[52] It functions as

---

50. Knierim, 'Food, Land and Justice', in *idem, Task of Old Testament Theology*, pp. 233-35; cf. G. von Rad, 'The Promised Land and Yahweh in the Hexateuch', in *The Problem of the Hexateuch and Other Essays* (trans. E.W.T. Dicken; New York: McGraw-Hill, 1966), pp. 79-83.

51. Hillers, *Micah*, p. 33; Allen, *The Books*, p. 290, sees this as the crowd or those who are of the same spirit. But for Allen this clearly does not mean the nation.

52. Westermann, *Basic Forms*, p. 201; Graffy, *A Prophet Confronts*; Murray, 'The Rhetoric of Disputation'. Cf. M. Sweeney, 'Concerning the Structure and

a response to the announcement of judgment. It is an attempt by the speaker (usually the prophet) to counteract an argument that is being espoused by those who oppose his message. It usually involves a quotation of the argument that is being refuted along with a statement of the position being defended. While 2.6-13 constitutes a response to the announcement of judgment, vv. 6-11 are the immediate response by the opponents to the message and 2.12-13 may represent a later response.

The coherence of ch. 2, however, encompasses aspects that are different. Verses 6-11, as a unit, appears to be distinct from what precedes. While the unit formed by vv. 1-5 focuses on the oppressors, the unit vv. 6-11 appears to focus on the disputation between prophet—as the messenger declaring the oracle against the oppressors—and those opposing the message. It has been argued that the false prophets are the ones opposing Micah[53] and are the ones quoted in 2.6. Perhaps the dispute is between the messenger and those against whom the accusation is brought (2.1-4).[54] They are the accused and the ones who stand to lose all. They have a vested interest in discounting the message. The fact that they oppose the message is not in itself indicative of their role. They are not necessarily false prophets and may not even be prophets.

Verse 6 is a citation of the opponents who are quoted as commanding the speaker not to preach (הטף; cf. Amos 7.16). The rationale is that disaster will not overtake the people. The opponents continue their argument (2.7) addressing the 'house of Jacob' with questions to verify the message. The first question introduces the other by asking about the legitimacy of the judgment against the house of Jacob (cf. Gen. 49; Exod. 19.3). The claim implicit in this is that such a thing cannot happen to God's chosen. Moreover, it appears that the opponents are claiming that God is not impatient (Num. 14.18-19; Neh. 9.17; Ps. 86.5; 103.8; Jonah 4.2). They are also questioning and in this way denying that acts of judgment are consistent with God's deeds. That God's deeds are saving acts on behalf of Israel is the presupposition that is actualized in the opponents' questions (cf. 6.6-7). The irony of the oppo-

---

Generic Character of the Book of Nahum', *ZAW* 104 (1992), pp. 364-77 (374-76). He identifies a disputation speech in Nah 2.2-3.19; *idem, Isaiah 1–39*, p. 519.

53.   Allen, *The Books*, p. 294; Waltke, 'Micah', p. 643; Renaud, *La Formation*, p. 88, suggests that there was a larger group of those opposing Micah than those targeted in 2.1-2.

54.   Wolff, *Micah*, p. 80; Shaw, *Speeches of Micah*, p. 79.

nents' position is that while they represent some aspect of 'truth', they represent only the parts that suit their perspectives (3.11; cf. Exod. 34.7).

The prophet counteracts the argument,[55] stating that the opponents are not upright. He cites as evidence the oppressive practices of the opponents and in so doing reiterates the basis for judgment. The opponents (identified as עמי) are depicted as oppressing the peaceful, innocent and harmless and stripping them of their clothes and home. However, the declarative statement which concludes the disputation indicates that the opponents may find acceptance among העם הזה, 'this people'. Typically, the prophet in his use of עמי (2.8aα, 9aα; cf. 3.5) identifies with the oppressed over against the oppressors.

I.B.1.a.2) *Response to the oracle—announcement of hope (2.12-13).* The positioning of 2.12-13 has been variously discussed. For example, Renaud argues that it be transposed to after 4.7.[56] Mays discusses how the oracle may be construed as a salvation oracle and the final in the series of redactional sayings concerning the exile.[57]

There is a question about what this text is saying. How are the verbs אסף אאסף used? First the typical meaning of the word אסף is 'to gather, remove'.[58] The use of the word in Zeph. 1.2, 3 clearly denotes 'to destroy', 'remove', and so on. This meaning is mainly in its contextual significance אסף מעל and more specifically, its occurrence with the dominant concept of destruction signaled by the use of כרת (Zeph. 1.3, 4) and ונטיתי ידי על-יהודה (Zeph. 1.4).

If the use is the same in both Mic. 2.12 and Zeph. 1.2, 3, further consideration must be given to the significance of the divine speech in this context—namely, whether it is a prophecy of hope, judgment or both. As a prophecy of both judgment and hope it would mean that Yahweh will remove or destroy Jacob, while he will gather the remnant of Israel. Does this mean that there are two distinct verbs being used to communicate two distinct ideas? It is probable that there are two ideas

---

55. Note the textual difficulty, that is, the LXX 'his word'. This rendering makes the opponents' question regarding God's treatment of the upright. The prophet's response would begin in v. 8 and pose a challenge first to the opponents' uprightness by offering competing evidence to their claim.

56. Renaud, *Structure*, pp. 20-25; *idem, La Formation*, p. 184.

57. Mays, *Micah*, pp. 4-5, 28, 73-76.

58. Feinberg, 'אסף', pp. 60-61.

being signaled by use of the two terms. In that case the first means
(אסף) 'to sweep away, remove' while the second means (קבץ) 'to
gather'. In the piel קבץ denotes gathering of that which is scattered, for
example, the gathering of the remnant (שארית) in Jer. 23.3 (cf. Isa.
40.11; 43.5; Jer. 31.10; Ezek. 34.13; Zeph. 3.19). If two different concepts are being communicated, then the first verb would take its clue
from 1.6-7 where judgment is announced against Jacob (cf. 1.8-9).

If the two distinct verbs are synthetically parallel it must be considered whether the concept being signaled is that of removing or scattering. The questions arise mainly in respect to אסף and its meaning in
relation to קבץ. Could this be an instance of antithetical parallelism? If
so, are the verbs parallel in this way exclusive of their synthetically
parallel objects? So Yahweh will remove Jacob—Jacob and Israel
meaning the same group. In this interpretation, 2.12 would stand in
contrast to 2.13.

Another point to be considered is whether the verbs are synthetically
parallel exclusive of their objects, such that the objects are indicative of
two distinct groups. In this case, rather than being dominated by the
first verb, the concept of the unit is dominated by the second, and the
multivalency of the first verb does not result in the multivalency of the
whole. This would mean that Yahweh promises to gather all of Jacob
on the one hand and a remnant of Israel on the other. Perhaps the parallelism incorporates the use of both verbs and nouns. In this case the
meaning is to 'gather' Jacob, and the remnant of Israel modifies Jacob.

It seems that the use of 2.12 presupposes the actualization of the exile
of the people: 'I will surely gather all of you, O Jacob. I will gather the
remnant of Israel.' Here the Yahweh speech is juxtaposed to the preceding without a messenger formula or any transitional introduction.
Further, the 1st person style of 2.12 is followed in 2.13 by a 3rd person
account of Yahweh leading the people. Thematic continuity unifies this
unit—namely, the gathering of the remnant. It shows continuity with its
surrounding units by its similarities with 1.16 and possibly 2.4. Conceptually, this unit is about hope inasmuch as it anticipates a time of
deliverance from the 'scattered' state of existence (cf. Isa. 41.21).
Further, it connects hope for the future with a promise for deliverance
of the people. In this way it answers the question about the fate of
Jerusalem/Israel—a fate that in 1.9 seems to be cast in the same light as
that of Samaria/Jacob. Thus, regarding the first aspect of the judgment
articulated concerning Jerusalem—namely, exile—the unit 2.12-13 indi-

cates that the judgment will not be the final reality for those who have been scattered.

The placement of this, however, can be most plausibly understood as a redactional addition. That it stands where it does may be to conclude the first part of the question concerning Jerusalem's fate, a fate influenced both by Jerusalem's sin and God's response (cf. 7.8-20).[59]

I.B.1.b. *Judgment speeches against Israel's leaders (3.1-12)* This is the unit that represents the second element in the focus on Israel's sin and the ensuing judgment. While the first (2.1-13) focuses on the oppression with regard to the land, this unit focuses on oppression with regard to the leaders (3.1-12).

I.B.1.b.1) *Transition formula (ואמר) (3.1aα)* The function of the transition formula may be to indicate the continuation of the dialogue and specially the disputation in 2.6-11. The 1st person address signals that the prophet is the speaker rather than the opponents (cf. 2.6). See discussion of 3.aβ [I.B.1.b.2)a)(1)] below.

I.B.1.b.2) *Against the leaders for their sins (3.1aβ-8)* The focus on the leaders includes attention to both the judicial leaders (3.1aβ-4) as well as the prophets (3.5-8) all of whom will receive further attention in (3.9-12). Each group of leaders in 3.1aβ is addressed with respect to their particular sins and the ensuing judgment. The result of this approach to the judgment is to emphasize the connection between the accusation and the judgment—each form of judgment corresponding to a particular form of sin or crime.

I.B.1.b.2)a) *The judicial leaders (3.1aβ-4)* That fact that the judicial leaders are the first to be addressed does not necessarily mean that their sins are more prominent than those of the other leaders.

I.B.1.b.2)a)(1) *Introduction—summons to hear (שמעו־נא) (3.1aβ)*. This unit is marked off from what precedes by ואמר. In its present position, it stands outside of the form of the unit it introduces. It has been variously interpreted, having been understood as a redactional element,[60] an autobiographical fragment,[61] or a simple 1st person statement similar to others of its kind occurring in the book of Micah (1.8; 2.7, 8; 3.3, 5).[62]

---

59. Mays, *Micah*, pp. 4-5, 28.
60. Willis, 'A Note on ואמר', pp. 50-54.
61. Lescow, 'Micha 1–5', 47-50; Mays, *Micah*, pp. 84-85.
62. Wolff, *Micah*, p. 95.

The judgment speech, then, begins with a summons to hear addressed to a group designated by the parallel expressions 'heads of Jacob' (יעקב ראשי) and 'leaders of the house of Israel' (קציני בית ישראל). Thus the accused are named by title and hence roles.[63] This is in contrast to 2.1 where the accused are designated by their 'sin' without citing their title. The only explicit indication of their status is the mention of their possession of power to do the evil that they plan (כי יש־לאל ידם, 2.2bβ).

The term ראש used in connection with קצין here designates those who have responsibility for justice. Semantically, ראש is used to designate 'head' of a family or tribe. More specifically, in Exodus 18,[64] Deut. 1.9-15[65] and 2 Chron. 19.4-11,[66] the title is used of the able men chosen to function as judges who were responsible to administer justice.

קצין, the other title used here as a synonym of ראש, is generally used to designate 'chief, ruler' (Judg. 11.6; Isa. 3.6). It is used in a military sense to refer to 'head of an army' (Josh. 10.24). On the basis of its Arabic cognate, it has been suggested that קצין has the connotation of 'judge'.[67] In Isa. 1.10 it has the general sense of political leader. Here in Mic. 3.1a the paired titles designate in the most general sense, 'leaders'. Their responsibility is to administer justice as indicated by the accusation in vv. 1b-3.

I.B.1.b.2)a)(2) *Judgment (3.1aβ-4)* The persons who are accused have been named in the introduction (3.1aβ) by their titles in the community. The judgment indicates that their title is indicative of their role and particular responsibilities. It is the violation of these responsibilities

---

63. David L. Petersen, *The Roles of Israel's Prophets* (JSOTSup, 17; Sheffield: JSOT Press, 1981), pp. 14-15, regarding role theory.

64. Knierim, 'Exodus 18', pp. 158-59; J.B. Barlett, 'The Use of the Word ראש as a Title in the Old Testament', *VT* 19 (1969), pp. 1-10; E. Hammershaimb, *Some Aspects of Old Testament Prophecy from Isaiah to Malachi* (Copenhagen: Rosenkilde & Bagger, 1966), p. 31; Roland de Vaux, *Ancient Israel: Social Institutions* (New York: McGraw–Hill), pp. 152-55.

65. Here ראשים is used synonymously with שפטים and שרים as titles, and שפט used to describe the responsibility.

66. G. Macholz, 'Zur Geschichte der Justizorganisation in Juda', *ZAW* 84 (1972), pp. 314-40; de Vaux, *Ancient Israel*, pp. 152-53.

67. Johannes P. van der Ploeg, 'Les chefs du Peuple d'Israel et Leurs Titres', *RevB* 57 (1950), pp. 40-61 (5); Gerard van Groningen, 'קצין', in *TWOT*, II, p. 807; Beyerlin, *Die Kulttraditionen Israels*, pp. 52-53.

that constitute the accusation (3.1ab-3) and the announcement of judgment (3.4).

I.B.1.b.2)a)(2)(a) *Accusation (3.1aβ-3)*. The accusation is formulated in a rhetorical question implying that the addressees know the answer to be indisputable. The question, by means of the construction ל + לא א + infinitive, expresses the idea of obligation and permission (cf. 2 Chron. 13.5).[68] According to Graffy, the rhetorical question is often used in disputation speeches to gain assent to what is being said.[69] An understanding of what the heads and leaders would be assenting to requires further examination of the obligation. The obligation is signaled by the verb ידע whose object is משפט. The term ידע denotes not merely an intellectual understanding of משפט but devotion to its execution.[70] Accordingly, Stansell argues that 'the formulation in 3.1, with its combination of "summons to hear" followed by a disputing, rhetorical question introduced by הלוא is a device of the wise men's disputation that Micah has apparently borrowed…'[71] This argument is, however, geared towards establishing the wisdom tradition (Prov. 2.9; 28.5) as the source of Micah's prophecy and understanding of the role responsibilities.[72] This connection to wisdom tradition is not to be discounted in much the same way that the Pentateuchal tradition is not to be discounted as Stansell so readily does. Both contribute to the understanding of this text. From the wisdom tradition it is clear that there is a responsibility —that practicing and understanding (בין) משפט is a characteristic and the responsibility of the 'good' person.

The Pentateuchal tradition (cf. Exod. 18.13-21 and Deut. 1.9-18) concerning the responsibility of judges readily suggests itself as a source

---

68. Cf. GKC, §150e and §114*l* Gen. 3.11; 29.15; 1 Sam. 2.27; 23.19; 1 Kgs 22.3; Amos 9.7; R. Williams, *Hebrew Syntax: An Outline* (Toronto: University of Toronto Press, 2nd edn, 1976), §284; Waltke and O'Connor, *Syntax*, p. 208, 'ethical dative'. Cf. also M.L. Brown, '"Is it Not?" or "Indeed!": *HL* in Northwest Semitic', *MAARAV* 4.2 (1987), pp. 201-209 (213-14).

69. Graffy, *A Prophet Confronts his People*, pp. 8-14. Here he discusses the form and function of the disputation speech.

70. Smith, *Micah, Zephaniah*, p. 72; Wolff, *Micah*, p. 98; Mays, *Micah*, pp. 78-79; Waltke, 'Micah', p. 657; Vuilleumier, 'Michée', p. 38; Keil and Delitzsch, *The Twelve Minor Prophets*, p. 450.

71. Stansell, *Micah and Isaiah*, p. 106.

72. Stansell, *Micah and Isaiah*, p. 105. Here he argues on the basis of the presence of wisdom vocabulary to which ידע is said to belong.

for understanding the nature of the responsibility as related to the heads and leaders. From these contexts, the responsibility is seen to be mainly judicial—to judge the cases and settle disputes equitably. However, in the case of Exod. 18.13-17 there is some dispute as to whether the division of responsibilities was a division between the religious and the civic.[73] This is not of primary concern here. What is of concern is that the responsibility for justice was viewed as sanctioned by God, the source of authority without which the role is nullified.

The accusation is expanded by a characterization of the leaders: 'You who hate good and love evil' (3.2a). The force of this is adversative indicating that although the leaders know their responsibility to administer justice, they do the opposite (cf. v. 9 which says that 'they abhor justice and pervert all that is just'). That the practice of the leaders is contrary to what is required is made evident elsewhere in prophetic literature, where to seek God is made synonymous with seeking good and made a prerequisite for the receipt of God's grace:

> [14]Seek good and not evil, that you may live;
> and so the Lord, the God of host, will be with you,
> just as you have said.
> [15]Hate evil and love good, and establish justice in the gate,
> it may be that the Lord, the God of Host,
> will be gracious to the remnant of Joseph (Amos 5.14-15; cf. Isa. 1.16-17; 5.19-20).

The accusation is therefore that they live in opposition to their responsibility.

As a unit, vv. 2b-3 further extend the accusation. The unit specifies the actions of the ראשים and קצינים. It depicts an imagery of violent and

---

73. Knierim, 'Exodus 18', pp. 163-64; *idem*, 'Customs, Judges, and Legislators in Ancient Israel', in Evans and Stinespring (eds.), *Early Jewish and Christian Exegesis* (Atlanta: Scholars Press, 1987), pp. 3-15; Martin Noth, *Exodus* (OTL; trans. J. Bowden; Philadelphia: Westminster Press, 1962), p. 150. There are those who argue that the sacral and civic functions were intermingled: Brevard S. Childs, *The Book of Exodus* (OTL; Philadelphia: Westminster Press, 1974), pp. 330-32; John I. Durham, *Exodus* (WBC, 3; Waco, TX: Word Books, 1987), pp. 250-52 (251). Cf. Harriet K. Havice, 'Concern for the Widow and Fatherless in the Ancient Near East: A Case Study in Old Testament Ethics' (unpublished PhD dissertation, Yale University, 1978), p. 48, who on the basis of 2 Chron. 19.5-11 argues that the administration of justice was the responsibility of the local court.

inhumane practices through its use of metaphorical language. In this instance, the figurative actions are named and the literal are implied.[74] The result is that the subject of the discourse is obscured behind the metaphor,[75] but the cruelty is brought into clear focus. The violence of the leaders' actions are made salient; and the metaphor of cannibalism thus illustrates the leaders' abuse of their responsibility. Furthermore, the inhumanity of the leaders illustrated by the metaphor is thus connected with the general statement of the accusation—you who hate good and love evil are just like those who ravage the people stripping them of their very existence.

The term גזל, used here to describe the leaders' abuse of their responsibility, has a variety of connotations. It is used in reference to depravity of justice (Isa. 10.2), of robbery (Gen. 31.31; Deut. 28.21; Judg. 21.23; 2 Sam. 23.21//1 Chron. 11.23; Job 24.9; Mic. 2.2), and of oppression (Deut. 28.29; Mic. 2.2). In its broadest sense, it 'denotes an illegal action which manifests power and overcomes a person or a thing'.[76] In 3.2b גזל governs two objects עורם and שארם—the skin and the flesh of the people.[77]

Verse 3 continues the depiction of the behaviors cited as examples of the leaders' hatred for what is good:

Who *devour* the flesh of my people;
strip their skin off of them;
break their bones;
and *chop* them as into a pot; like meat into a caldron (my translation and emphasis).

The language is metaphorical and as such depicts the outrageous acts of abuse being committed. The violence is described using the verbs אכל,

74. Laurence Perrine, *Literature: Structure, Sound and Sense* (New York: Harcourt Brace Jovanovich, 4th edn, 1983), pp. 570-71, 1461.

75. Thomas B. Dozemann, *God on the Mountain* (SBLMS, 37; Atlanta: Scholars Press, 1989), pp. 30-32. See his discussion of S.J. Brown, *The World of Imagery: Metaphor and Kindred Imagery* (New York: Russel & Russel, 1966), pp. 49-40.

76. Schupphaus, 'גזל', pp. 456-58; cf. Oswalt, 'גבר', pp. 148-49.

77. MT lacks an immediate antecedent to the 3rd person plural suffixes in v. 2b. Therefore various proposals have been offered including: Keil and Delitzsch, *The Twelve Minor Prophets*, p. 450, who propose the antecedent to be בית ישראל in v. 1a. Others propose a transposition of v. 2b to follow v. 3. 'My' would then be the referent of the suffixes; cf. Hagstrom, *The Coherence*.

פשט,[78] פצח and פרש, all of which are used metaphorically, in this instance, to illustrate the ravaging of the people.

By identifying the objects of the violence (by means of the 3rd person plur. pron. suff.), this part of the judgment speech makes reference to those being abused. They are identified as עמי (the prophet being the referent of the 1st person pron. suff.). Notably, this group is not identified as עני, אביון, דל, רש, עשק or any of the terms typically used in reference to the poor[79] and disadvantaged.[80] This is not to say that the group called עמי was not as disadvantaged as those typified by the vocabulary of the concept of the poor. The absence of the typical semantic field is simply the absence of the semantic signals and does not indicate the absence of the concept.[81] Insights into the nature of the group identified by the term עמי is implied in the focus of the accusation on the leaders' abuse of their responsibility. The very language of responsibility presupposes the object of responsibility—in this case עמי. More specifically, the language of 2.1 already suggests the dichotomy between those with power and those over whom they exercised that power. From this perspective the distinction in 3.3 is between those responsible for justice and those for whom they are responsible. From the perspective of both the Pentateuchal (e.g. Deut. 15) and prophetic (Isa. 1.16-17; Amos 2.6-8; 5.12) traditions it is the disadvantaged who were of special concern to receive justice.[82] To this extent, the accusation is that the leaders are abusing their responsibility to the עמי who, by virtue of their lack of power, are disadvantaged and thus identifiable with groups who are typically identified by the 'language of the oppressed'.

---

78.   Victor P. Hamilton, 'פשט', in *TWOT*, II, p. 741. The term is used to denote violent acts (Gen. 37.23; Ezek. 16.39; 23.26; Mic. 2.8) including dismemberment (Lev. 1.6; 2 Chron. 29.34; 35.11), although it is used also of changing one's clothes (Lev. 6.11, 23; Neh. 4.23).

79.   Cf. Miscall, 'The Concept of the Poor', pp. 30-33.

80.   Miscall, 'The Concept of the Poor', pp. 30-33.

81.   See Chapter 4 of this study for my discussion of various types of indicators.

82.   Havice, 'Concern for the Widow'; Jeffries M. Hamilton, *Social Justice and Deuteronomy: The Case of Deuteronomy 15* (SBLDS, 136; Atlanta: Scholars Press, 1992); C.F. Mariottini, 'The Problem of Social Oppression in the Eighth Century Prophets' (unpublished PhD dissertation, Southern Baptist Theological Seminary, 1983), p. 112; Itumeleng J. Mosala, *Biblical Hermeneutics and Black Theology in South Africa* (Grand Rapids: Eerdmans, 1989), pp. 112-13.

(b) *Announcement of judgment (3.4).* The announcement of judgment is introduced by אז (vis-à-vis לכן in vv. 6, 12) followed by the imperfect. This construction is typically used to point to the future as the time frame for the events described.[83] Verse 4 presupposes the conditions described in vv. 1b-3 both in the fact of the impending judgment and in the correspondence between the judgment and the nature of the sin depicted in the accusation.

The text focuses on the reaction of Yahweh to the leaders' cry, זעק. The term usually denotes a loud cry made at times of distress with the purpose of receiving immediate assistance.[84] Notably, the judgment is not that the leaders will experience distress nor that they will cry out. The judgment presupposes the distress as the logical and chronological precondition of the cry. God's silence as the cause of the distress has lead to speculations about the nature of the distress. Mays, for example, speculates that the general suffering that the leaders inflicted on the people will be inflicted on them;[85] however, Waltke identifies the distress specifically as that of the exile and the accompanying adversities.[86] While it is possible that the judgment refers to a specific time of distress, it may also refer to the inevitability of the cry rather than a particular anticipated future distress. The inevitability of the distress would be the unfolding of the 'act-consequence' pattern.

It is therefore the reaction of Yahweh to the 'cry' of the leaders that constitutes the judgment—that is, Yahweh's silence. Semantically, the judgment consists of two parallel expressions. The first of these is: 'Then they will cry out to Yahweh but he will not answer them'. The action of the leaders (זעק) is striking because the 'cry for help' is typically a cry for justice which is made by the underprivileged,[87] and which constitutes an obligation to the hearers to offer assistance (cf. Deut. 22.23-27). Stansell argues that it is not uncommon for oppressors to cry to God for assistance (Judg. 3.9, 15, 6.6-10; 10.10; cf. Hos. 7.14;

---

83. DeVries, *From Old Revelation to New*, pp. 3-4. He sees the adverb as representing the 'transitional use of the futuristic אז'; thus Mays, *Micah*, p. 80; Wolff, *Micah*, p. 100. Cf. GKC §107c3, after אז the imperfect is used to indicate the future (Gen. 24.41; Exod. 12.48; Ps. 51.21).

84. R. Albertz, 'צעק', in *THAT*, II, p. 573.

85. Mays, *Micah*, p. 80.

86. Waltke, 'Micah', p. 662.

87. Havice, 'Concern for the Widow', pp. 51-52; Cf. Gen. 4.10; 2 Kgs 4.1; 8.1-6; 6.26-30; Job 16.18.

8.2; Joel 1.14). However, in these instances cited by Stansell, the cry is made by the people as a nation who had done evil. The idea is that the people had lived contrary to the 'will' of God. Noteably, these texts do not have the the oppressor vs. oppressed connotation. The most that can be claimed on the basis of these texts is that even those who were not pleasing to God cried out to God in their distress and received help. Thus it cannot be said that God always refuses to hear the cries of those who practiced 'evil'. Clearly this is not the argument of 3.4 and the tradition that it reflects.

The text presupposes that God's response to the cry for help is conditioned by the actions of the distressed. Having abused their responsibilities, the heads and leaders out of their distress will cry out to Yahweh; but Yahweh will not respond to them. This idea is reflected elsewhere:

> If you close your ear to the cry of the poor,
> you will cry out and not be heard (Prov. 21.13).

That Yahweh's lack of response to the זעק is to be construed as judgment, presupposes that it is atypical. Typically, Yahweh would answer:

> The eyes of the Lord are on the righteous,
> and his ears are open to their cry.
> The face of the Lord is against evil doers…
> When the righteous cry for help, the Lord hears,
> and rescues them from all their troubles (Ps. 34.15-18; cf. Exod. 3.7).

The condition under which Yahweh responds is clearly suggested—that the distressed are 'righteous'. It is this conditional aspect of Yahweh's response that is at issue in Mic. 3.4a. The response of Yahweh is not apathy suggested by a passivity toward the cry for help. It is a deliberate action of refusal to respond. This deliberateness is made explicit in v. 4bα: 'but he will hide his face from them at that time'. There is only one other such references where God's 'hiding his face' is accompanied by reference to God's not answering 'cries'. In this instance, the hiding of the face results in the not hearing:[88]

> See, the Lord's hands is not too short to save,
> nor his ears too dull to hear.
> Rather, your iniquities have been barriers

---

88. Samuel E. Balentine, *The Hidden God* (Oxford: Oxford University Press, 1983), p. 69.

between you and your God,
and your sins have hidden his face from you
so that he does not hear (Isa. 59.1-2).

The phrase סתר פניו belongs to the larger context of the 'hiddenness of God' motif. '[It] is semantically distinctive within the vocabulary of the Old Testament. Not only is it a phrase used with the verb סתר, it is also an expression used almost exclusively with reference to the hiding of God's face.'[89] It is often found in the Psalms and Prophets in laments and judgment speeches,[90] and denotes Yahweh's anger expressed in the lack of compassion.[91]

The scope of the judgment is qualified by two indicators: מהם and בעת ההיא. What these restrictive qualifiers indicate is the deliberate aim of the judgment—the limited application of the hiddenness of Yahweh.[92] It is not simply that Yahweh will hide his face from all of Israel for all times. מהם restricts the extent of the judgment to the leaders. The other restriction on the judgment is further presented in the temporal indicator—בעת ההיא. It indicates that the hiding of Yahweh's face is not permanent but limited to the specific time denoted by the phrase and its complementary expression—אז (3.4).

The cause of Yahweh's act of judgment is then reiterated in 3.4bβ— הרעו מעלליהם. This points back to 3.1b-3 connecting the 'sins' of the leaders with Yahweh's action. Conceptually, it suggests that Yahweh does not arbitrarily hide his face, but has a reason for such an abandonment of the leaders (vis-à-vis Ps. 104.29). In support of this observation are other instances where the cause of Yahweh's hiding his face is clearly articulated as the people's 'sins': חטאותיכם, עונתיכם (Isa. 59.2); כל ערתם (Jer. 33.5); כפשעיהם, כטמאתם (Ezek. 39.24); כל-הרעה (Deut. 31.18).[93]

89. Balentine, *The Hidden God*, p. 113.

90. Balentine, *The Hidden God*, p. 47.

91. Thomas W. Mann, *Divine Presence and Guidance in Israelite Traditions: The Typology of Exaltation* (Baltimore: The Johns Hopkins University Press, 1977), pp. 257-58; cf. also G. Wehmeier, 'סתר', in *THAT*, II, p. 175.

92. In contrast to Mays, *Micah*, p. 80, who views בעת ההיא as redactional and thus there is no qualifier of Yahweh's face-hiding activity. Cf. DeVries, *From Old Revelation to New*, p. 36, according to whom the phrase in Mic. 3.4 is a futuristic transition (Isa. 33.23; 35.6, 7; 41.1; 58.8; 60.5; Jer. 2.2; 31.13; Ezek. 32.14; Hab. 1.11; Zeph. 3.9, 11).

93. Balentine, *The Hidden God*, p. 66.

With the correspondence of the accusation and the judgment exemplified in the syntax and concept of the text unit, vv. 1b-4 may be summarized as follows: the leaders are judged because they abused their responsibility to carry out justice. The idea of accountability is implied in the text. Leaders are accountable to Yahweh, yet they failed the people. That they are judged illustrates a world-view in which they are neither the highest authority nor exempted from accountability. Havice discusses this order of accountability, noting that concern for the underprivileged is found in the hierarchical world-view of the ancient Near East. In this world-view, each person exists in a hierarchical relationship to all others. In this relationship the two primary reciprocal duties are loyalty and obedience owed upwards to one's superior, and beneficence owed downwards to one's inferior.[94]

The judgment in v. 4 implies such a hierarchy. The leaders failed the people by their injustice toward the people, a failure which threatened the very existence of the people. Yahweh abandons the leaders in their distress, thus threatening their existence.[95]

I.B.1.b.2)b) *Against the prophets (3.5-8).* As the second judgment speech of the first main unit of ch. 3, the sub-unit vv. 5-8 continues the presentation of the correspondence of sin and judgment. Set off from the preceding sub-unit by the use of the messenger formula כה אמר יהוה, this oracle is addressed to the prophets. They are identified by the title נביאים (v. 5a) and their deeds expressed in relative participial clauses (v. 5aβ-bα)—in apposition to נביאים—and the relative clause introduced by ואשר (cf. 3.3).[96] Through parallel use of the titles they are further depicted as having the same or similar functions as seers (חזים) and diviners (קסמים, v. 7).

I.B.1.b.2)b)(1) *Introduction—messenger formula (כה אמר יהוה) (3.5aα).* Typically the messenger formula is an authorization formula indicating the validity of the messenger and message. However, its presence here has been a point of dispute. The dispute is centered on the non-generic use of the formula. This is most salient in the postponement of the message and the presence of עמי where עמו would be expected. It seems that the עמי is used here by the prophet as messenger. The prophet continues as speaker in v. 8. The message of Yahweh appears in v. 6. Despite this explanation, various emendations have been proposed to

---

94. Havice, 'Concern for the Widow', p. ii.
95. Cf. Miller, *Sin and Judgment*, p. 32.
96. GKC §§116w and 151i regarding vv. 5bα; see also §159-60.

achieve a more typical and smoother reading. These include the deletion of the formula,[97] and replacement of the formula with reference to
the woe oracle (הוי).[98] The function of the messenger formula is supported by v. 8 which in its tone and content is disputational, suggesting
the need for an authorization formula. The need consists in the incredibility of the message and the incredulity of the accused.

I.B.1.b.2)b)(2) *Judgment (3.5aβ-7)*. The responsibilities of the prophets
define the nature of the judgment pronounced against them. Both the
accusation (3.5ab-b) and the announcement of judgment (3.6-7) build
on the assumption that they have the responsibility to lead the people
and not to deceive them by means of false prophecies.

I.B.1.b.2)b)(2)(a) *Accusation (3.5aβ-b)*. Verse 5 has the dual function
of describing the accused and stating the accusation. The accusation is
focused on the prophets—נביאים—who are accused of leading the people astray (v. 5aβ). The means by which they lead the people astray
is not readily understood. Clearer understanding of the accusation is
achieved through understanding the semantics of the unit as well as the
structure of the argumentation.

First the semantic 'who lead my people astray', תעה (hiphil participle) The verb in the qal denotes, 'to wander, lose one's way' (Gen.
21.14; Exod. 23.4), 'stagger' (Isa. 28.7). In the hiphil—with people as
object—there are various means by which people are led astray: by
harlotry (Hos. 4.12); lies (Amos 2.4); wickedness (Prov. 2.26; 28.10).
As a form of punishment Yahweh leads astray both the people (Isa.
30.28; Jer. 50.6) as well as the leaders (Isa. 63.17; Ps. 107.4).[99] Leaders
also mislead the people (Isa. 3.12). More specifically, the prophets are
known and condemned for misleading the people (Jer. 23.13, 14, 32;
Ezek. 13.10). In Jer. 23, it is the prophets who mislead the people by

97.   Lescow, 'Micha 1–5', p. 48, replaces the formula with ואמר.
98.   K. Budde, 'Micha 2 und 3', *ZAW* 38 (1919–20), p. 20, argues to replace על
with הוי; Mays, *Micah*, pp. 81-82, sees the formula as redactional and thus proposes
that v. 5 began with the definite plural participle; Hillers, *Micah*, p. 44, reads הוי על
in place of על. Stansell, *Micah and Isaiah*, prefers the deletion of the messenger
formula on the basis of the typical usage of הוי with participle, 2.1-5; and the
impersonal style of v. 5; Ramsey, 'Speech-Forms', pp. 45-48 (55), sees 3.5-8 as a
possible woe oracle altered on analogy of Jer. 14.15 or 23.15.
99.   Stansell, *Micah and Isaiah*, pp. 75-76; Wolff, *Micah*, pp. 101-102; Keil and
Delitzsch, *The Twelve Minor Prophets*, pp. 451-52; Waltke, 'Micah', p. 662; Mays,
Micah, p. 82.

various means—for example, by prophesying by Baal (23.13), practicing evil (23.14) and fabricating dreams (23.32).

Conceptually, in 3.5 the way in which the prophets lead the people astray is juxtaposed to the initial accusation by means of an attributive relative participle. Two elements are fundamental to understanding the accusation, namely, understanding the means by which the people are mislead (e.g., self-delusion, fabrication of message); and recognizing the presuppositions of the prophets' claim to authenticity.

The first means by which the prophets mislead the people is signaled by the phrase הנשכים בשניהם. Typically this is taken to mean 'bite with their teeth', that is, 'when the prophets are fed'. The motivation for the prophecy would then be personal gain rather than loyalty to Yahweh. The nature of the prophecy, then, is made dependent on the receipt of compensation[100]—that is, food. But the accusation goes beyond the framework suggested by this interpretation.

This understanding of the nature of the accusation necessitates a reassessment of three elements: (a) use of the verb נשׁך, (b) the phrase הנשכים בשניהם and (c) its meaning in relation to 3.5bβ. There are some questions about the meaning of נשׁך. Its interpretation is largely based on a presumed antithetical parallel expression in 3.5bβ.[101] But the term most typically denotes the bite of a snake (Gen. 49.17; Num. 21.8; Amos 5.19; 9.3; Prov. 23.32). On the basis of these occurrences, it may be argued that the interpretation of the term נשׁך as 'to eat' is unprecedented or at least falls short of its meaning or significance in this passage. In agreement with Deane, it is here argued that the parallelism does not dictate a forced interpretation of the term.[102] But it must also be noted that the typical meaning is also not a dictate of its particularity in this text. The semantic field weighs heavily on the infratextual[103] meaning even if the term has been resignified in its present context.

---

100. Mays, *Micah*, p. 82; Wolff, *Micah*, p. 102; Smith, *Micah, Zephaniah*, p. 74; Waltke, 'Micah', p. 663.

101. Keil and Delitzsch, *The Twelve Minor Prophets*, p. 452, cite the alternative way of interpreting the phrase but argue in support of interpreting the term on a perceived antithetical parallel phrase; Cheyne, *Micah*, p. 31, citing 1 Sam. 2.13-16; Orelli, *The Twelve Minor Prophets*, p. 200, citing Isa. 9.14-15; Bennett, *The Book of Micah*, p. 33.

102. W.J. Deane *et. al.*, 'Micah', in H.D.M. Spence (ed.), *The Pulpit Commentary* (New York: Funk & Wagnalis, 1950), p. 36.

103. Knierim, *Text and Concept*, p. 3.

More than the semantic analysis is demanded in this instance. For a fuller understanding, one must examine the particular tendency of the current text as well as the intertextual aspects of the theme of prophets misleading the people.

In ch. 3 the parallelisms are all synonymous or synthetical (vv. 2-3, 6-7, 8, 9, 10, 12). There is no other instance in this unit of antithetical parallelism being used. This is not to discount the possibility of its use here but to encourage the consideration of a more viable alternative— synthetical parallelism. In this case, the waw of the independent indefinite relative, וַאֲשֶׁר, would not signal antithetical relationship of the two segments,[104] but a synthetical relationship of the means by which the prophets mislead.

Any antithesis, then, is between the message of 'peace' on the one hand and of 'war' on the other. Inasmuch as they are explications of the accusation, that is, that the prophets lead astray, the focus is not as much on this contrast as it is on the circumstances that give rise to the message—namely, the self-reliance of the prophets. Both messages have the effect of misleading the people. In considerating the nature of the accusation, the present author interprets the sub-unit to mean that the prophets make themselves the source of the prophecy rather than relying on Yahweh as source. This explains the correspondence of the accusation and the judgment. The judgment is Yahweh's withholding of revelation through prophetic vision. The resultant shame (indicating the prophet's reliance to some extent on Yahweh) necessitates the consideration of this alternative.

Under the circumstances described by v. 5bα, the prophets proclaim 'peace'—שָׁלוֹם. The term קְרָא is the term typically used to introduce a quote. Wolff argues that the quotation is a device of indicating guilt, and is consequently the justification of judgment.[105] In this respect שָׁלוֹם becomes the quote. Yet to say that they proclaim 'peace' does not uncover the significance of the accusation. The term שָׁלוֹם signals more than 'peace' as understood as the absence of 'war' although this meaning is certainly suggested in the parallel use of the term in v. 5bα with מִלְחָמָה in v. 5bβ.[106] In general it means wellbeing, security, prosperity.

---

104. Contrast Waltke, 'Micah', p. 662.

105. H.W. Wolff, 'Das Zitat im Prophetenspruch', *Gesammelte Studien zum Alten Testament* (Munich: Chr. KaiserVerlag, 1964), pp. 36-129; cf. Graffy, *A Prophet*, p. 105; Stansell, *Micah and Isaiah*, p. 76.

106. John I. Durham, 'שָׁלוֹם and the Presence of God', in John Durham *et. al.*

It became the content of the proclamation about which the prophets disputed and as such the litmus test of true and false prophecy.

Verse 5bα calls to mind Jer. 23.23-32 and other texts where the proclamation of 'peace' is a false proclamation. The force of the text is that the prophets' prophecy of peace is deceitful and as deadly as the bite of a snake. That the quote here possibly had the meaning of declaring false prophecy, is supported by texts in which the prophets are depicted as deceiving the people (Jer. 6.14//8.11; 14.13; 23.16-17, 23; 28.9), and in which the proclamation of 'peace' is made in the absence of peace (Jer. 12.12; 30.5; Ezek. 13.9-10). In the latter texts, God is said to be opposed to the practice of delivering false prophecies. Seen with these references, v. 5bα may be interpreted to mean that the prophets deceitfully proclaim 'peace'. This interpretation takes 'bite with their teeth' to be a metaphor for the deadly consequence of proclaiming peace when judgment is impending.[107]

Verse 5bβ also explicates the accusation against the prophets. Here the means of misleading the people is signaled by the relative clause, ואשר לא־יתן על־פיהם. Again as in v. 5bα, the understanding of this clause influences the understanding of the accusation. Typically, the clause is taken to mean 'whoever puts something into their mouths— give them something to eat'. This is thus rendered in accordance with the presumed antithetical parallelism of vv. 5bα and 5bβ.[108] However, there is another possibility based in large part on the intertextual use of the expression. Wolff[109] notes that the typical semantic field used to represent the idea 'to put something in the mouth' is either שׂים בפה (Exod. 4.15; Num. 22.38) or נתן בפה (Deut. 18.8; Jer. 1.9, and so on), rather than על־פה (נתן). The latter as found in Mic. 3.5bβ and Gen. 45.21 is typically used to express the idea of 'according to a wish'. According to this interpretation, the prophets were demanding that the

(eds.), *Proclamation and Presence: Old Testament Essays in Honor of Gwynne Henton Davies* (Macon, GA: Mercer University Press, corrected edn, 1983), pp. 272-93 (280-81); Mays, *Micah*, p. 83.

107. A.S. van der Woude, 'Micah in Dispute with Pseudo-Prophets', *VT* 19 (1969), pp. 244-60; cf. Smith, *Micah, Zephaniah*, p. 74.

108. Wolff, *Micah*, p. 102, cites this interpretation but also proposes an alternative; Allen, *The Books,* p. 311; Hillers, *Micah,* 45; Keil and Delitzsch, *The Twelve Minor Prophets*, p. 452; Miller, *Sin and Judgment*, p. 33; Mosala, *Biblical Hermeneutics*, p. 135; Mays, *Micah*, p. 80; Ewald, *Commentary on the Prophets*, p. 307; Vuilleumier, 'Michée', p. 39; Renaud, *La Formation*, p. 129.

109. Wolff, *Micah*, p. 102.

people compensate them. The accusation here is not so much that the prophets are taking compensation—food—but specifically that they made the content of their message dependent upon the fulfillment of their demands.

A further difficulty here is the meaning of the phrase 'according to their demand': (a) giving as opposed to not giving at all, or (b) content of the giving where the alternative is giving quality and quantity as demanded as opposed to giving but not the quality and quantity demanded. In the occurrences in Gen. 41.40 and 45.21 the references are to the content of the command. In Num. 3.51 (cf. 2 Kgs 23.35) both nuances are present. Thus it is possible that in v. 5bβ both nuances are present: the alternative of giving as opposed to not giving and the content of the giving as demanded. However, in light of v. 10, in which the content of the demand is in focus, the first nuance seems to be the primary one. What is suggested is that the prophets were compelling people to compensate them. This further suggests that there were those that did not compensate the prophets. The concept of the accusation may be reconstructed thus: the prophets were not coerced into taking compensation and thus succumbed to abusing their role. They were the instigators of the abuse.

The consequences of not giving according to the demand of the prophets are to be understood in this line of argument—the 'declaration of war/hostility'. The accusation is that the prophets deceitfully proclaimed 'peace', but still declared war against whomever did not give according to their demands. So whether or not one gives the message is false inasmuch as it comes from the prophets' whim and corruption rather than from their reliance on God. It is in this way that they lead the people astray.

I.B.1.b.2)b)(2)(b) *Announcement of judgment (3.6-7)*. The judgment is the withholding of visions—of revelation. This in essence means the nullification of the role of the prophets as messengers of Yahweh, since their sanction to be prophets came from God. The judgment uses the metaphor of night and its characteristics. This is presented through pairs of parallel expressions: night without vision (מחזון)//darkness without divination (מקסם); sun will go down//day shall be dark (cf. Amos 5.18). In the first pair, חזון and קסם are used in the most general sense of types of revelation. It is not a polemic against קסם[110] as a prohibited means of

110. R.L. Alden, 'קסם', in *TWOT*, II, p. 805.

inquiry. The implicit assumption of the legitimacy of the prophets—that is, against whom the accusation was uttered—is central to the plausibility of the judgment. They at some point relied on Yahweh as the source of their message. However, they had become self-reliant. Their shame came when they sought Yahweh for revelation, and Yahweh did not give it to them. They then were left without a verifiable message. Thus the picture is of prophets who tried to be both self-reliant and dependent on Yahweh as they saw fit. The assumption in the text seems to be that they were not true or false but both since the validity of the prophets depended on the content of the prophecy with relation of its source.[111] Therefore, the judgment of withholding revelation from the prophet would be their nullification and falsification as prophets of Yahweh.

Verse 7 is a further expansion of the judgment—the seer will be ashamed and the diviners disgraced. Here the cessation of revelation is primary and the shame secondary in effect, though nonetheless a significant part of the judgment. This shame is presented in the paired expression using the synonyms בוש[112] and חפר. In many instances in the Old Testament, shame—a feeling distinct from guilt—is a form of social control. It is associated with failure or feelings of inadequacy to fulfill expectations and responsibilities. According to L.M. Bechtel, the effectiveness of shame as a form of social control is directly proportional to the extent to which the social structure is group dominated. One of the main effects of shame is to deter and control unacceptable behavior.[113]

Here in v. 7 the shame may be the prophets' response to their failure. In this respect, the shame presupposes the prophets' awareness of their failure to live up to their role responsibility—to guide the people. There is also the possibility of the community's awareness of that failure. Such awareness may be presented in the picture of the audacious prophets

111. J. Lindblom, *Prophecy in Ancient Israel* (Philadelphia: Fortress Press, 1962), p. 213.

112. F. Stolz, 'בוש', in *ThWAT*, I, pp. 269-72; H. Seebass, 'בוש', in *TDOT*, II, p. 52; cf. J. Pedersen, 'Honour and Shame', in *idem, Israel: Its Life and Culture* (London: Oxford University Press, 1962), II, pp. 213-44.

113. L.M. Bechtel, 'Shame as a Sanction of Social Control in Biblical Israel: Judicial, Political and Social Shaming', *JSOT* 49 (1991), pp. 47-76 (49-50); Cf. Margaret Odell, 'The Inversion of Shame and Forgiveness in Ezekiel 16.59-63', *JSOT* 56 (1992), pp. 101-12 (102-105).

replaced by that of humiliated prophets. The shame is a sharp contrast suggesting more the internal awareness of failure. These were prophets who instigated the corruption of their office. Why would they be ashamed if they had no dependence on Yahweh as the sanction of their authority in the community?

Elsewhere, shame is expected as a response to the abuse of responsibility (Jer. 6.13-15//8.9-10), and condemnation results if shame is not exhibited. In this instance, the condemnation does not come because of the lack of shame. Shame comes as a result of and in conjunction with the condemnation. Shame here is not repentance for misleading the people, it is the product of punishment.

The depiction of the prophets' humiliation continues with reference to their behavior—they 'cover the lips'. This behavior is associated with mourning (Ezek. 24.17, 22), ritual uncleanness of lepers (Lev. 13.45) and uncleanness due to sin (Lam. 4.13-15). The idea here is that shame will be manifested in the behavior of the prophets who will be castigated and removed from the position of power to one of ostracism. The reason for the consternation and the judgment is introduced by the כי-clause—'there is no answer from God (אלהים vis-à-vis יהוה in vv. 4aα, 11bα-β). Having relied on their own devices, they now find that when they seek God they do not receive vision/revelation.

The shame further suggests that they were seen as authorities by their group—those to whom God gave 'answer', מענה. That they have no answer—the purpose of their role—showed that they are no longer sanctioned as prophets. Thus, having rejected God as the source of their message, they are rejected by God as God's messengers. This rejection signaled their nullification as compared to the death expected (cf. Jer. 6.15; 8.12; 14.15; Deut. 13.5; 18.20).

Verse 8 functions as justification of the speaker's message both because of the incredibility of the message and the incredulity of the hearer. Unlike vv. 2-3, 5, 10-11, the justification is not of the fact that judgment is impending, but of the authority of the speaker to proclaim the message. The prophet in v. 8 gives an assertion of his legitimacy. The tenor of it is disputational, observable first in the strong adversative particle (ואולם) that introduces the assertion (cf. Job 2.5; 5.6-8; 13.3; also Gen. 28.19; 48.19; Num. 14.21; 1 Kgs 20.23). This particle connects v. 8 with the preceding unit, vv. 5-7.[114] Secondly, the disputational

---

114. Waltke, 'Micah', p. 667, sees v. 8 as constituting a separate unit. Mosala,

tenor is observed in the claim to legitimacy (3.5; cf. 2.6-11). The speaker characterizes himself by a series of attributes which connote preparedness and willingness—authority to do what is required of him as messenger. However, this is not necessarily a report of a call as some such as Mays presume.[115]

The first of these attributes, כח, is used to refer to physical strength. Here it may indicate 'spiritual dynamism' (cf. Isa. 40.26, 29, 31).[116] In the use here, as in Isa. 40.26, כח and רוח יהוה are not distinct attributes. רוח יהוה is used as an explication of כח. Thus, as used in v. 8, the source of כח is רוח יהוה. The second attribute cited is משפט. The consideration of the term merits its own extensive analysis. Here, however, the consideration will be limited to its immediate context. The prophet characterizes himself as endued with the same responsibility as the heads and leaders (cf. 3.1b)—the responsibility of equitable and wise administering of justice.

Finally, גבורה generally suggests 'vigor, might', often in reference to preparedness for war.[117] It has been suggested that the attribute is to be understood as the speaker's 'courage' to stand up to the heads and leaders with the accusation that he proclaims.[118] In contrast to the speaker, the prophets he accuses lack this courage.

Verse 8b offers the purpose of the endowment. The purpose is to be a messenger in service of Yahweh's purpose and not one's own purpose (2.1, 6-11; 3.2-3, 5). Notably, the נגד + ל (infinitive construct) indicates the purpose of the prophet's endowment. The objects of נגד—פשע[119] 'crime' and חטא[120] 'sin'—are used in parallel with each other (cf. 1.5, 13) and are qualified by 'Jacob' and 'Israel' respectively. Thus, the

---

Biblical Hermeneutics, pp. 126, 135, 148, places v. 8 as the first verse in the unit vv. 9-12.

115. Mays, *Micah*, pp. 84-85.

116. Waltke, 'Micah', p. 667; Wolff, *Micah*, p. 104.

117. H. Kosmala, 'גבורה', in *TDOT*, II, p. 369.

118. Wolff, *Micah*, p. 105; Waltke, 'Micah', p. 667; Keil and Delitzsch, *The Twelve Minor Prophets*, p. 453; Allen, *The Books*, p. 314.

119. Knierim, *Die Hauptbegriffe für Sünde*, pp. 113-15; *idem*, 'פשע', pp. 488-95. Cf. Koch, *Die Sünde im Alten Testament*, pp. 27-28; contrast L. Köhler, *Theologie des Alten Testaments*, p. 158; KB, pp. 981-82. Norman H. Snaith, *The Distinctive Ideas of the Old Testament* (London: Epworth Press, 1944), pp. 63-65. He argues that sin is rebellion rather than transgression and, accordingly, פשע as used in the eighth-century BCE prophets is more accurately translated 'rebellion'.

120. R.P. Knierim, 'חטא', in *THAT*, I, pp. 541-49, 'to err'.

prophet sees his responsibility to proclaim, generally speaking, the 'sins' of Jacob//Israel. While these terms are generally translated crime and sin respectively, their meaning here is suggested by the accusations cited by the prophets: abuse of their responsibility by their practice of injustice (3.2-3, 9-11) and misleading the people (3.5-6). What is clearly evident here is that both are community oriented.[121] However, they are also the consequence or manifestation of an internal state. This is evident in the correspondence depicted between the internal state and the ensuing behaviors: planning evil and then carrying it out (2.1); in hating good and loving evil (3.1b, 2-8).

Summarily, vv. 5-8 is a judgment speech against prophets who by their self-reliance have falsified themselves and thus lead the people astray. The judgment is that they will not be given vision—revelation—from Yahweh, and thus will be humiliated and ostracized. This withholding of the message constitutes the end of the sanction of the messenger and thus signals the death knell of their prophetic role.

I.B.1.b.3) *Against Jerusalem for its leaders' sins (3.9-12).* Like the two preceding sub-units, this is a judgment speech consisting of the three characteristic parts of this genre. Its coherence is the judgment on the city because of the leaders' injustices. The accusation picks up the concerns articulated in 3.1b and v. 8a, this is, signaled by the use of the term מִשְׁפָּט. As in 3.2 and 5, relative participles are used in apposition to the titles to describe and accuse those named. It seems that v. 9a suggests a broader scope than the judicial leaders (cf. the heads, priests and prophets of v. 11). This will be discussed later in the discussion of v. 11. The accusation is presented first in general terms. As is typical of ch. 3, this is followed by an expansion of the accusation. Here the expansion is a specification of the accusation by the type of activity (v. 10) then by the groups and their specific responsibilities (v. 11). Verse 11 then makes explicit the misconception which constituted the basis of the security of the addressees. Finally, the announcement of judgment reiterates the dependence of the impending judgment on the accusation.

I.B.1.b.3)a) *Introduction—summons to hear (שִׁמְעוּ־נָא) (3.9a).* The introduction consists of a 'summons to hear' and the identification of the addressees. Here as in 3.1-5 they are the heads and leaders.[122]

---

121. Knierim, 'Hamartiology', pp. 424-28; Wolff, *Micah*, p. 105.
122. See above for the discussion of the responsibilities of the addressees.

I.B.1.b.3)b) *Judgment (3.9b-12)*. The focus on Jerusalem is achieved through the mention of Zion and identifying the leaders as those of Jerusalem in both the accusation (3.9b-11) and the announcement of judgment (3.12).

I.B.1.b.3)b)(1) *Accusation (3.9b-11)*. The general accusation is that the heads and leaders 'detest, abhor' (תעב) justice. The term תעב is variously used to denote abhorrence (Job 9.31; 19.19; 30.10; Ps. 107.18) and the detesting or exclusion for ritual and/or ethical reasons (Deut. 7.26; 23.8 [Eng. 7]; cf. Amos 5.10).[123] The accusation reflects the tendency towards the practice of injustice already described in 3.1b—hate good and love evil. Its place in the semantic field characterized by such terms as שׂנא, supports this connection. Moreover, the pairing of the general accusation in v. 9 that justice is abhorred with the specification of the accompanying actions alludes to the correspondence between the internal state and its ensuing actions.

Here תעב is paired with עקשׁ, 'to pervert', which has as its object כל־הישׁרה, 'all straight, right, just' (cf. Job 33.27; Prov. 10.9; 28.18). The accusation is that the leaders abhor justice—the practice of the equitable administration of justice, and so on—and pervert all that is right and just. The specific ways that this tendency toward injustice is manifested are the mistreatment of the people, the leaders accepting bribes and the leaders fostering a false basis of security.[124]

In the first part of the expansion of the accusation, Jerusalem is brought into focus, thus setting the tone for the rest of the unit. This focus is achieved through the thrice-repeated reference to Jerusalem in the 3rd fem. pron. suff. in v. 11 and another thrice-repeated reference in v. 12 by means of parallelism. The parallel use of Zion (v. 10a) and Jerusalem (v. 10b) suggests the religious and political significance of Jerusalem.[125] These references establish the focus of the leaders as related to the city of Jerusalem—the physical representation of a religious and political ideology.

Verse 10 is the specification of the practices of the leaders that exemplify their perversion of justice. This example is described in reference to the building of Jerusalem—'who build Zion with blood (דמים) and Jerusalem with wickedness (עולה)'. It has been argued that the reference here is to the harsh building program that resulted in

123. Ronald Youngblood, 'רעב', in *TWOT*, II, p. 976.
124. Wolff, *Micah*, p. 106.
125. Waltke, 'Micah', p. 671.

fortifications and large public buildings (2 Kgs 20.20-21; 2 Chron. 32.27-29).[126] This background provides the basis for understanding the accusation, in that it points to the harsh and cruel measures—forced labor, heavy taxation and bloodshed—by which the building of the city was accomplished. This, therefore, explicates the specified action as an example of the perversion of justice. The action is qualified by parallel expressions בדמים and בעולה, signifying the means by which the action was executed.

The term דמים refers both to spilled blood (Gen. 4.10; Exod. 22.1; Ps. 5.7)[127] and blood-guilt (Ezek. 7.23; 22.1; Hos. 4.2; Hab. 2.12).[128] The connotation of the term here is violence, bloodshed and cruelty. Its contextual synonym, עולה, usually denotes violence of various sorts including murder (2 Sam. 3.34) and oppression (Hab. 2.12; cf. Hos. 10.9; 2 Sam. 7.10). Its use as antonym further suggests its contradistinction to terms such as צדקה/צדק (Lev. 19.15; Isa. 26.10), ישר (Deut. 32.4; Ps. 107.42) and משפט (Deut. 32.4; Ezek. 33.14-16; Ps. 43.1). Similarly, its use as synonym suggests its affinity with terms such as ענה (2 Sam. 7.10), רשע (Isa. 26.10; Ezek. 18.24), and פשע (Ezek. 33.12).[129]

The accusation leveled against the leaders is that they built Jerusalem by means of violence and cruelty. The specifics of this could be understood in light of the labor practices and taxation to which the populace was subjected in order to finance the building of Jerusalem. The charge of violence is followed by a further explication of v. 9b in the form of naming the groups being accused (v. 11). The titles are all qualified with reference to Jerusalem, meaning that those being charged are limited to the city—not all heads, prophets and priests. Thus, while the accusation is that the leaders pervert the entirety of what is 'just', the reference is limited to the leaders of Jerusalem, perhaps with Jerusalem functioning as a metonym for the whole nation.

This interpretation takes ראשים as the main term which is further expanded by two synonyms כהנים and נביאים. What may be indicated here is the full range of leaders not simply prophets and priests, but all who have the responsibility to provide leadership to the people. Jeremiah

---

126. Waltke, 'Micah', p. 671; Wolff, *Micah*, p. 106; Mays, *Micah*, p. 89.

127. Wolff, *Micah*, p. 107.

128. B. Kedar-Kopfstein, 'דם', in *TDOT*, III, p. 241, proposes that some of the leaders had the specific responsibility of dealing with matters of blood-guilt but that they neglected this responsibility (2 Chron. 19.10).

129. G.H. Livingston, 'עול', in *TWOT*, II, 652-54.

6.14//8.10 and Lam. 4.13 illustrate this use of prophet and priest together to indicate the range of leaders (ומנביא ועד־כהן):

> For from the least to the greatest of them,
> everyone is greedy for unjust gain;
> and from prophet to priest,
> everyone deals falsely (Jer. 6.14).

This nuance is to be considered while noting the specification of the roles. What is thus indicated is the full range of functions involved in leading the people.

The groups are characterized by their accepting of bribes for the performance of their duty. This practice is condemned by law (Exod. 23.8; Deut. 16.19; 27.25),[130] and more specifically to the ראשׁים it is identified as a prohibition for one who holds that office (Exod. 18.21). Similarly, part of the qualification is that the 'heads, judges' hate bribes (Deut. 1.17). Here they are accused of taking bribes (שׁחד). The priests responsible for teaching[131] compromise the integrity of their office by selling their service (מחיר). The prophets also compromise their office by making their prophecy dependent on the receipt of payment (כסף). It is believed that such dependency undercuts one of the fundamental characteristics of prophecy—that it be 'inherently new and unpredictable'.[132] To prophesy for a bribe would mean control of the message. However, according to Johnson, the fact that the prophets were consulted indicates that they had some measure of control over their power.[133] The charge is not that they have control, but that they use their control to exploit their services. The dominant concept is that despite their role responsibilities the leaders—the full gamut of them—abuse their responsibilities.

Nonetheless, a caveat must be noted with reference to the tendency of over-generalizing the accusation. The accepting of a fee is not what is being condemned. The fee was a means of sustenance for these groups. It was customary for prophets and seers to receive gifts for services

---

130. Cf. Mays, *Micah*, p. 89, for further references.

131. Aubrey R. Johnson, *The Cultic Prophet in Ancient Israel* (Cardiff: University of Wales Press, 1962), pp. 5-7.

132. M.J. Buss, 'The Social Psychology of Prophecy', in J.A. Emerton (ed.), *Prophecy: Essays Presented to Georg Fohrer on his Sixty-fifth Birthday* (Berlin: W. de Gruyter, 1980), pp. 1-11 (6-7).

133. Johnson, *Cultic Prophet*, pp. 23, 31.

rendered (1 Sam. 9.7-10; 1 Kgs 14.3; 2 Kgs 5).[134] What is condemned is the perversion of the practice resulting from making the performance of the duty dependent on the receipt of compensation. The lead term in this instance שׁחד, to which מחיר and כסף are juxtaposed, has this specific connotation (Exod. 23.8; Deut. 16.9; Isa. 1.23; 5.23).[135] The taking of bribes is prohibited. The reason for the prohibition against the accepting of bribes is stated in the book of Exodus:

> You shall take no bribe,
> For a bribe blinds the eyes of the officials,
> and subverts the cause of those who are in the right (Exod. 23.8).

It is not only the poor who are of concern here, although it is usually the poor who lack the economic means with which to secure a bribe. The underprivileged come into focus as those whose cause is potentially subverted. This says nothing of their guilt or innocence, nor that of those who could afford to purchase a favorable judgment. The assumption is that bribery biases the judgment toward the purchaser. So what is at issue is not that the judgment will be rendered in favor of the powerful as opposed to the powerless. Such an assumption would equate the powerful with the guilty and the powerless with the innocent. At issue is that a bribe favors the one giving the bribe whether that person is rich or poor, innocent or guilty. The prohibition therefore aims at combating the purchasing of judgment, because such a purchase could result in acquittal of the guilty and the indictment of the innocent. Generally speaking, it seeks to safeguard the integrity of the judgments and guidance.

In v. 11b the belief of the leaders is quoted—they rely[136] on Yahweh saying: 'Is not Yahweh in our midst! Then no evil will befall us!' As previously mentioned, such quotations often represent an element that is to be refuted. The claim is that Yahweh's presence guarantees security. It therefore indicates the underlying reason for the flagrant abuses —exemption from misfortune—and the apparent disbelief that they would be subject to punishment by Yahweh. Stansell points out that what is being referred to here is the Jerusalem cult tradition, specifically the Zion tradition, in which Zion/Jerusalem was believed to be the

---

134. Johnson, *Cultic Prophet*, pp. 23-24.
135. Victor Hamilton, 'שׁחד', in *TWOT*, II, p. 914.
136. Cf. Wolff, *Micah*, p. 108.

dwelling place of God and thus inviolable.[137] The fact of the judgment indicates that the leaders have deluded themselves. The irony is that they deliberately mislead the people (3.5) and somehow unknowingly mislead themselves in the process.

I.B.1.b.3)b)(2) *Announcement of judgment (3.12)*. Like v. 6, v. 12 begins with לכן signaling the judgment as consequence of the infractions of the leaders. Here the reason for the judgment precedes the announcement of the judgment. The reason is simply בגללכם, 'because of you', the antecedent being the leaders (v. 9a) as characterized in the accusation (vv. 9b-11). Thus, the 'because of you' points beyond the title to the attributes of those bearing the title. The judgment comes not because of their role but because of their abuse of their role.

The judgment, however, is not focused on nullification of the role. In vv. 5-8 the judgment did not follow what is expected in view of Deuteronomy 16—that is, death does not follow what is expected in light of the pattern of ch. 3. In relation to the פשע, the judgment seems disproportionate. The leaders are indicted yet the scope of the punishment is the entire city. In contrast to the destruction of the city for the sin of the few, Isa. 1.21-26 says that the wicked are punished for their sins as a way of purifying the city. Thus, the correspondence seems to be in the existence of the city and the means by which it came into being (cf. Ps. 127.1). The city was built by violence and thus will be destroyed. Furthermore, the judgment addresses the misconception of the leaders who gave the false hope of inviolability despite their rampant practice of injustice. The judgment nonetheless represents the collective retribution for the sins of the few, that is, the leaders' sins result in judgment upon all of Jerusalem.[138]

The destruction is described in the usual parallelism of ch. 3, each component presenting an aspect of the impending destruction. The terms Zion, Jerusalem, temple mount, all point to the significance of the city

137. Stansell, *Micah and Isaiah*, p. 63, contrasts Micah's and Isaiah's particularities with respect to the Zion tradition. He notes that Isaiah had a more favorable view of Zion (Isa. 1.21-26; 29.1)—punishment toward purification—than did Micah (for whom punishment = destruction); cf. Mays, *Micah*, pp. 90-91, Wolff, *Micah*, p. 108; Allen, *The Books*, p. 319.

138. See Richard Adamaik, *Justice in the Old Testament: The Evolution of Divine Retribution in the Historiography of the Wilderness Generation* (Cleveland: John T. Zubal, 2nd edn., 1985), p. 85, regarding collective retribution in the pre-exilic prophets.

as political and religious center. The images of destruction—cultivated field, heap of ruins and forest—all suggest uninhabitable conditions.[139]

In conclusion, the coherence of the text is demonstrated in its adherence to the generic form of the judgment speech. Through this form the presence of various concepts and the pattern of correspondence between sin and judgment are signaled. The interrelationship of ch. 3 to the preceding is indicated in its shared concern that Israel will be judged because of its sins. The use of the typical vocabulary for sin also serves as an indicator of the relationship of chs. 1 and 3. See Figure 1 above for the interrelational aspects.

I.B.2. *Future: announcement of hope—establishment of Yahweh's reign (4.1–5.14)*

This unit is constituted in its concern with the future as a time of Yahweh's reign. The extant form and function of the oracles show the overall concern about the remote future and the imminent future as a means to it.[140] As the final unit of the first dispute with Israel concerning its fate, this unit addresses the question implicit in ch. 1 and specifically 1.9. Is the fate of Jerusalem the same as that of Samaria whose wounds were incurable? It has already been suggested in 2.12-13 that there is a future existence for Israel beyond the devastation of exile. This, however, is not an assertion on the part of the text that the sin of Israel is any less meritorious of judgment than that of Samaria. The text does not compare the sins in this way but reflects a perspective in which the nature of the judgment matches the nature of the sin.

Structurally, the unit begins with a temporal indicator or futuristic transition, והיה באחרית הימים (4.1),[141] and employs various transitions throughout—ביום ההוא נאם־יהוה (4.6; 5.9), עתה or ועתה (4.9, 11, 14).[142]

---

139. Wolff, *Micah*, pp. 108-109; Waltke, 'Micah', p. 673; Mays, *Micah*, p. 92.

140. Note that here the use of the terms 'imminent' and 'remote' in no way suggests a degree of certainty of their actualization. They are used with respect to chronological perspectives. The remoteness of the future is thus relative to the less distant future. Both, however, are regarded as time frames within history rather than at its end.

141. See DeVries, *From Old Revelation to New*, pp. 64-74, for discussion of the various temporal formulas and their variety of uses and significance to the organization of texts.

142. DeVries, *From Old Revelation to New*, pp. 28, 32, 47, classifies all of these as temporal transitions; contrast Mays, *Micah*, p. 105, who sees עתה in 4.9 as a rhetorical and literary device with no temporal nuance.

Even so, the structure and its coherence are not clearly discernible. This to some extent is due to the presence of these temporal indicators. For while they signal a transition, their presence, if not examined along with the conceptuality of the unit and any logical continuity of the sub-units, may obscure the larger unit to which the smaller units belong. Recognizing the potential for this confusion, Renaud, for example, proposes that the unit exhibits a chiastic structure: A 4.1-4; A' 5.8-14; B 4.6-7; B' 5.6-7; C 4.8-14; C' 5.1-5. He argues that 4.8-14 and 5.1-5 both begin by naming a city and that these units share the theme of the eschatological age.[143] The significance of the mention of the cities in these units is left uninterpreted. He ignores the transition formula in 5.9 in order to maintain the chiastic structure. Furthermore, while 4.6-7 and 5.6-7 are paired on the basis that they share the theme of the remnant, the distinctive conceptuality of each is not taken into account in the proposed structural arrangement. These two units approach the discussion of the remnant from markedly different vantage points. On the one hand, both are concerned with the existence of the remnant. On the other hand, the unit 4.6-7 discusses the remnant from the vantage point of restoration and Yahweh's reign over them in Zion, while the unit 5.6-7 discusses the remnant from the vantage point of their rise to power in exile. Furthermore, in light of its formulaic introduction, 4.6-7 is concerned with the remnant as a part of the remote future. In contrast to this, 5.6-7 is concerned with the imminent future as the precursor to the remote future.

Willis's proposal is based on his observation of a symmetry constituted in the alternation between doom and hope in each of the seven units: 4.1-5, 6-8, 9-10, 11-13; 4.14–5.5; 5.6-8, 9-14.[144] He, however, contends that the coherence of the whole (which includes 3.9-12) is evident in the concern for the goals and results of Yahweh's leadership—the common historical background of desolation; and the present doom in contrast to the future exaltation.[145]

The present writer proposes that chs. 4–5 constitute a coherent unit comprised of two sub-units: 4.1-5 and 4.6–5.14 (which is further divided

---

143. Renaud, *Structure*, pp. 18-19; Contrast Willis, 'Structure, Setting', p. 191; *idem*, 'Micah 3–5', pp. 200-201, for a further discussion of the arguments concerning the divisions of the unit.

144. Willis, 'Structure, Setting', p. 191; *idem*, 'Micah 3–5', p. 198.

145. Willis, 'Micah 3–5', pp. 204-206, 211.

into 4.6-7, 4.8–5.8, 9-14). This unit (that is, chs. 4–5) is not a contradiction of the previous unit nor is its placement suggestive of any intent to contradict or reverse the announcement of judgment found in the immediately preceding unit. A contradiction of the judgment would resemble that evidenced in the disputations of the previous units (that is, 2.6-11; 3.11; cf. 3.5) offering an alternative to judgment or else denying the validity of its announcement.[146] The fundamental presupposition of chs. 4–5, as is also the case for 2.12-13, is the presence of desolation. As such it cannot be said that the futuristic orientation—essentially the announcement of hope—caters to a minimization of the present crisis, or a reinterpretation of the present as being less significant in light of the future. Inasmuch as the text points to the future as a time of restoration, it also embraces the present as reality and as that from which the future will emerge. Its realistic nature, then, is that it takes its cue from the present. Hope for the future presupposes the present as a time that is less than ideal. For example, the present is a time of exile; the hope held out to the people is restoration from that exile. The present desolation of Jerusalem is that it is in ruins—an event that was believed to be impossible because of Yahweh's presence there; the hope is exaltation of Zion as the center of Yahweh's activity.[147] Thus, as the justice of judgment is seen in the correspondence of sin and judgment, so the reality and realism of hope is seen in the correspondence of the hope and the present circumstances.

The function of 4.8–5.8 is to address the circumstances of the present that must be surmounted to achieve the future that is announced. The association of the announcement of Zion's exaltation with the present circumstances that precede that exaltation is also found in Isa. 2.2–4.6.[148] In that context, the purification of Zion and the salvation of the remnant in Zion are brought together. It is in this respect that a contrast

146. Cf. van der Woude, 'Micah in Dispute', who proposes that 4.1-5 originated in the same group as 2.12-13. He classes both of these as direct contradictions of Micah's message of judgment against Israel.

147. See the discussion of 3.11 above. Cf. Ollenburger, *Zion*, pp. 21-22, 168 n. 2, who supports the idea that the 'significance' of Zion is Yahweh's presence there and not because the place itself has any inherent mystical quality apart from this presence.

148. Cf. Sweeney, *Isaiah 1–39*, pp. 87-88. He categorizes Isa. 2–4 as a prophetic announcement concerning the cleansing of Zion. The cleansing is geared toward the role that Zion will play in Yahweh's world order.

may be spoken of with reference to the realities portrayed by the present text. Even so, the distinctiveness of the past, present and future at once hold them together as chronologically if not also logically dependent.

Whether primary or secondary, a contrast is indicated in the role of the leaders in both sections on judgment and hope. In chs. 2 and 3, those in powers are portrayed as the source of the problem. They abuse their power and this in essence is the sin that leads to the judgment on the nation. In chs. 4 and 5, it is promised that Yahweh will establish universal reign in Zion, fulfilling the role of teacher, judge and reconciler. However the relationship of promise and hope is mediated by judgment.

I.B.2.a. *Introduction—Yahweh's reign in Zion (4.1-5)*. It is important to note that this unit's conceptual background is the establishment of Yahweh's universal reign in Zion. However, it is this observation that has been the subject of discussion concerning the conceptuality of the text and its parallel in Isa. 2.2-4.[149] In the present context, the unit may serve to address the issue of the fate of Zion, the dwelling place of Yahweh, as linked with the fate of Israel. Nonetheless, the perspective of the reign is universal in the sense that Zion is established as the center of Yahweh's activity, to which all nations go as a result of that established rule. This interpretation of the unit sees the link with 1.2, 3-4, as part of the contextual framework. Yahweh summons all peoples in order to bear witness against them. Until now, the focus has been on Israel throughout chs. 2–3. Here in 4.1-5, the universal framework is pulled to the foreground again and provides the context for understanding the hope offered to Israel. This hope is partly constituted in Yahweh's promise of universal rule. The unit functions as an introduction to chs. 4–5 in the sense of providing the framework for understanding the distinctive parts.[150]

---

149. For a discussion of Isa. 2.2-4//Mic. 4.1-4 see: H. Wildberger, *Jesaja* (BKAT, 10.1-3; Neukirchen–Vluyn: NeukirchenerVerlag, 1972–82); Renaud, *La Formation*, pp. 160-63; Wolff, 'Schwerter zu Pflugscharen—Missbrauch eines Prophetenwortes? Praktische Fragen und exegetische Klärungen zu Joël 4, 9-12, Jes 2, 2-5 und Mic 4, 1-5', *VT* 44 (1984), p. 280. Sweeney, *Isaiah 1–39*, pp. 96-99, on the structure of Isa. 2.2-4.

150. Cf. Allen, *The Books*, p. 329; Waltke, 'Micah', p. 686.

I.B.2.a.1) *Introduction—temporal formula (והיה באחרית הימים) (4.1aα).*
This unit is marked off by the phrase והיה באחרית הימים. The phrase is
often found in later interpolations to exile and postexilic prophecies
where it is used to signal a turning point (Hos. 3.5; Jer. 23.20; 30.34;
Ezek. 38.16 where the phrase serves as introduction). It usually comes
at the end of a passage as a means of indicating a future time. Its use as
an eschatological term is late, that is, arising from the postexilic period
(e.g. Gen. 49.1; Num. 24.14; Jer. 23.20; 30.34; Hos. 3.5; cf. Ezek.
38.16).[151] In this context, the nuance of the phrase may not necessarily
be eschatological but indicative of a remote future, and a time within
history. This interpretation makes sense of the attention to the present
circumstances, if these are seen as necessary to the actualization of that
future (4.8–5.8).

I.B.2.a.2) *Announcement of the promise (4.1aβ-4).* This announcement
brings the future status of Zion into focus without identifying conditions for the actualization of the promise. It also indicates a particular
time frame and those events that will happen in that time frame as guaranteed by Yahweh.

I.B.2.a.2)a) *Promise (4.1aβ +b).* The unit begins with a statement of the
promise v. 1aβ +b and ends with its own concluding formula (כי־פי
יהוה צבאות דבר) that serves as an authentication of the immediately
preceding promise. In its present position, the promise signals a turning
point from the desolation of Jerusalem/Zion announced in 3.12. Unlike
the heap of ruins and wooden heap depicted in 3.12 (עיין and לבות יער),
the future for Zion is announced as one of exaltation. This exaltation is
presented in three aspects. The first concerns 'the mountain of the
house of the Lord' (הר בית־יהוה; cf. 2 Chron. 33.15). Whether the difference in designation of the phrase in 3.12 (הר בית) is significance, as
suggested by Wolff, the similarity in focus indicated by the shared terminology is undeniable. Both passages are concerned with the fate of
Zion. Their concern—not the designation—is the point of difference.

In 3.9-12, Zion's fate is connected with the sin of the leaders of
Jerusalem. As such, Zion as a place of corruption becomes a place of
ruins. In the present text (4.1-5), the fate of Zion is one of exaltation

---

151. Wolff, *Micah*, p. 119; DeVries, *From Old Revelation to New*, p. 92, argues
that within Isaiah and Micah, the 'the introductory rubric...actually predicts an
eschatological bliss'.; see also *idem, Yesterday, Today, and Tomorrow*; contrast
Allen, *Micah*, p. 324, who argues that the phrase refers to a chronological time
within history and not to the end of time.

and centrality as the location of Yahweh's reign. The centrality of Zion is signaled by such formulations as 'it will be established (נכון) as the head of the mountains (בראש ההרים)' and 'raised above the hills'. It has been suggested that this is an indirect polemic against other divine mountains which would now be in the shadows of the 'mountain of the house of the Lord'.[152] The centrality is further signaled by the promised pilgrimages of many peoples/nations to Zion (4.1b).

I.B.2.a.2)b) *Aspects of the promise (4.2-4)*. The second aspect of the future in relation to Zion's exaltation is in vv. 2-4. The effect of the exalted status of the mountain, which until now has not been referred to by the name 'Zion', is that 'many peoples will flow to it'.[153] This will be contrary to the situation of the people passing by and hissing at the ruins.

I.B.2.a.2)b)(1) *Pilgrimages to Zion (4.2)*. The pilgrimages will be deliberate both with respect to the peoples'/nations' knowledge of the identity of the place to which they go—the house of the God of Jacob—and the benefit that they hope to receive—not just by seeing or even touching the mountain. The purpose will not be to bring gifts (cf. Hag. 2.6; Isa. 60; Ps. 72). Instead, the nations are self-motivated (נעלה)[154] to make pilgrimages to Jerusalem and are fully cognizant of their intention —to be taught the ways of Yahweh and in turn to live accordingly (cf. Zech. 8.20-22).

The י-clause in v. 2b indicates the nations' motivation to make their pilgrimages to the house of the God of Jacob (cf. Pss. 46.8, 12; 76.7; 84.9) now called Zion (ציון)/Jerusalem. They will come to receive instruction because Zion is reputed to be the place from which the law/ the word of God goes forth—not the teaching of the priests (cf. 3.11) but Yahweh's own word.

I.B.2.a.2)b)(2) *International peace (4.3-4)*. The third aspect of the future is announced in vv. 3-4. Yahweh will establish justice among the nations. Yahweh will judge or render arbitration between the nations (v. 3a) which will result in 'peace'. The resultant peace is indicated by the fact that the nations themselves will reshape their weapons of war

---

152. Wolff, *Micah*, p. 120.

153. The words are seen here as synonyms and not meant to be distinguished. Cf. Isa. 2.3, כל־הגוים.

154. Cf. Jer. 31.6, Ps. 122.4 and Zech. 14.17 for instances of עלה used with the connotation of pilgrimage to Jerusalem.

into farming tools. The peace is also indicated in the cessation of international warfare and of the devotion to warfare. That there will be no fear further suggests that peoples will be confident of that peace (v. 4). Such confidence is guaranteed by Yahweh—because Yahweh has spoken.

The concluding formula reflects back to 3.5—a situation where the receivers of the message could have no confidence in the message because of the source. The prophets are accused of declaring peace and war according to how they are rewarded. Here in 4.5, the confidence that there will be peace lies in Yahweh as the creator of the future of which peace will be characteristic. This concluding formula is connected directly with the preceding aspect of the promise articulated in vv. 3-4 and not necessarily the conclusion of the unit (4.1-4).

I.B.2.a.3) *Conclusion (4.5).* Verse 5 shows elements of distinction between it and vv. 1-4—namely, its 1st person address and statement contrasting the speaker (collective) and the nations.[155] The יכ-clause at the beginning of v. 5 signals a logical continuation of thought between v. 5 and vv. 1-4, while the concluding formula in v. 5b—לעולם ועד—indicates a conclusion of that unit of thought. This conclusion offers the reason for Yahweh's established rule in Zion—the peoples (העמים) live (הלך) in reliance on their own gods. It also presents a contrast in both time frame and circumstances. With regard to time frame, the contrast is between the future and the 'now' of the speaker's reality. By means of this contrast, it is apparent that while the nations will seek out Yahweh in order to walk (הלך) in his way (4.2), that time has not yet arrived. With regard to the contrast of circumstances, it is related to the contrast in time frame. The particular circumstances are that the nations are not following Yahweh. However, from the text's perspective, the fundamental reason for Yahweh's establishing his reign is to bring all nations to live according to his ways. In v. 5b the speaker claims

155. Van der Woude, 'Micah in Dispute', takes this as further indication that this unit is the work of false prophets. However, this argument is based on a presupposition regarding the relationship of judgment and promise. According to this presupposition, these are mutually exclusive and as such cannot be announced by the same prophet. The juxtaposition of judgment and promise in the same book is then viewed with suspicion. See Chapter 6 below for further discussion. Cf. Hagstrom, *The Coherence*, p. 60, who proposes that the speaker may be the assumed audience of the book.

continual devotion to Yahweh. What is the significance of this claim in a context where Israel is condemned for sin?

I.B.2.b. *Toward the actualization of the promise/future (4.6–5.14)*. This unit depicts the path toward the actualization of the future announced in the introduction (4.1-5). It also signals that Yahweh has a plan to achieve the announced future. The introductory formula—ביום ההוא נאם־יהוה—combines the temporal transition formula and the oracular formula, and the accompanying divine oracles mark the beginning (4.6-7) and end (5.9-14) of the unit (4.6–5.14). What is further characteristic of these units is their specification of the future that is already indicated by the temporal transition formula in 4.1. The phrase 'in that day' (ביום ההוא) in these two instances, therefore, points to the same time frame as the באחרית הימים. As such they indicate that in the time frame of the exaltation of Zion and the ensuing peace there will be a restoration of a remnant to Zion as well as a cleansing of the cultic and military implements (5.9-13). Directly linked to this cleansing will be the punishment of all the nations who do not obey Yahweh's word (5.14; cf. 4.5 vis-à-vis 4.2).[156]

I.B.2.b.1) *Future restoration of the remnant (4.6-7)*. The focus of the unit is the restoration of a remnant (שארית) to Zion. The term שארית has various nuances and is not used exclusively of Israel.[157] Although it may have theological significance, it is not inherently theological. Furthermore, it may signify both hope and doom.[158] The latter nuance is evident in instances where the term is used to indicate total annihilation of a people in the sense that there will be no remnant after the destruction (cf. Isa. 14.30; 15.9, in relation to the nations; Jer. 6.9; 15.9, in relation to Israel). As to the hope aspect, the term may indicate the

---

156. While the following scholars agree that the temporal formula refers back to the time frame introduced in 4.1, this observation does not at all influence their understanding of the structure of the text. See Wolff, *Micah*, pp. 123, 152; Allen, *The Books*, p. 329; Mays, *Micah*, pp. 100, 125; Hagstrom, *The Coherence*, pp. 60, 68; Hillers, *Micah*, p. 54, while recognizing that it points to the future no discussion is given to whether or not that future is the time frame introduced in 4.1.

157. For detailed presentations of the term's occurrences and nuances see, Gary Cohen, 'שאר', in *TWOT*, II, pp. 894-95; H. Wildberger, 'שאר', in *THAT*, II, p. 847; cf. Gerhard F. Hasel, *The Remnant* (Berrien Spring, MI: Andrews University Press, 1972); E. Jenni, 'Remnant', in *IDB*, III, pp. 32-33; Mays, *Micah*, pp. 101-102; Wolff, *Micah*, pp. 123-24.

158. Mays, *Micah*, pp. 101-102.

survival of persons, as in the case of Israel. However, this survival may have 'no reference to a distant future and little theological elaboration (e.g. Isa. 36.4; Hag. 1.12, 14; 2.2)'.[159] The fact of survival, as compared to total annihilation, is the hope signaled in the particular references to the remnant in the book of Micah (that is, 2.12-13, 5.6-7).

While it has been argued that the remnant in the book of Micah is the 'faithful',[160] this argument is not consistent with the text. The promise incorporates three aspects. First, Yahweh will gather the lame, exiles and afflicted (הצלעה v. 6aα-b; cf. Gen. 32.32; Zeph. 3.19b). Yahweh initiates this restoration of the people (Isa. 11.1, 16; Jer. 23.30). Yet, Yahweh, as indicated in the 1st person address, is here identified as the cause of their present desolation (ואשר הרעתי),[161] and the one who will in turn assemble (אקבצה) the people to be formed into a remnant (cf. Jer. 31.10). Nowhere in this immediate context is the reason for the desolation articulated. Such reasons are seen in chs. 2–3. Thus, with respect to the remnant, the announcement of promise does not deny the involvement of Yahweh in the desolation of the present while attributing to Yahweh the hope constituted in the prospect of a better future. Yahweh, as indicated by this 1st person account, is involved in both the desolation (the scattering) and the hope (the gathering) (cf. Ezek. 34; Jer. 31.10).

Second, Yahweh will make the remnant (שארית)—the 'outcasts' (הנהלאה)—into a strong nation (4.7; cf. 5.6-7; Jer. 31.8). This remnant will not be marginalized by virtue of the weakness of those by which it is constituted—namely, the lame and the afflicted (cf. Ezek. 34.13, 16).[162] Instead, the remnant will be made into a nation. Finally, the promise is that Yahweh will forever rule over this nation in Zion (cf. Ps. 146.10). With this promise of eternal rule over the remnant in Zion, the remnant is presented as involved in the future announced in 4.1-5.

159. Mays, *Micah*, pp. 101-102, argues that in this present text the remnant is created by Yahweh's saving activity and not by judgment. It designates 'the eschatological goal of Yahweh's way with Israel'. Cf. Cuffey, 'Coherence of Micah', p. 410.

160. Cuffey, 'Coherence of Micah', pp. 410-11, cites as parallel uses of the 'faithful remnant' passages such as Isa. 7.3; 10.21.

161. For other uses of the term רעע with Yahweh as subject, cf. Exod. 5.22; Josh. 24.20; Jer. 25.6.

162. Note that while the imagery of the flock is used in Ezek. 34 and Mic. 2.12-13, it is absent from Mic. 4.6-7.

I.B.2.b.2) *Resolution of present circumstances (4.8-5.8).* The promised future is contingent upon the present and its resolution of its various circumstances. Both the circumstances and their resolutions are depicted as the work of Yahweh. Furthermore, the present itself affirms that actualization promise unfolding the future from the particular aspects of the present.

I.B.2.b.2)a) *Introduction (4.8).* With the emphatic use of the pronoun (ואתה) and vocatives, v. 8 signals a modification of focus—tower of the flock, hill of the 'daughter of Zion' (cf. 4.10, 13). Its focus is the promise of restoration of Zion to its former dominion[163]—that is, the restoration of the extent of the kingdom as the center from which Yahweh will execute divine rule.[164] The assumption of this oracle is the loss of Zion's dominion (cf. 3.12). Furthermore, it presupposes that Zion has not yet been restored to its former dominion. In this respect, the promise of 4.8 speaks of a time before the actualization of Yahweh's reign in Zion.

As an introduction to 4.9–5.8, 4.8 indicates a preliminary step in the actualization of Yahweh's reign, a step to occur within the imminent future. What follows then presents the various aspects of the present whose resolution contributes to the actualization of the remote future.

I.B.2.b.2)b) *The present reality toward resolutions (4.9-5.8).* The reality of the present becomes the focal point in so far as the actualization of the future is born out of the present realities. The series of three units—whose concern with the present is indicated by the temporal transition (4.9, 11, 14) shows by the use of עתה and ועתה—culminates in promises the actualization of which would address each of the present situations.

I.B.2.b.2)b)(1) *Captivity and deliverance (4.9-14).* The captivity is both an adversity and a signal of the actualization of the promise of the future in that it is a necessary precursor to the deliverance.

I.B.2.b.2)b)(1)(a) *General statement (4.9-10).* The unit is marked off by the introductory עתה followed by rhetorical questions addressed to 'daughter of Zion' (cf. v. 10). These questions inquire after the reason

---

163. Renaud, *La Formation*, p. 184, sees v. 8 as a significant shift from Yahweh's reign to the Davidic kingdom and its capital, a more nationalistic and monarchic stance; Waltke, 'Micah', p. 690; Hagstrom, *The Coherence*, p. 61; contrast Mays, *Micah*, p. 103, denies that the promise is nationalistic and constituted only of political hopes.

164. Cf. Mays, *Micah*, p. 103, who proposes that the former kingdom refers to the kingdom itself and possibly to its status as independent state.

for the outcry (רוע; cf. 2 Kgs 25.1, 3-7, 8).[165] Yet the context already suggests the answer. There is no king or counselor in their midst. Wolff suggests that here both king and counselor refer to Yahweh (e.g. Isa. 5.19; 19.17; Jer. 28.29; 32.19).[166] By this means, the distress of the people is linked (by analogy) to the misconception concerning Yahweh's presence (cf. 3.11)—namely, 'If Yahweh is in our midst then no misfortune can befall us'. Reconstructed on the basis of Wolff's argument, the text would suggest that the presence of Yahweh does not mean the absence of desolation. However, contrary to Wolff, I propose that the questions more likely refer to the rule of a powerless king whose inability to fight off the Babylonians results in captivity of the people.[167]

Instead of being comforted, the people are commanded to writhe and groan like a woman in labor (cf. Isa. 13.8; Jer. 4.31; 13.21; 22.23; Ps. 48.7). Introduced by the clause כי עתה, the motivation for their travail takes the form of three impending occurrences: the going from the city; the dwelling in an open country; and the going to Babylon. All these are part of the distress of being taken into exile. So the distress of having the equivalent of no king is compounded by the distress of the people's exile. All this is to be endured before the travails of labor yield the product, namely, redemption from the hands of the enemies (v. 10). The condition indicated by the proposition שם 'there'—that is, in Babylon—is therefore imposed on the fulfillment of the promise.

I.B.2.b.2)b)(1)(b) *Expansion (4.11-14).* The two aspects of the distress are introduced in 4.9-10 as the lack of effective leadership and the captivity of the daughters of Zion by an enemy. What follows in the next two sections expands on these two aspects.

I.B.2.b.2)(1)(b)α. *National subjection and victory (4.11-13).* As in 4.9, the 'now' (ועתה) in v. 11 signals the beginning of this unit. It is also addressed to the daughters of Zion and progresses from the distress to the resolution of the distress. In this instance, the distress is constituted by the nations assembled against Zion, while the resolution is Zion subduing the nations. In 4.10 the reference is to one nation, Babylon. The significance of this may have more to do with the concern it introduces than an exclusion of Babylon from the assembled nations. The refer-

---

165. Wolff, *Micah,* p. 139.

166. Wolff, *Micah,* p. 139.

167. Wolff, *Micah,* p. 105, says that the king could refer to a powerless king who cannot help his people. He further discounts the likelihood that king and counselor refer to Yahweh.

ence to 'many nations' connotes the enemies of Israel generally and not a particular nation or particular circumstance. In accordance with those plans, all the nations used as agents of God's plans will be subdued. While 4.11-13 functions to show the resolution of the problem of Israel's enemies as part of the restoration promised in 4.8, this resolution belongs to the imminent future and not to an eschatological age.[168]

The irony of the distress is revealed in v. 13, that is, that even the nations did not assemble of their own accord, but were brought against Zion by Yahweh for Yahweh's purpose (cf. Isa. 14.24-27). So in this instance, Yahweh brings nations to war and commands Israel to beat people into pieces with iron horns and bronze hooks, and by this means to subdue the nations (cf. Jer. 9.21; 51.33). This scene is in stark contrast to the future peace of Zion where the swords are beaten into plowshares and the spears into pruning hook (4.3). However, 4.11-13 is to be seen not as a characteristic of the future, but as part of the present that forms the path to that future.

I.B.2.b.2)b)(1)(b)β. *National threat—humiliated leader (4.14).* While this unit is introduced by 'now' as in 4.9, 11, the discerning of its relationship to those units is complicated by its apparent change of addressee from בת־ציון to בת־גדוד[169] and by the absence of the resolution. It reflects back to 4.9-10, which expressed concern about the leader, and 4.11-13, which provided the depiction of the assembled nations. As in the case of 4.11-13, this unit picks up on the distress of its preceding unit and expands on that distress. In the future the assembled nations will be subdued; but now they have besieged the city and humiliated the judge of Israel (cf. 2 Kgs 25.4-7). The image is of a ruler being humiliated with the very implement of his rule—the staff. However, the forecast of a future resolution is absent from 4.14. This forecast of the future in the other two units is introduced by a command addressed to the daughters of Zion. In 4.14 the command introduces the distress.

I.B.2.b.2)b)(2) *Resolutions (5.1-8).* The promised resolution corresponds to the distress in that the leadership, the enemies, and the captivity are addressed in this unit. Thus, while the first part of 4.8–5.8 (4.9-14) is introduced by the focus on temporal aspects, this second part

---

168. Contrast Mays, *Micah*, p. 107.

169. Hagstrom, *The Coherence*, p. 63, sees בת־גדוד as a variation of בת־ציון used to emphasize the distress of the siege. Cf. his citation of various arguments regarding the uses.

$(5.1-8)^{170}$ is focused on the parties involved (the ruler, the enemy, the remnant). Likewise, in this unit, as in the preceding one, there is an overlap between the constitutive units such that the following promise picks up a situation presented in the preceding units. So while 5.1-3 already promises security, 5.4-5 addresses the issue of security specifically with regard to Assyria. That security will incorporate the subduing of Assyria in Assyria. In 5.6-7 it is promised that the remnant in the lands of their captivity will subdue their captors.

Concerning the connection of 5.1-3 and the unit begun in 4.8, Hagstrom says that

> the deliverance in v. 10f-h corresponds with the return in 5.3cd. Thus, read in context לכן serves not only to link 5.1/5.2-3, but also to link 5.2-3 back to the entire sequence from 4.8; 5.2-3 then function to explain the why behind the present distressful situation and to establish when the future kingdom is to be expected.[171]

I.B.2.b.2)b)(2)(a) *Promised leadership (5.1-3)*. The unit is introduced by the emphatic use of the pronoun (ואתה) addressed to Bethlehem-Ephrathah.[172] As in 4.8, the use of the pronoun focuses on the addressee as a central part of the promise. Here the promise is that a ruler will come from Bethlehem. The promise concerns the rise of a ruler within the history characterized in the text as a time of distress and not necessarily within the eschatological age.[173] This ruler's rise to power will be to address the situations of distress related to the lack of an effective leader in Israel (4.9, 14). However, there will be a delay in the actualization of the rise of this leader.

In its use of לכן, v. 2 indicates that the present distress is already factored into the promise. Yahweh will give up Israel until a specified time, that is, the appointed time and the return from exile. In this way,

---

170. Most propose a different division of the text than presented here: 4.14–5.3 (Mays, *Micah*); 4.9–5.5 (Nielsen, *Oral Tradition*); chs. 3–5 (Wolff, *Micah*); Waltke 'Micah' 4.8–14; 5.1-5 (Renaud, *Structure*).

171. Hagstrom, *The Coherence*, p. 65.

172. Cf. Wolff, *Micah*, p. 143, who cites the following references as indicators of the connection to David's hometown: 1 Sam. 17.12; 16.18; 17.58; Ruth 1.2.

173. Its messianic character is the role to be played by the ruler and not the ruler's eschatological significance. This is not a messianic promise in the sense of foretelling the birth of Jesus Christ. It introduces the reason for the delay of the actualization of the promise.

this unit resembles the preceding units in its combination of distress and promised resolution.

Unlike the preceding units, the promise is introduced first, and is followed by a discussion of the longevity of the present distress. Finally, there follows an expansion of the promise in the form of a characterization of the promised ruler (5.3). The leader is thus characterized as the one who will 'feed his flock' by his reliance on God (cf. 2.12-13).[174] Furthermore, there will be peace in Israel because of the greatness of the ruler. This sense of security reflects back in a contrasting way to the insecurity characteristic of the time of the humiliated and powerless ruler in Israel and in this way completes the unit.

I.B.2.b.2)b)(2)(b) *Victory over Assyria (5.4-5).* The demonstrative (זה) at the beginning of v. 4 suggests an antecedent. Such an antecedent could be found in the immediately preceding unit which focuses on the establishment of the new ruler in Bethlehem and the promise of security for Israel (4.3). As such, this unit is an expansion describing the effects of this new leader as related to the nations (4.11-13) and Assyria in particular. While it may be suggested that the two units, vv. 1-3 and vv. 4-5, do not share the same focus or are not of the same style—thus making possible the conclusion that the two originated in different times and for different purposes—Mays notes that the redactor conforms vv. 4-5 to the concerns of the present text.[175] It is in this respect that the connection with the preceding is to be seen.

Concerning Assyria, when they invade, Israel will be prepared. By means of the sword Israel will subdue and rule Assyria. The text presupposes the power of Israel (the once weak nation) over Assyria (the great nation). Thus, a reversal of fortune is indicated in the depiction of Israel's rule over Assyria. As in 4.11-13, Israel will be victorious over its enemies. Here, however, this victory is not characterized or qualified as a part of God's plan. That it is a plan of God is indicated in the larger context and logical progression in chs. 4–5.

A further presupposition of the text is the establishment of the national borders. This is not the picture of the people living in open country (cf. 4.10). According to the information available on this period, the struggles with Assyria predate the Babylonian exile. Thus the actualization of the promise concerning Assyria would be a precursor to the

---

174. Contrast the self-reliant leaders in ch. 3, esp. 3.5-7. Cf. Willis, 'Micah IV 14–V5', p. 536.

175. Mays, *Micah*, p. 119.

promise of deliverance from Babylon. Here, as in 4.12-13, the use of weapons of war is clearly depicted and is in contrast to the international peace promised in 4.1-4. There peace or security will come about by Yahweh's arbitration between the nations. Here peace and security are achieved through war. These are aspects of the text that further support the conclusion that they belong to and depict a time prior to the actu- alization of Yahweh's reign in Zion.

I.B.2.b.2)b)(2)(c) *Remnant's rule in captivity (5.6-8)*. While this unit has often been taken as a parallel of 4.6-7, there seems to be one impor- tant connection with 4.10 which says that the daughters of Zion will go to Babylon. In 4.6-7 the promise is to assemble the scattered and to make them into a remnant and a strong nation. Here in 5.6-8, though it is not yet assembled in Zion, the remnant is already a reality. Its reality is its existence among the nations. Furthermore, their existence is de- picted by metaphors, suggesting that its presence among the nations is not controlled by the nations or the remnant but by God (cf. 4.11-13).[176]

One important aspect of the depiction of the remnant is the imagery of it as dew and showers. This suggests that the time of their stay among the nations will be brief (5.6). The other aspect of the remnant's presence among the nations is that it is not a peaceful presence but a ravaging and destructive one (5.7-8). The promise is that in its scattered state among many nations, the remnant will subdue those nations (cf. 4.11-13).[177] This is hardly the picture presented in 4.6-7 of a weak and lame people who will be made but is not yet strong. Nor is it the picture of a peaceful coexistence of nations. Again, the text suggests that this promise is a precursor to the actualization of the reign introduced in 4.1-4 and further characterized in 4.6-8 and 5.9-14.

I.B.2.b.3) *Future purification (5.9-14)*. The introductory formula—וְהָיָה בַיּוֹם־הַהוּא נְאֻם־יְהוָה—refers back to the time frame introduced by 4.1. It introduces an oracle attributed to Yahweh by the oracular formula. This entire unit concerns the parties of the established reign. While there is no mention of the nation by name, the focus of this unit is the cleansing of the nation. It is presumed that Israel is the nation who will be gathered in Zion (4.6-7).

First, the military implements will be destroyed: the horses, chariots and strongholds (v. 9). Second, the cultic aspects are destroyed: the

176. Cf. Wolff, *Micah*, p. 155.
177. Mays, *Micah*, pp. 121, 13, interprets 5.8 as a prayer addressed to God; cf. Wolff, *Micah*, p. 157.

forbidden means of divination, sorcerers and soothsayers (cf. Jer. 27.9; Deut. 18.10-11); the prohibited cultic images (cf. Exod. 20.4; Deut. 5.8; 7.5, 25; 16.22; 1 Kgs 14.23; cf. Jer. 1.16; Pss 115.4); and the very cities of the cultic practices. Micah 5.12b cites the reason for the destruction of the images—namely, that the people will no longer worship them.

Finally, the disobedient nations will also be destroyed as a part of the preparatory cleansing toward the actualization of Zion's future. The relationship of this verse to its unit is sometimes seen as problematic. However, if it is seen as purification of the parties who will coexist in the world order inaugurated by Yahweh's reign, then the problematic nature of the verse is somewhat reduced. The nations who do not follow the teachings of Yahweh will not survive to challenge the promised peace. Their destruction is then as much a part of the actualization of Yahweh's reign as the creation and exaltation of the remnant, in that both are promised as aspects of the reign.

In this way, the first part of the book of Micah comes to a close suggesting that the fate of Israel continues into the future. However, that fate is shaped within the larger context of Yahweh's reign while being influenced by the actions of Israel. The nations—the accused against whom Yahweh has a case (1.2)—are brought into focus in chs. 4–5 as part of Yahweh's larger plan in history (and for Israel). Thus they are presented as a part of the universal framework of Yahweh's activity in history.

Chapter 5

LEVELS OF COHERENCE: CHAPTERS 6–7

II. *Second Dispute (6.1–7.20)*

II.A. *Introduction—Dispute (6.1-8)*
This unit introduces chs. 6–7 using the form of a dispute whose concern is Israel's misconception about Yahweh. There are three elements within this introductory unit, namely, 6.1-2, 3-7 and 8.

II. A.1. *Introduction—summons to hear (6.1-2)*
This introductory portion of 6.1-8 consists of three summons (vv. 1a, 1b, 2). It introduces vv. 3-8 and functions to identify the scope of the text with regard to the parties involved—Yahweh, Israel, the natural elements and the messenger—and also with respect to the nature of the message being communicated—a dispute (ריב, v. 2) between Yahweh and Israel, Yahweh's people (vv. 2, 3, 5, 8).

II.A.a. *General* שמעו־נא *(6.1a).* Verse 1a (שמעו־נא) presents difficulties in that it lacks an explicit addressee. Addressees are clearly identified in all the other instances where the 'summons to hear' is used (שמעו, 1.2 and 6.2; שמעו־נא, 3.1, 9). This lack of an explicit addressee has led to several proposals including: the people[1] and the book's audience.[2] Wolff argues that v. 1a is a redactional transition used by the final redactor to connect the preceding chapters with what follows.[3] Even so, Wolff recognizes that the summons to hear introduces the word of Yahweh to the people as a whole vis-à-vis specific groups (3.1, 9).[4]

---

1. Allen, *The Books*, p. 364.
2. Wolff, *Micah*, pp. 167, 172; Waltke, 'Micah', p. 727; Renaud, *La Formation*, p. 302, argues that v. 1 is an editorial addition. Cf. Mays, *Micah*, p. 128, who is vague in saying that 'v. 1a addresses a general audience'; Hillers, *Micah*, p. 77, refers to the prophet's 'audience'.
3. Wolff, *Micah*, p. 167.
4. Wolff, *Micah*, p. 169.

Another question raised by v. 1a is the question concerning the speaker. It is generally agreed that the prophet is the speaker.[5] Whether v. 1a is spoken by the prophet or is a redactional transition, this study must account for it as part of the extant text. The introduction is seen to have a dual function in the extant text—that is, to introduce the unit, vv. 1b-8, as well as the larger unit, chs. 6–7. To say this, however, is not to minimize the tension presented by the multiple summons. This means that v. 1a calls upon the particular audience to whom it is addressed and for whose particular context its constitutive elements are brought together. Thus, it is here argued that the dual function of v. 1a must be recognized in the analysis of vv. 1b-8 and especially with respect to the presumed scope of v. 8.

II.A.1.b. *Specific—call to action (6.1b-2)*. Another difficulty posed by v. 1a is its juxtaposition to v. 1b-2. If the prophet is the speaker in v. 1a introducing the word of Yahweh, then it seems most probable that the speaker in v. 1b is not the prophet but Yahweh. However, this conclusion is not unanimous among scholars. Thus, it has been argued that v. 1b represents the words of the prophet to the people,[6] in which case the people are called upon to present their case (קום, singular imperative).

Thus, it is not merely a question of the speaker in the introduction, but of the conceptuality of the unit it introduces. To say, along with the majority of scholars, that Yahweh is the speaker does not constitute a solution to the question of the conceptuality of the unit. An examination of this generally held conclusion reveals that it is based on the juxtaposition of vv. 1b-2 and v. 1a and the infratextual tension in v. 1b-2. Thus, v. 1a is taken as an introduction to vv. 1b-2 and what follows.

II.A.1.b.1) *Participants (6.1b-2a)*. The dispute includes named participants, that is, Yahweh as the plaintiff and the natural elements as witnesses. The absence of addressees in this unit results in the lack of a named defendant. However, in 6.2b in the articulation of the reason for the dispute, the defendant may be identified as עמו. Even so, there are

---

5.   Ewald, *Commentary on the Prophets*, p. 326; Smith, *Micah, Zephaniah*, p. 118; Mays, *Micah*, p. 128; Hillers, *Micah*, p. 77; Waltke, 'Micah', p. 727; Hagstrom, *The Coherence*, p. 109; Vuilleumier, 'Michée', p. 70.

6.   Ewald, *Commentary on the Prophets*, p. 331; cf. Allen, *The Books*, pp. 364-65.

other factors to suggest that the case ensues from a prior accusation against Yahweh (cf. 6.3).

II.A.1.b.1)a) *Yahweh (6.1b)*. Regarding vv. 1b-2, there are several contributing factors to the apparent multivalency of the concept. The first factor is the addressees. Even among those who identify Yahweh as speaker in v. 1b, there is no consensus as to the identity of the addressees. Mays[7] argues that v. 1a is a redactional element used to establish a link with vv. 2-5. He further argues that Yahweh is summoning the people to participate in the trial which Yahweh is convening.

Part of the difficulty of the unit is the verb-preposition construction. The verb קוּם (sing. impv.) with רִיב may denote preparation to act in which case the emphasis is not on the first but on the second verb (Gen. 27.19, קוּם לֵךְ; Jer. 1.17, וְקַמְתָּ וְדִבַּרְתָּ; cf. also Num. 22.20; 1 Kgs 17.9; Jon. 1.2).[8] In vv. 1b-2a, it is not so much that the addressees are summoned to arise as that they are summoned to present their case. Others argue that Yahweh is summoning the prophet as Yahweh's envoy.[9] However, that Israel is accused by Yahweh is not, as Waltke[10] presumes, sufficient reason to deny that Israel is being addressed. It is that very fact that is the supporting factor. Israel is summoned to appear and to render testimony to support her charge against Yahweh (v. 2; cf. v. 3b, עֲנֵה בִי).

II.A.1.b.1)b) *Natural elements (witnesses) (6.1b+2a)*. Inasmuch as אֵת in the construction ...רִיב אֶת־ is usually understood as an adversative (Jer. 2.9; Judg. 8.1; Neh. 5.7; 13.11, 17),[11] it may be argued that the mountains are not depicted as witnesses but as the accused. However, it is being argued that this context does not support an adversative nuance of רִיב אֶת־. One example is seen in the LXX reading πρoς as adopted by Wellhausen (אֶל) and others who follow him.[12]

Wolff argues that the mountains (הֶהָרִים) and hills (הַגְּבָעוֹת) 'are a poor doublet with v. 2 mountains (הָרִים) and foundations of the earth

---

7.   Mays, *Micah*, p. 131.

8.   L.J. Coppes, 'קוּם', in *TWOT*, II, p. 793.

9.   Waltke, 'Micah', p. 727, argues that Israel in this case cannot be the addressees since they are the accused; cf. also Smith, *Micah, Zephaniah*, p. 119; Halévy, 'Michée', p. 291; Renaud, *La Formation*, p. 302; Huffmon, 'Covenant Lawsuit', p. 287; Hillers, *Micah*, p. 77.

10.   Waltke, 'Micah', p. 727.

11.   Limburg, 'The Root רִיב', p. 301; Wolff, *Micah*, p. 173.

12.   Wellhausen, *Einleitung in das Alte Testament*, p. 146.

(מסדי ארץ)'.[13] Thus, to eliminate this difficulty of the conceptuality of mountains as the accused, Wolff proposes that the mountains are used as 'cipher of nations'[14] who are summoned in 1.2 and 5.14. In the latter case, they are depicted as not giving heed. The mountains in parallel with 'earth and all who dwell in it', are the subject of Yahweh's wrath.[15] Wolff's suggestion is not to be completely discounted. However, while it is possible that the nations are elsewhere subject to wrath, it seems that the infratextual[16] aspects govern in such a way that the current text does not speak or even allude to the nations. Thus, while it may not be so in other instances (e.g. Nah. 1.5), the analogy of nations and mountains is remote in this context. A more plausible argument is that the nations are called to witness Yahweh's dispute with Israel not in the sense of legal witnesses, but as observers of Yahweh's dealing with Israel and hence the possibility of Yahweh's dealing with them[17]—but even this is conjectural.

Another central aspect to the conceptuality of this unit (vv. 1b-2) are the witnesses. In light of the explicit reference to the mountains as addressed in v. 2a, it has been argued that the natural elements in v. 1b are called upon as witnesses. However, this conclusion has come about through observation of the intertextual data. Here as in other instances, natural elements (earth, mountains, and so on) are summoned as witnesses (Deut. 4.26; 30.19; 31.28; Isa. 1.2; cf. Deut. 32.1; Ps. 50.4).

The mountains are summoned as witnesses because of their characteristics. The text presupposes a cosmology in which the mountains are enduring, if not permanent. They are witnesses to the covenant,[18] and are therefore aware of the conditions of the covenant.[19] They are here (v. 2a) summoned to hear Yahweh's case against Israel his people (עם־עמו). The mountains are characterized as 'enduring foundations of the earth' (האתנים מסדי ארץ) and function in the same way as the heavens and earth.

13. Wolff, *Micah*, p. 171.
14. Wolff, *Micah*, p. 169.
15. Wolff, *Micah*, p. 173.
16. Knierim, *Text and Concept*, p. 3.
17. Cf. Hagstrom, *The Coherence*, p. 24, where he discusses the distinction between 1.2-4 and 6.1-2.
18. Huffmon, 'Covenant Lawsuit', p. 292.
19. Huffmon, 'Covenant Lawsuit', p. 292, regarding the analogy to Hittite international treaties.

There are those who prefer the reading האזינו, thus creating a parallel
with שמעו (Mic. 1.2; cf. Deut. 32.1; Isa. 2.1; Hos. 1.5).[20] They tend to
see two sets of witnesses, mountains—their height and power—and the
foundations of the earth—imperturbable and constant. The emendation,
evidently a harmonization, signals an alternative conceptuality which
itself is similar to the one it emends. Both have undeniable plausibility.
In the present context, the textual support is skewed toward the former
option—the mountains and enduring foundations of the earth.

In this unit, the addressees are not only clarified, but the reason for
the summons is made explicit—Yahweh has a controversy with Israel
his people and intends to contend with them. This signals the parties in
the case: Yahweh as plaintiff and Israel as the defendant (the accused).
Israel has not brought Yahweh to trial; but it is Israel's accusation
against Yahweh that has prompted Yahweh's dispute with Israel. The
exact accusation is not made explicit by the text. However, it is implicit
in Yahweh's accusation against Israel (v. 3).

II.A.1.b.2) *Reason for the summons (כי) (2b).* The כי-clause functions
as qualifier of the immediately preceding summons. However, this כי-
clause which establishes the scene may also function as qualifier of the
larger unit (vv. 1b-2a). This connection is signaled by the use of ריב in
all three segments: v. 1b (קום ריב את־ההרים), v. 2aα (שמעו הרים את־דרים)
יהוה) and v. 2bα (כי ריב ליהוה עם־עמו) (Cf. Isa. 1.2b the כי-clause
qualifying the summons.)[21]

Conceptually, the qualifier both expands v. 1b by giving a reason for
the summons to action—that is, a dispute—and anticipates the process
which follows in vv. 3-8. Verse 2bβ uses יכח in a synthetical parallel
expression to expand the qualifier. This verb is used most typically with
the judicial human arbitrators (Gen. 31.36-55) and God as plaintiff (Isa.
1.18; Hos. 4.4; Ps. 50.8, 21). Underlying this judicial nuance is the goal
to discipline and educate,[22] as seen in its parallel use with יסר 'to in-
struct, discipline'.[23] Perhaps it is partly this nuance, 'to educate, correct',
that may account for v. 8. Notably, v. 8 appears to function by way of

---

20. Wellhausen, *Einleitung in das Alte Testament*, p. 146; Wolff, *Micah*,
p. 164; Waltke, 'Micah', p. 728.

21. Hos. 4.1bα, כי ריב ליהוה עם־יושבי הארץ; 12.3a [Eng. v. 2] וריב ליהוה
עם־יהודה.

22. Paul R. Gilchrist, 'יכח', in *TWOT*, I, pp. 376-77; cf. Huffmon, 'Covenant
Lawsuit', pp. 286-95.

23. Paul R. Gilchrist, 'יסר', in *TWOT*, I, pp. 386-87.

correcting a misconception—a misconception presumed by the questions in vv. 6-7.

The כי-clause also clarifies the parties and specifically qualifies the relationship between them. It is Yahweh who has a controversy with Israel. This qualification is important given the ambiguity of the construction and the ambivalence resulting from the summons (vv. 1a, 1b, 2a). What follows in vv. 3-8 primarily concerns ישראל, identified in synthetical parallelism with עמו, יהוה being the antecedent of the 3rd person pron. suff. So the scene is depicted in which Yahweh not only has a dispute, but the party with whom Yahweh has the dispute is significant to the nature of the dispute.

It is for this reason that it is important to note the concept of 'people of יהוה'. In the book of Micah, עמי occurs mostly in prophetic speeches against the leaders (2.8, 9; 3.3, 5).[24] In these instances, עמי is not the object of Yahweh's wrath but of Yahweh's concern. Also in these instances, עמי is neither identified with all of Israel nor identified as the 'poor or oppressed' as is the case in Isaiah (Isa. 3.15; 10.2). However, this association is nonetheless implicit in the book of Micah. By contrast, in Mic. 6.1-8 the people are referred to three times: עמו, v. 2bα; עמי, vv. 3a and 5a.[25] In these instances, the reference is to the people Israel,[26] not to a group within the whole with whom the prophet expresses solidarity. Furthermore, as in other passages, they are the object of accusation (1.3; 5.13). Thus, in contrast to other occurrences in the book of Micah, עמי or עמו designates the entire nation of Israel as the elect people of Yahweh.

It is further noted that the concept of relationship between Yahweh and Israel is thus brought into focus by the textual signals עמי or עמו and אליהיך. This is election language (Deut. 7.6; 14.2; 26.18; cf. Exod. 19.5; Amos 3.1-2), that is, the concept of the people as the possession of Yahweh:

> For you are a people holy to the Lord your God; the Lord your God has chosen you to be a people for his own possession, out of all the peoples that are on the face of the earth (Deut. 7.6).

24. Stansell, *Micah and Isaiah*, pp. 117-20 (118). He includes 2.4 and 1.9 but recognizes that 1.9 does not occur in accusation of the leaders.

25. Stansell, *Micah and Isaiah*, pp. 117-20, he attributes ch. 6 to a later addition and therefore does not consider 6.3, 5.

26. Cf. Amos 7.8, 15; 8.2.

It is in this perspective of vv. 1a-2b that vv. 3-8 are to be understood. The conceptuality of the unit is signaled by the term ריב. Its anticipation of the immediately following unit is seen in its use of עמו. The term עמו points to the relationship of the participants within the present context—that relationship in which the grounds for dispute exist (v. 3). It is that relationship which provides the evidence used by both participants to argue their cases (Yahweh in vv. 4-5 and Israel in vv. 6-7) and which then governs the conclusion of the dispute (v. 8).

II.A.2. *Argumentation (6.3-7)*

Yahweh, the first to speak in the dispute, presents the accusation (v. 3) and evidence to disprove it (vv. 4-5). This is then followed by a response on behalf of the people (vv. 6-7) and a resolution, that is, an attempt to prove the case by clarifying the misconception intrinsic to Israel's charge against Yahweh (v. 8).

II.A.2.a. *Yahweh's argumentation (6.3-5).*

As plaintiff Yahweh articulates the case against Israel. This includes an accusation (6.3) and a refutation of the accusation (6.4-5).

II.A.2.a.1) *Accusation against Israel (6.3).* The vocative עמי followed by the 1st person style signals a unit different from the 3rd person style of the purpose clause in v. 2b. Verse 3 constitutes the entire accusation. Conceptually, the question presupposes a charge against Yahweh— namely, that Yahweh has acted in an adverse way toward Israel or has in some way caused the state of weariness out of which Israel makes such a charge.

II.A.2.a.1)a) *Questions—accusation proper (6.3a).* In a more general sense, this question (מה־עשיתי) is used to demand an accounting of the addressees (עמי) as to the cause of the present adverse circumstances. It usually presumes the innocence of the speaker of having caused the adversity. Thus for example, David, after Saul's scheme to kill him and a narrow escape, goes to Jonathan for help as he had previously done with an inquiry—...מה עשיתי מה־עוני:

> What have I done? What is my guilt?
> And What is my sin before your father,
> that he seeks my life? (1 Sam. 20.1).

Other instances also share the feature of the unjustified charge. In 1 Sam. 17.29 David, accused by Eliab of being malevolent, asks for the basis of Eliab's accusation. Also to be considered is 1 Sam. 26.18, where David inquires of Saul why he (Saul) pursues David.

> Why does my lord pursue after his servant?
> For what have I done? What guilt is my hand? (1 Sam. 26.16)[27]

The intratextual[28] aspect of the text consists of an ontology according to which adversity begets adversity, and an unfounded malevolence or charge should be accounted for and not simply ignored. Also presupposed is that the question is preceded not only by reflection on circumstances but also by a conclusion that the speaker is innocence.

Here in 6.3 there is no indication of the circumstances of the charge made by Israel. Therefore, one must rely on textual and conceptual indicators to better understand the charge. The pairing of v. 3aα and v. 3aβ allows for possible clarification of the charge—v. 3aβ ומה הלאתיך.[29] The particle מה has been interpreted as 'in what'[30] which seems to presume במה (cf. Exod. 22.26; Gen. 15.8; Judg. 16.5).[31] It is possible that the question is aimed at the manner in which Yahweh has burdened Israel. In this instance מה is used as exclamatory question (cf. 2 Kgs 4.48; Num. 23.8) and can be read in the sense of 'how'.[32] It is here argued that there is a quasi-rhetorical element present which both assumes the incredulity of the charge against Yahweh and at the same time challenges Israel to support its charge.

Thus an analysis of the verb used here is informative of the incredulity of the charge against Yahweh. The verb לאה, 'to be weary', is often used in reference to physical weariness (Gen. 19.11; Jer. 12.5), psychological weariness in the sense of discouragement (Job 4.5), annoyance and disgust (Job 4.2), and with particular reference to the weariness due to the excess of that which caused the weariness (Isa. 47.13; Jer. 6.11; 15.6).[33] Included among these is the motif of God's

---

27. Cf. also 1 Sam. 29.8; contrast Judg. 8.1 where the question is addressed to the accused.

28. Knierim, *Text and Concept*, p. 3, defines 'intratextual' as that which lies beneath the text and is presupposed by it.

29. As mentioned below in the Appendix the LXX may have included an additional question as a device of intensification and on analogy to other instances where being weary or over-burdened occurs in parallel expressions.

30. Smith, *Micah, Zephaniah*, p. 119.

31. Waltke and O'Connor, *Syntax*, §18.3d-e.

32. Waltke and O'Connor, *Syntax*, 18.3f-g; GKC §148a.

33. A. Bowling, 'לאה', in *TWOT*, I, p. 464.

disgust with Israel's sacrifices (Isa. 1.14).

The noun form תלאה is used of Moses' potential weariness in leading the people—that is, unless he shares the leadership responsibility (Exod. 18.8). It is also used in Moses' characterization of the hardship suffered in Egypt and en route to the land (Num. 20.14) and of the people's view on sacrificing (Mal. 1.13). Its synonym is יגע, 'toil, grow or be weary'. It is in reference to יגע that the other instances of Israel being wearied by their own practices are talked about (Isa. 55.2; 57.10). In other instances it is Israel who wearies God by calling evil good:

> You have wearied the Lord with your words.
> Yet you say, 'How have we wearied him?'
> By saying, 'Everyone who does evil is good in the sight of the Lord, and he delights in them'. Or by asking 'Where is the God of justice?' (Mal. 2.17)

In Isaiah there is a glimpse of the possible charge against God although this passage is multivalent:

> 22Yet you did not call upon me. O Jacobs;
> but you have been weary of me, O Israel!
> 23You have not brought me your sheep for burnt offerings,
> or honored me with your sacrifices.
> I have not burdened you with offerings,
> or wearied you with frankincense.
> 24You have not bought me sweet cane with money,
> or satisfied me with the fat of your sacrifices.
> But you have burdened me with your sins;
> you have wearied me with your iniquities (Isa. 43.22-24).

Here יגע is synthetically parallel with עבד, 'to work, serve', the latter when in hiphil having the meaning of 'burden with toil as a slave' (cf. Exod. 1.13).[34] Also significant for the present study is the interpretation of this text. The present author interprets the text to mean that Yahweh recognizes that Israel is weary of Yahweh and has sacrificed to Yahweh. The multivalency of the text allows for the interpretation that God desires sacrifices but have been denied them by Israel. This is supported by the language of Isa. 43.23 '[you have not] *honored* me with your sacrifices'. In this line of thought, Yahweh is seen to give the reminders

---

34. Walter C. Kaiser, 'עבד', in *TWOT*, II, pp. 639-41.

that Yahweh has not enslaved Israel to offering sacrifices and that Israel's sins are burdensome to Yahweh.[35]

Some scholars argue that the text speaks to a particular historical situation recognized by Deutero-Isaiah. In that situation, Israel was unable to sacrifice to God and therefore missed out, since sacrifice was the means of grace to Israel.[36] On the contrary, others argue not for the impossibility of offering sacrifices to Yahweh but for Israel's unwillingness to do so since the people were sacrificing to other gods. Israel is thus depicted as wearied by that practice. Thus, the text is seen in the tradition of the critique of sacrifices as found in Amos 5.21-25, Isa. 1.10, and so on.[37]

Although sacrifice is required for sin, God is burdened by sacrifices (cf. Isa. 1.17). In the intertextual framework, the relationship of the extant Isa. 1.17 and 43.22-24 is in tension with ch. 6 of Micah. With these as part of the intertextual[38] framework, the charge lying behind 6.3—the intratextual component—must therefore not be discounted.

Concerning 6.3, it cannot be said that Israel knowingly (cf. v. 8) violated Yahweh's requirement. As evidenced by Isa. 43.22-24, the charge presupposed by 6.3 may point to a continual dispute between Yahweh and Israel. It may further signal a misconception on the part of Israel about what Yahweh demands. Apparently, for Israel, Yahweh demands excessive and costly sacrifices. Thus the question in v. 3a accuses Israel of charging Yahweh with burdening Israel. It is, therefore, not a request on the part of Yahweh for Israel to enumerate all that Yahweh has done. Rather, it is a challenge to explain how the saving acts of Yahweh have been burdensome.

Some scholars have interpreted this verse to mean that Israel has no complaint.[39] Such an interpretation needs to be reassessed because of

35.   G.W. Grogan, 'Isaiah', in Frank E. Gaebelein (ed.), *The Expositor's Bible Commentary* (12 vols.; Grand Rapids: Zondervan, 1986), VI, p. 261.

36.   George A.F. Knight, *Deutero-Isaiah: A Theological Commentary on Isaiah 40–55* (New York: Abingdon Press, 1965), p. 104.

37.   Christopher R. North, *The Second Isaiah: Introduction, Translation and Commentary to Chapters 40–55* (Oxford: Clarendon Press, 1964), pp. 127-30, offers as support Jer. 7.20 among others; *idem, Isaiah 40–55* (London: SCM Press, 1956), pp. 76-77.

38.   Knierim, *Text and Concept*, p. 3, considers intertextuality as having to do with 'the coherence of separate literary works'.

39.   Limburg, 'The Root of ריב', p. 302; Allen, *The Books*, p. 365; Waltke, 'Micah', pp. 729-30.

its presuppositions concerning God's relationship with Israel, the text's concept and the resignification of traditions. The presuppositions maintain that God is irreproachable, and that Israel's behavior is always reprehensible. However, the very nature of v. 8 presupposes the need to clarify a previously known or at least communicated piece of information. It is not a new requirement. The intertextual framework of the various concepts evidences the need for clarification. Whether the multivalency of a particular concept is due to diachronic or synchronic aspects, they were at some point brought together toward a particular purpose—that is, they were recontextualized and reconceptualized (resignified).[40] The challenge of concept-critical analysis is then to identify what unifies the whole—that is, that governing concept to which all others are supporting arguments and in light of which all the others are reconceptualized as they are recontextualized.

II.A.2.a.1)b) *Challenge to Israel (6.3b)*. The understanding of v. 3b has therefore to take into account the preceding discussion. The expression ענה בי is typically used of bearing witness (Job 9.14; 2 Sam. 1.16) and specifically as testimony (1 Sam. 12.3). This is Yahweh's challenge to Israel to present evidence to support its accusation against Yahweh. This is to be distinguished from 'putting God to the test'[41] (Exod. 17.1-7) or God's testing Israel to determine its faithfulness (Exod. 16.4; Deut. 8.2). Yahweh's speech continues with Yahweh's presentation of evidence to counter Israel's charges.

II.A.2.a.2) *Refutation of the accusation (6.4-5)*. Verses 4-5 then begin with a כי-clause with an adversative nuance. This is typically achieved with כי אם (1 Sam. 8.19) or כי (Gen. 18.15; 19.2) following a negative sentence; or as in this instance, the question presupposes the negative response.[42] The כי-clause syntactically connects v. 3 and vv. 4-5.[43] Thus, the extent to which v. 3a is rhetorical is to be determined by the tenor of the Yahweh speech in vv. 4-5. Is it therefore a reason for the demanded response? Or is it a refutation of the implied claim that Yahweh has wearied his people (עמו)? The clause appears to presuppose both the demand and the refutation.

40. Knierim, *Text and Concept*, p. 6.

41. M.R. Wilson, 'נסה', in *TWOT*, II, p. 581, for further characterization of the 'testing' motif.

42. Wolff, *Micah*, p. 175; GKC §163a-b.

43. Waltke, 'Micah', p. 729, who sees a threefold connection, that is, signaled by syntax, phonology and theme.

It has been often noted that there is a word play between v. 3
(הֶלְאֵתִיךָ) and v. 4 (הֶעֱלִתִיךָ).[44] As significant as this observation may be,
the concept of the unit goes beyond the apparent linguistic connection.
The coherence of this unit is constituted in its recollection of the acts of
Yahweh on behalf of Israel. There are several elements to be addressed
in this respect. Why the recollection? Why these specific elements of
the recollection?

II.A.2.a.2)a) *The evidence—Yahweh's saving acts (6.4-5bα).* The
recollection[45] of Yahweh's saving acts on behalf of Israel occurs in various contexts in the Old Testament. Without specification of any acts,
Deut. 8.2 has an entreaty to remember God's leading. It simply states
the purpose, namely, to humble Israel and so to test its faithfulness.
Another instance of this recollection/Torah story is Isa. 1.2, where it
occurs in a Yahweh speech accusing Israel of committing crimes.
Jeremiah 2.4-8 is another example. Toward a clearly articulated purpose, it recalls Egypt, the guidance through the wilderness and the entry
into the promised land. The goal was to refute an apparent claim that
the forefathers of Israel had found wrong in Yahweh which resulted in
their turning away from Yahweh (cf. Deut. 32.7-14). The recollection
of Yahweh's saving acts is integral in prophetic reviews of Israel's
history (Amos 2.10; 3.1). In the present context, the recollection of the
saving acts of Yahweh is a presentation of evidence against Israel.
What is the evidence?

II.A.2.a.2)a)(1) *Exodus and guidance (6.4).* The first element of the
recollection is the Exodus from Egypt (6.4a) and the guidance through
the wilderness. The latter is represented as the provision of leadership
during the wilderness journey (6.4b).

II.A.2.a.2)a)(1)(a) *Deliverance from Egypt (6.4a).* Here the Exodus is
expressed in two ways, as in the language seen in Deuteronomy (7.8;
13.5).[46] The first is seen in v. 4a 'I brought you up' (cf. Amos 2.10; 3.1;
9.7; Hos. 11.1; 12.13; Jer 2.6; 7.22; 11.4) and with particular reference
to the rescue 'from the iron furnace' in Jer. 11.7. The second way is
seen in various references to the deliverance from Egypt (Hos. 2.15;

44. Mays, *Micah*, p. 134; Wolff, *Micah*, p. 175; Allen, *The Books*, p. 366;
Smith, *Micah, Zephaniah*, p. 121; Renaud, *La Formation*, p. 302; Orelli, *The
Twelve Minor Prophets*, p. 213.

45. Sanders, *Torah and Canon*, pp. 76-79, terms this recollection 'Torah Story'.

46. J. Wijngaards, הוציא and העלה: A Twofold Approach to the Exodus', *VT*
15 (1965), pp. 98-101.

12.9; 13.4; Isa. 11.16). The characterization of the deliverance with the clause in v. 4aβ—'I redeemed you from the house of slavery' (ומבית עבדים פדיתיך)—is significant here in light of the charge against Yahweh —Yahweh has wearied us. The inclusion here of the clause thus portrays a misconception on the part of those making the charge—e.g. you accused Yahweh of burdening you yet it is Yahweh who delivered you out of Egypt the place where you were burdened. What Yahweh has done for you is to rescue you from adversity and not create such adversity for you.[47]

II.A.2.a.2)a)(1)(b) *Provision of leadership (through the wilderness) (6.4b)*. The benevolence of God did not end with the deliverance from Egypt. In the persons of Moses, Aaron and Miriam, God provided guidance for the journey from Egypt up to Moab.[48] There is no explicit mention of the wilderness wandering although this would have illustrated that it was Israel who was constantly rebellious. Instead, the recollection focuses on the benevolence of Yahweh with no mention of Israel's ways, though such recollection of Israel's sins are found elsewhere (1 Sam. 12).

II.A.2.a.2)a)(2) *Protection and fulfillment of promise (call to remember) (6.5)*. Verse 5 is a call to remember and points to the acts of God that took place in the plains of Moab up to the entrance into the land.

II.A.2.a.2)a)(2)(a) *Balak–Balaam incident (6.5a)*. This part of the journey is characterized by God's intervention to prevent Israel from being cursed, despite Balak's persistence (Num. 22–24). The significance of this incident is that God intervened in such a way that Israel would not be cursed and thus be destroyed. At issue is not simply the act of the curse but its potency. Balaam is characterized as having great power. This is evidenced in Num. 31.16 where the counsel of Balaam resulted in Israel's rebellion against God.[49]

---

47. Note here that this is particular to the present context. The Pentateuchal context allows for another interpretation. The journey to Egypt and the deliverance are all in line with the promise to deliver Israel to the land. In this view, the oppression in Egypt becomes the precondition of the Exodus. To this extent then the concept of Yahweh creating adversity for Israel may not be foreign in the Pentateuchal canon. Cf. Knierim, 'The Interpretation of the Old Testament', in *idem*, *Task of Old Testament Theology*, pp. 57-138 (130-34).

48. See Appendix for the discussion regarding the significance of the mention of the three.

49. Martin Noth, *Numbers* (Philadelphia: Westminster Press, 1968), p. 173.

In Josh. 24.9 the recollection of the Balak–Balaam tradition represents the outcome as Yahweh's refusal to listen to Balaam. It is implied that contrary to the resistance depicted in the Numbers 22–24 account, Balaam intends to curse Israel. Deut. 23.4-5 likewise represents Yahweh as resisting Balaam's request. Here the reason for Yahweh's act is made explicit:

> Nonetheless the Lord your God would not hearken to Balaam;
> but the Lord your God turned the curse into a blessing for you, because
> the Lord your God loved you (Deut. 23.4-5).[50]

What is significant in the recontextualization of the Balak–Balaam tradition in Mic. 6.5 is that Yahweh has preserved Israel even in the face of extinction, as Yahweh had done in the Exodus.

II.A.2.a.2)a)(2)(b) *Entrance into the land (6.5bα).* The final part of this recollection—the evidence offered in support of Yahweh's case—is fragmented. The mention of Shittim and Gilgal points to the final phase of the journey into the land—Shittim being the last stop before crossing the Jordan, and Gilgal the first after arriving in the land (Josh. 4.19). The significance of this recollection is perhaps to recall the miraculous crossing. This is paired with the Balak–Balaam tradition in much the same way as the Exodus and guidance traditions are paired. This component of the recollection indicates that the promise of the land has been fulfilled.

II.A.2.a.2)b) *Statement of purpose (למען) (6.5bβ).* Thus the history is summarized from the deliverance from Egypt to the entrance into the land, all characterized here as צדקות יהוה. This phrase (צדקות יהוה) is a technical way of speaking about Yahweh's deeds (Judg. 5.11; 1 Sam. 12.7; Ps. 103.6).[51] But the purpose is not simply to remember (זכר) acts. The remembering is such that one's behavior is to be amended. So in this case, the purpose of the recollection is that Israel sees Yahweh as being innocent of the charge of burdening them.

In summary, the Yahweh speech uses the form of recitation to present its argument against the underlying charge that Yahweh has wearied Israel. Yet the intertextual framework indicates that this charge is neither new nor unfounded. The questions in v. 3 may or may not be

---

50. Cf. Neh. 13.2.

51. See Sanders, *Torah and Canon*, pp. 16-17, regarding the significance of the term to designate 'Torah story'.

rhetorical; however, it would seem that such questions and challenges, as in 1 Sam. 12.7, may have a rhetorical flare. To say this, however, is to say at once that the questions reflect the speaker's point of view. Thus Yahweh's view, as presented in this text, would be that there is no evidence to support the charge, and that the evidence demonstrates that Yahweh has acted on Israel's behalf in ways beneficial to Israel. Thus, the concept here is that of Yahweh's benevolence and involvement in the entirety of Israel's existence. The concept of the burdensome nature of Yahweh's involvement with Israel is neither addressed nor allowed as a viable perspective. Yet this perspective presents itself when the text is brought into its intertextual framework.

II.A.2.b. *Israel's argumentation (presentation of evidence) (6.6-7)*. It is important to note at the beginning of the analysis of this sub-unit that, as discussed above, its form has been the subject of debate. Here I consider that the generic form of a text or close resemblance to such a form, while it facilitates understanding of the concept of the text, may depart from its typical generic function. Thus while vv. 6-7 may be or resemble a temple entrance liturgy, its presence here suggests a recontextualization as well as a reconceptualization.[52] The prophetic critique of sacrifices is not the primary conceptuality of the unit. This nuance is secondary to the text's portrayal of sacrifices as the means of pleasing God. If present, the element of critique is in Israel's questions. Therein lies the view of sacrifices as being burdensome.

II.A.2.b.1) *General inquiry (6.6a)*. The question במה suggests the necessity of bringing something to Yahweh.[53] There are several passages that indicate the necessity of bringing something before Yahweh including: Exod. 23.15 (לא־יראו פני ריקם); 34.20; Deut. 16.16 (ולא יראה את־פני יהוה ריקם)[54] (cf. 1 Sam. 6.2-4). It is this inquiry paired with the response that has lead to the unit's classification as entrance liturgy. The vocabulary portrays the stance of the questioner in relation to Yahweh. Verse 6aα, 'with what shall I come before Yahweh', opens

52. See J.A. Sanders, *Canon and Community* (Philadelphia: Fortress Press, 1984), pp. 21-22 resignification and the process of canonization; Knierim, *Text and Concept*, p. 6, on recontextualization and reconceptualization.

53. Smith, *Micah, Zechariah*, p. 125.

54. Note that the requirement is given with a specific occasion in mind, the feast of unleavened bread.

the section (cf. Deut. 23.5 [Eng. v. 4]; Isa. 21.14; Ps. 95.2). The following part of the inquiry, v. 6aβ, further characterizes the mode of appearing before Yahweh. This is signaled by the term כפף, 'bow down', as for example the effect of suffering (cf. Pss. 145.14; 146.8).[55] The portrait is that of humility if not humiliation. So the general question is asked.

II.A.2.b.2) *Specific inquiry (6.6b-7).* Verse 6b is the questioner's proposed answer to the general inquiry. While it has been said that this is satirical in nature, one cannot for this reason minimize the questions' significance to the conceptuality of 6.1-8. This sub-unit is connected with the preceding in its function. This is to be understood as the response to the challenge to present evidence against Yahweh (ענה בי, v. 3b). This understanding is facilitated in light of other instances in which the language of being wearied by Yahweh, or Yahweh being tired, is connected with the offering of sacrifices and belongs to the tradition of critique of Israel's cultic practices. Thus, for example, in Isa. 1.10-17. God addresses the leaders of Sodom and Gomorrah telling them of God's weariness of their sacrifices—according to Isa. 1.11, 13, bringing offerings is futile (מנחת־שוא) and incense is an abomination (תועבה). However, this pejorative attitude is qualified (signaled by נלאיתי שנאה in Isa. 1.14). The cause of the weariness is that the sacrifices are accompanied by evil. Thus the command to:

> ...learn to do good; seek justice; correct oppression;
> defend the fatherless, plead for the widow (Isa. 1.17).

Yahweh's words to his people are further conditioned by the people's disobedience of Yahweh's law:

> ...your burnt offerings are not acceptable
> nor your sacrifice pleasing to me (Jer. 6.19-20).[20]

Similarly, the acceptability of sacrifice is conditioned by obedience in Jer. 7.2-26. Here, however, the contrast to what God requires is made explicit in reference to the commandments given to Israel when God brought them out of Egypt. What God said then still stands. Thus the argument proceeds that sacrifices (עולה וזבח) were not commanded but obedience was (שמעו בקולי):

> This command I gave them,
> Obey my voice, and I will be your God

55. Wolff, *Micah*, p. 177.

and you shall be my people;
and walk in all the way that I command you,
that it may be well with you (Jer. 7.21).[56]

In 1 Sam. 15.22 the specific situation is the disobedience of Saul to completely destroy the Amalekites. One of the conceptual components is the dynamics of obedience and sacrifice. The perspective is not that of Saul but that of Samuel evaluating the act of Saul. Furthermore, the evaluation is expressed in rhetorical questions establishing that God does not have as great a delight in sacrifices (החפץ ליהוה בעלות וזבחים) as God does in obedience (שמע). The narrative moves the evaluation from the specific to the general—better is obedience than sacrifice (שמע מזבח טוב). Here obedience and the offering of sacrifices are not mutually exclusive. What is being condemned is neither sacrifices nor obedience, but the misappropriated priority. Saul had placed his priority in the element that ought to have been secondary. Thus the text presupposes that Saul was trying to please God in sacrificing to God. Fundamentally, the evaluation of sacrifices vis-à-vis obeying God is, according to the narrative, prompted by Samuel's perception of Saul's misconception about sacrifices.

Though the nature and extent of the prioritizing is variously expressed, this ordering of priority with reference to God and sacrifices is basic to the critique of sacrifices in prophetic literature. Amos 5.21-25 uses aversive language to describe Yahweh's attitude toward cultic practices (לא ארצה שנאתי, מאסתי, and so on). The sacrifices mentioned include: עלה, מנחה, and שלם. The entirety of Israel's cult is placed in contrast to משפט וצדקה. This passage qualifies the rejection of the cult by its repeated use of the second masculine plural pronominal suffixes attached to the rejected elements (מריאיכם, מנחתיכם, עצרתיכם, חגיכם, שלם).[57] These qualifications indicate that the rejection is not of all cultic practices everywhere but of Israel's[58] and perhaps under the circumstances prompting the critique. The Amos text also uses the technical

---

56. While it seems that Jeremiah is violating a cultic law by telling the people to eat the burnt offering, M. Fishbane, *Biblical Interpretation in Ancient Israel* (Oxford: Clarendon Press, 1991), pp. 306, 529, recognizes that this text is aggadic hyperbole, and as a form of aggadic exegesis does not subvert the divinely revealed law.

57. Also the singular forms שריך and נבליך. The apparatus suggests reading יכם in place of the singular form.

58. Mays, *Amos*, p. 109.

language for favorable sacrifice, that is, רצה:[59] לא ארצה, 'I will not be
pleased with' (Amos 5.22; cf. Ezek. 20.41; Mal. 1.10, Ps. 51.18 [Eng.
v. 16]; Jer. 14.12; 2 Sam. 24.23); לא ירצה, 'it will not be favored' (Lev.
7.18; 19.7; 22.23, 27).[60]

As in Jer. 7.21-26 the precedence for the rejection of sacrifices is the
relationship of God and Israel in the Exodus and wilderness experi-
ences. The cultic practices are seen as an insignificant basis for God's
saving acts on behalf of Israel. This critique of sacrifices and the cult at
large is also evidenced in Isa. 43.2-24. Here the critique of sacrifices
uses the same vocabulary as found elsewhere to identify the objects of
critique, that is, עלה, זבח and מנחה. However, when compared to Amos
5.21, 1 Samuel 15; Jer. 7.21 and Isa. 1.11-17, the critique is of the abundance or unacceptability of sacrifices. On the contrary, the multivalency
of that text allows for the interpretation that this critique is Israel's.
Israel is weary of Yahweh and does not sacrifice.[61] Here the element of
contrast is different. It is not sacrifice vs. justice, but sacrifice vs. the
preponderance of sin. The later indicates that sacrifices in some way are
desired by Yahweh.

There is no specification as to the nature of the efficacy of the sacrifices. Here the charge that Yahweh has wearied Israel is answered by
the allusion to the necessity of sacrifices. Thus, the weariness of the
people is portrayed in contrast to the 'new thing' (Isa. 43.19) that
Yahweh is doing. Israel is wearied by Yahweh and does not sacrifice—
compared to Isa. 1.4, 14, 24, where it is Yahweh who is weary of sacrifices. These reflect different significations of a tradition to particular
community concerns.

Together these texts illuminate 6.6-7. First, they (esp. Isa. 43.22-24)
suggest that the complaint that God has wearied Israel is not as anoma-

---

59.   William White, 'רצה', in *TWOT*, II, p. 859; KB, pp. 1280-81. Cf. Knierim,
Text and Concept, p. 35 n. 26. He states that 'the Hebrew word highlights pleasure,
agreement, and favor, whereas "acceptance" may be a connotation depending on
the favorable response by someone who "accepts" someone else's approach or gift'.
He thus prefers *Wohlgefallen* ('favor') as the translation of רצה. In this interpretation Knierim agrees with R. Rendtorff, *Leviticus* (BKAT, 3.1; Neukirchen–Vluyn:
Neukirchener Verlag, 1985); while disagreeing with G.J. Wenham, *The Book of
Leviticus* (NICOT, 3; Grand Rapids: Eerdmans, 1979); B.A. Levine, *Leviticus* (JPS
Torah Commentary; Philadelphia: Jewish Publication Society, 1989).
60.   H.W. Wolff, *Joel and Amos* (Hermeneia; Philadelphia: Fortress Press,
1977), p. 263.
61.   Grogan, 'Isaiah', pp. 261-62.

lous as it may be if the unit vv. 1-8 is seen in isolation from its intertextual framework. Second, the presentation of sacrifices in vv. 6-7 as the evidence of the way in which Yahweh wearied the people is also illuminated intertextually. Among other things, it means that there was some misconception about the place of sacrifices in the life of Israel. This misconception was not with respect to the efficacy of the sacrifice nor with whether or not sacrifices should be offered. The misconception was concerning the place of sacrifices in relation to other requirements and specifically justice as a communal responsibility.

II.A.2.b.2)a) *Types and quantity of sacrifices (6.6b-7a)*. One cannot overlook the sacrifices mentioned nor the question of their significance. Like others wherein the sacrifices are critiqued, this text mentions sacrifices. The עלה, 'burnt offering', is mentioned vis-à-vis other types of sacrifices, for example, מנחה and זבח שלמים.[62] This type of sacrifice, עלה, uses the entire sacrifice.[63] It is a gift to the deity[64] brought voluntarily by the worshiper, but nonetheless with an awareness of the need to rectify a broken bond. But to say that the עלה is gift does not yet answer the question of its significance. Gray argues that in the prophetic critique of sacrifices (Hos. 6.4-6; Amos 4.4; 5.21-25; Isa. 1.10-17; Mic. 6.6-8; Jer. 7.21) the sacrifices are gifts—that is, a means of gratifying the worshiper. According to Gray, it is this giving of sacrifices to curry Yahweh's favor that is repudiated.[65] However, the repudiation may be due to another reason—the unrepentant worshiper.

The general statement is then specified. Here scholars have noted an exaggeration of the requirements with reference to both the quality and

---

62. With regard to the types of sacrifices see Walter Eichrodt, *Theology of the Old Testament* (OTL; Philadelphia: Westminster Press, 1961), I, pp. 144-46; Gerhard von Rad, *Old Testament Theology* (San Francisco: Harper & Row, 1962), I, p. 256.

63. See Knierim, *Text and Concept*, regarding the requirements and accompanying conceptuality.

64. Norman Snaith, 'Sacrifice in the Old Testament', *VT* 7 (1957), pp. 300-17 (309); Eichrodt, *Theology of the Old Testament*, I, pp. 144-45, מנחה as gift and p. 146, עלה as petitionary sacrifice; von Rad, *Old Testament Theology*, I, p. 256, מנחה in P as gift-sacrifice; Knierim, *Text and Concept*, p. 21.

65. George B. Gray, *Sacrifice in the Old Testament* (New York: Ktav, 1971), pp. 41-42; cf. von Rad, *Old Testament Theology*, I, p. 251. He notes that Lev. 1–5 focuses on procedures while Deuteronomy mostly addresses the question of significance.

quantity of the sacrifices mentioned.[66] An examination of the text reveals that the questions focus on the quantity and significance of the sacrifices. Thus, the mention of 'calves a year old' (עגלים בני שנה) represents a specific type of עלה. The calves בני שנה point to more than young calves. This is not an indication of calves younger than one year, but those that already have lived one year. The phrase, though much debated, may represent not only the age requirement but the relative value of the sacrifice.[67] One-year-old calves already signify the owner's investment in caring for them, since calves could be sacrificed as early as seven days after birth (Lev. 9.3; 22.27). Accordingly, one-year-old calves were very economically valuable.[68] Thus, the בני שנה requirement of the עלה and other sacrifices (cf. Num. 6.14; 7.15; 28.3) does not necessarily signify the innocence of the animal.[69] No other requirement is cited in Mic. 6.6b, but the text presupposes that this sacrifice meets the requirement for being favorable.

Verse 7 then continues the question with the language of the favorable nature of the sacrifice (cf. Lev. 19.7; 7.18; 22.23, 27). However, here it is not the priest's pronouncement that is in question, but Yahweh's attitude towards the sacrifices. Inasmuch as v. 7 is a further expansion of the inquiry of v. 6 about coming before Yahweh (קדם, piel), it should be noted that it now quantifies the sacrifices mentioned by use of the terms אלף and רבבות (cf. 1 Kgs 3.4). More is involved here than a quantitative change in sacrifices cited. Compared to the עגל in v. 6, the sacrifices mentioned here are איל (cf. Gen. 22.13; 1 Sam. 15.22; Isa. 1.11) and נחלי־שמן.[70]

It is not the catalogue found in Isa. 43.22-24 nor in Amos 5.21-25. No mention is made of זבח שלמים nor of מנחה. The emphasis here appears to be the quantification of certain sacrifices rather than the specific categories. It is the quantification that suggests Israel's sarcasm (or possible hyperbole) used to demonstrate the reason for the underlying charge against Yahweh—Yahweh has wearied Israel.[71] However, this is

---

66. E.g. Mays, *Micah*, p. 136.
67. Gray, *Sacrifice in the Old Testament*, pp. 349-51
68. Osborn, 'Nature of True Religion, p. 77.
69. Cf. Gray, *Sacrifice in the Old Testament*, p. 350.
70. See the discussion below with regard to the LXX reading.
71. See Wolff, *Micah*, p. 178, according to whom this quantification suggests a caricature of what is becoming more and more nonsensical, especially the great size of sacrificial offerings.

the perspective of an observer. The quantifications are better understood
from the perspective of the questioner. Thereby, it suggests the burden
alluded to in v. 3 and the frustration of not understanding what pleases
God. Verses 6-7 presupposes that sacrifices are required by God.

II.A.2.b.2)b) *Purpose of the sacrifices (6.7b).* The latter part of this unit
further qualifies the significance of the enumeration of the sacrifices.
The conception behind the offering of the sacrifices is the means of
dealing with sin. This is made explicit in v. 7b. The question is typically
presumed to deal with the deplorable practice of human sacrifice and to
signal the incredulity of the question. However, the question, though it
may point to an extreme—ultimate and condemnable—sacrifice, also
stands along other texts in which the offering of the firstborn does not
have this pejorative nuance.

Some scholars, including Anderson, suggest that the intensification is
due to increased awareness of the unworthiness and obligation.[72] It may
not be presumed, as Wolff has,[73] that the question portrays the sheer
despair of the intention to give oneself fully to acts of propitiation, thus
going beyond all legal possibilities provided by the Yahwistic cult. One
must take into account the various laws concerning offering of the firstborn (Exod. 13.2, 15; 22.28; 34.20; Num. 18.15)[74] together with instances where human sacrifice is condemned (Deut. 18.10; Lev. 18.21;
20.1-5). In this intertextual framework, the apparent misconception
leading to and underlying the line of question is therefore elucidated.
Thus it seems that the text itself represents a conflation of traditions—
that conflation itself being the essence of the misconception.[75]

The use of נתן in 1 Sam 1.11 of Hannah's vow to 'give' Samuel to
Yahweh is often favorably interpreted in contrast to 1 Kgs 16.34, Josh.
6.26 and Jer. 7.31. Thus Fishbane has argued that Num. 18.15 may
represent the earliest stratum of the cultic rule. Exodus 28.28-29 (cf.
13.2) is then a softening of that rule.[76] The polemic against the donation
of persons may have been due to socio-political factors as well
as theological factors. In the Micah passage, then, the use of נתן may

---

72. Anderson, 'Micah 6.1-8', p. 193.

73. Wolff, *Micah*, p. 179; cf. Waltke, 'Micah', p. 732.

74. Fishbane, *Biblical Interpretation*, pp. 184-85.

75. See Osborn, 'Nature of True Religion', pp. 74-78, regarding the presence
of different conceptions in the text unit.

76. Fishbane, *Biblical Interpretation*, p. 186; Eichrodt, *Theology of the Old
Testament*, I, p. 149, sees a principle of substitution indicated in these passages.

be interpreted in light of the optional nature of the donation of the sacrifice.

Notably, the question is not whether the firstborn is to be a 'transgression offering'. Verse 7 consists of synthetically parallel expressions governed by the verb נתן—'my firstborn for my crimes' (פשעי)[77] //'the fruit of my body for the sin of my soul' (חטאת).[78] The vocabulary of v. 7b recalls other passages in the book of Micah where they are synthetically paired (1.5; 3.8b). In each case they refer to Israel. Here the mention of פשע and חטאת is not toward condemnation of Israel's crimes and sins as in the other occurrence in the book. Here פשע and חטאת are mentioned in reference to what the questioner must do in order to please Yahweh. The questioner presupposes the presence of פשע and חטאת and the need for dealing with them and, furthermore, presumes that offering sacrifices is desired or at least acceptable (cf. Isa. 43.22-24).

In summary, vv. 6-7 as a unit is the response to the challenge of v. 3b (ענה ב'). It seeks to give evidence in support of the charge against Yahweh—namely, that Yahweh has wearied Israel—and to clarify the basis of that charge. Seen intertextually, the unit appears as a conflation of traditions—first, about the necessity of offering sacrifices; second, about the requirement of the particular types and quantity of sacrifices; and third, about the purpose of the sacrifice. Conceptually, the unit alone does not represent a critique against sacrifices. This critique is seen intertextually and in conjunction with the following unit (6.8). Even so, to call vv. 6-7 a critique is to say too much about the nature of the unit. Verses 6-7 represents a misconception about sacrifices as Yahweh's requirement. In the addressing of that misconception, sacrifices are brought into focus, thus suggesting that Israel's own ways have wearied Israel.

II.A.3. *Resolution (6.8)*
In light of the above discussion the place of v. 8 should first of all be noted. Infratextually, v. 8 functions as the final statement of the dispute

---

77. Knierim, 'Hamartiology', pp. 424-27; *idem*, 'פשע', pp. 488-95, as crime; *idem*, *Die Hauptbegriffe für Sünde*, pp. 113-16; in contrast to Snaith, *The Distinctive Ideas*, pp. 63-65, who see פשע as rebellion; cf. N. Seebass, 'פשע', in *ThWAT*, VI, p. 791; contrast Köhler, *Theologie des Alten Testaments*, p. 158, according to whom the term denotes 'rebellion'; see *HALAT*, III, pp. 981-82.

78. See Knierim 'חטא', pp. 541-49.

between Yahweh and Israel. It clarifies the apparent misconception underlying Israel's charge against Yahweh, a misconception further demonstrated by the questions in vv. 6-7. As such, v. 8 is limited in scope to Israel and to the issue of what pleases Yahweh.[79]

II.A.3.a. *Basis of the dispute (הגיד לך) (6.8a)*. The address הגיד לך אדם points to more than the addressee, אדם. It also points to the prior disclosure of that which is misconceived by the questions in vv. 6-7. What has been made known is termed טוב, recalling 3.2—the accusation of the leaders' hating what is good and doing the opposite of what is required of them (cf. Amos 5.14-15; Isa. 1.16-17; 5.19-20). The address further suggests that the hearer has the capacity to know (ידע) what is good (טוב)—in contrast to evil (רע). Thus, because it was made known, the hearer would be cognizant of the good.[80]

The text gives no indication as to when the disclosure/revelation was made. It could be the prophetic declarations to Israel to seek good and not evil (Amos 5.14-15; Isa. 1.16-17). Some argue that the reference is being made to Law and especially Deuteronomy.[81] Before proceeding with the discussion of what constitutes the 'good' revealed, it should be noted that the very response presumes the accusation in v. 3 to be unfounded and hence the entire dispute resolvable by clarification of what is previously known. The whole concept of this clause is that there has been a need to reiterate what has already been made known, thus making explicit that this is not a new requirement. The connection with vv. 3-7 seems to be conceptual. Israel is weary because of its own doings and misunderstanding of Yahweh's requirement. Yahweh does not require a multitude of sacrifices.

The vocative אדם has led to various theories about the scope of the declaration—universal (all humanity)[82] or particular (Israel).[83] The use

79. It must also be said that the assertion is not a denial of potential universal applicability of v. 8.

80. George W. Buchanan, 'The Old Testament Meaning of the Knowledge of Good and Evil', *JBL* 75 (1956), pp. 14-20, argues that the knowing of good and evil is associated with a specific age, that is, 20 years. However, in 6.8 it is not age that constitutes the basis of the knowledge. Likewise, it is not experience that brings this knowledge. Instead, it is Yahweh's specific disclosure.

81. Cheyne, *Micah*, p. 51.

82. Waltke, 'Micah', p. 733; Smith, *Micah, Zephaniah*, p. 127; Ewald, *Commentary on the Prophets*, p. 332.

83. Mays, *Micah*, p. 141; Hillers, *Micah*, p. 79.

of אדם is an insufficient basis for asserting universality, especially in light of the vocabulary typical of covenant relationship—חסד and אלהיך—of which the עמי in vv. 3 and 5 is a counterpart (cf. Deut. 7.6; 14.2; 26.18; Exod. 19.5). Intratextually, this declaration is particular to Israel.

II.A.3.b. *Clarification of Yahweh's demands (6.8b).* The declaration equates or at least explicates טוב with what Yahweh seeks (דרש) of you (אדם as antecedent). The verb דרש (parallel בקש, piel) has a wide range of meaning: 'to seek', 'to inquire' and 'to require'. The basic meaning, 'to seek', is used to indicate the implementation of something, for example 'justice' (Isa. 1.16-17), 'peace' (Jer. 29.7; 38.4), 'good' (Deut. 23.7 [Eng. v. 6]; Amos 5.14-15). It is also used in Gen. 9.5 of Yahweh's diligent pursuit of vengeance, and of legal inquiry in Deuteronomy 12–34.[84]

The construction כי אם functions as an adversative indicating a restrictive nuance (cf. Gen. 40.14; Job 42.18).[85] This restrictive sense designates the elements introduced by it as standing in contrast to those preceding it. Thus, the sacrificing is placed in contrast to the elements enumerated in v. 8. The declaration sets out two components which are in essence the 'good' that was revealed. The first deals with community relationships and the second with the relationship of God and Israel, the people of God.

II.A.3.b.1) *Toward the community (6.8bα).* Concerning relationships within the community, it is not simply 'justice' (משפט) but the practicing of it (עשות משפט) that is required (cf. דעת משפט, 3.1). The term משפט itself deserves its own discussion, a task that has been variously undertaken and upon which the present study depends. The term is already used in 3.1, 9, where it is used with reference to the leaders and by inference to the marginalized. Here it is sufficient to indicate that it is the practice of 'justice' that is required.[86] It should be further noted that the requirement of משפט is usually associated specifically with leaders. They are responsible for משפט though not only they but all who are in the position to execute it. However, it is not simply the strict implementation of law devoid of concern for those involved in the process.[87]

---

84.   S. Wagner, 'דרש', in *TDOT*, III, pp. 293-307.

85.   Waltke and O'Connor, *Syntax*, §39.3.5d; GKC §163d.

86.   Anderson, 'Micah 6.1-8', p. 194.

87.   Moshe Weinfeld, *Social Justice in Ancient Israel and in the Ancient Near East* (Minneapolis: Fortress; Jerusalem: Magnes Press, 1995), pp. 25-27.

עשׂות משׁפט is juxtaposed with the following אהבת חסד. Two aspects of this deserve attention, namely, the specific semantics of the expression and the conceptual relationship with the preceding phrase. First, אהב 'to love'[88]—as opposed to שׂנא 'to hate'—denotes favorable disposition toward its object. In 3.1 the leaders are said to hate good and love evil and in 3.9 to abhor justice. As in those instances, there is an explicit reference to the inward state out of which behavior is produced. While one does not guarantee the other, the conceptuality of ch. 3, for example, presupposes that behavior is indicative of an inward state, such that injustice reflects the abhorrence of justice and the hatred of good. Thus, it is the practice of justice (עשׂות משׁפט) that is required. What is the relationship of the two phrases? Do they signal two different requirements or two aspects of one requirement? To answer this question one must first understand the meaning of both phrases—עשׂות משׁפט and אהבת חסד. Here חסד, the object of אהב, is itself as complex a term as משׁפט with which it is paired. חסד is usually the object of the verb עשׂה.[89] According to Glueck, חסד may denote 'loyalty' born out of people's obligation to each other, for example, God's loyalty to the covenant relationship and mutual obligation among persons.[90] Sakenfeld, in discussing the 'secular' uses of the term, prefers to translate the term as 'loyalty' noting that this may also refer to relationships of superiors to inferiors and not simply mutuality of relationship as previous presumed. In contrast to Glueck, Sakenfeld argues that חסד is not necessarily obligatory.[91] In some instances חסד refers to acts of kindness (e.g. 2 Sam. 2.5; Ruth 1.8-9; 2.11-12).[92]

Notably, the occurrence of the demand for חסד vis-à-vis sacrifices is not unique to 6.8. This also occurs in Hos. 6.6 where it is suggested that

---

88. Cf. Konstantin Zobel, *Prophetie und Deuteronomium* (Berlin: W. de Gruyter, 1992), pp. 23-24.

89. K. Sakenfeld 'Love (OT)', in *ABD*, IV, p. 377; *idem, Meaning of Hesed in the Hebrew Bible: A New Inquiry* (Missoula: Scholars Press, 1978), pp. 16-21; cf. N. Glueck, *Hesed in the Bible* (trans. A Gottschalk; Cincinnati: Hebrew Union College Press, 1967), pp. 35-36, 70-71; Gordon R. Clark, *The Word Hesed in the Hebrew Bible* (JSOTSup, 157; Sheffield: JSOT Press, 1993).

90. Glueck, *Hesed*; cf. W.F. Lofthouse 'Hen and Hesed in the Old Testament', *ZAW* 5 (1933), pp. 29-35.

91. Sakenfeld, *Meaning of Hesed*.

92. H.J. Stoebe, 'חסד', in *THAT*, I, pp. 599-622; L.R. Harris, 'חסד', in *TWOT*, I, pp. 305-307.

חסד is to be directed toward God.[93] Nonetheless, the element of the requirement is usually placed in contrast to sacrifices (cf. Amos 5.21-24; Jer. 7.21-26; Isa. 1.10-20).[94]

To whatever extent חסד typically denotes an obligation, in v. 8 its occurrence with אהב suggests more that a mere obligation. With respect to relationships within the community, חסד is used of Israel to connote a community responsibility. It gets its validity from the community itself, the covenant community. Thus, חסד itself may be compelled by the nature of a relationship. Generally speaking, it neither necessitates nor presupposes love. As such, Israel may have been loyal to the covenant relationship without loving that loyalty. This is not to qualify or quantify the existence of loyalty by the presence or absence of love. Nonetheless, it is to suggest that the quality of חסד varies relative to the presence of love. So, in 6.8 the demand is not to simply to fulfill an obligation within the community, but to love the commitment to preserve the community in much the same way as one is to love good. It does not imply that the nature of the various relationships within the community determines the nature of חסד. It suggests that the nature of the required חסד is that of love—regardless of the specific relationships. Conceivably, it is possible that one hates חסד in the same way the one hates good. So the requirement's broad statement indicates that indiscriminate nature. According to Glueck,

> *Hesed*, which formerly existed only between those who stood in a fundamentally close relationship toward one another, undergoes considerable expansion in meaning. Every man becomes every other man's brother, *hesed* becomes the mutual or reciprocal relationship of all men toward each other and toward God.[95]

The juxtaposition of עשׂות משׁפט and אהבת חסד raises the question as to the relationship between the two. Are these parallel expressions as found elsewhere (Pss. 33.5; 89.15; 101.1; Jer. 9.23; Hos. 12.7)?[96] This question itself recognizes the possibility of משׁפט and חסד being more than two mutually exclusive phenomena. Each may be essential to the other though not simply as means (משׁפט) to an end (חסד).[97] The rela-

93. Sakenfeld, *Meaning of Hesed*, pp. 172-73.
94. Sakenfeld, *Meaning of Hesed*, pp. 172-73. What is required usually 'involves behavior towards one's fellowmen'.
95. Glueck, *Hesed*, p. 61.
96. Weinfeld, *Social Justice*, p. 36.
97. Thus Wolff, *Micah*, p. 181.

tionship may be constituted in their inherent nature. They both presuppose a relationship between persons. If this relationship is defined by the presence of משפט and חסד it is characterized by efforts to ensure its own wellbeing.

The text does not suggest that either is necessitated by the other. Therefore, it is conceivable that one may practice justice (משפט) as an ethical obligation without any sense of love or devotion. Likewise, justice (משפט) may be practiced without a sense of obligation. Thus, practicing justice may or may not be indicative of loyalty any more than loyalty may be indicative of justice. Still, the love of loyalty may be a predisposing factor to the practice of justice. Some scholars suggest that the v. 8 does not articulate three requirements but three aspects of the same thing. Accordingly, Mays argues that the requirement is 'to do justice', while 'to love mercy' and 'to walk humble with God' are more general ways of expressing the same thing.[98]

II.A.3.b.2) *Toward God (6.8bβ)*. The other component of the demand of God on Israel is that Israel 'walk humbly' with God. To walk, לכת, qualified by the adverbial modifier הצנע has been traditionally translated 'humbly'.[99] On the basis of the text's shared vocabulary with the Dead Sea Scrolls, Hyatt proposes that the term הצנע is to be translated 'skillfully, wisely'.[100] While the vocabulary is absent, Deut. 10.12-20 in conceptuality attests to the 'humility' required of humans in reference to God. In this respect the humility has more to do with the life of Israel than with the attitude in the immediate situation—that is, the arrogance in charging Yahweh and the sarcasm in the inquiry in vv. 6-7. What is required is devotion to God in the humility of circumspection born out of the recognition that God is God, as well as the humility that comes from knowledge of God's choosing Israel and becoming the God of Israel (אלהיך).

In summary, v. 8 declares to Israel that, based on God's disclosure to Israel, she knows what is good. Verse 8 is a clarification of God's requirement for Israel reiterated in response to Israel's misconception of what is required in order to please God.

---

98. Mays, *Micah*, p. 142.

99. Osborn, 'Nature of True Religion', p. 78; Keil and Delitzsch, *The Twelve Minor Prophets*, p. 497.

100. J. Philip Hyatt, 'On the Meaning and Origin of Micah 6.8', *ATR* 34.4 (1952), pp. 232-39 (237).

II.B. *Concerning Israel's Fate (6.9–7.20)*
This unit is the major unit of chs. 6–7 and is the counterpart to 2.1–5.14. It discusses both the judgment and the hope aspects of Israel's existence.

II.B.1. *Present: judgment on Israel (6.9–7.6)*
The present is characterized by judgment but is the precursor to the future.

II.B.1.a. *Judgment speech (6.9-16).*[101] As with the judgment speeches in ch. 3 this speech articulates the accusation (6.10-12) as being intricately connected to the announcement of judgment (6.13-16).
II.B.1.a.1) *Introduction (6.9).* The introduction in v. 9 is composed of three elements. First is a report formula introducing Yahweh's proclamation to the 'the city' (v. 9aα). Second is a parenthetical remark addressed to Yahweh concerning the prudence of heeding Yahweh's name (v. 9aβ).[102] Third is the summons to hear addressed to the tribe and the assembly of the city.[103]
II.B.1.a.2) *Judgment (6.10-16).* The judgment focuses on the behaviors from which the impending judgment ensues.
II.B.1.a.2)a) *Accusation (6.10-12).* The accusation comprised of rhetorical questions follows in vv. 10-12. Willis argues that the function of 6.9-16 is to complete the lawsuit begun in 6.1 and which is interrupted by 6.6-8. His argument is based on the observation that the announcement of judgment is the typical ending of the lawsuit.[104] Willis's argument

101. The order of the MT is followed thus leaving v. 12 in its current position rather than transposing it to after v. 9a or v. 9b. There are various textual difficulties that confront the interpretation of this text unit. While these are recognized, the reiteration of the difficulties and the various proposals for a solution will not be done here. Such details may be found in Hagstrom, *The Coherence*, pp. 93-94. Cf. Wolff, *Micah*, pp. 186-87; Mays, *Micah*, p. 143. See the Appendix below.

102. The wisdom language of the text has been noted with reference to the similarity to the theme of 'the fear of Yahweh'. Wolff, *Micah*, p. 191, sees this remark as a redactional addition whose intent is to offer a confession before God. Cf. Mays, *Micah*, pp. 145-46.

103. Wolff, *Micah*, p. 192, argues that the tribe and the assembly are two distinct groups. The tribe refers to Judeans from the settlements who came to Jerusalem to trade. The assembly of the city would then refer to the residents of the city who assemble for a particular purpose.

104. Willis, 'Structure, Setting', p. 261; contrast Hagstrom, *The Coherence*, pp. 95-96.

minimizes the function of the introduction in v. 9. As in 3.1, 9, the summons to hear focuses attention on a specific group within the larger group already introduced in the dispute. In this case the tribe and assembly of the city are the focus as a part of the people of God, Israel.

It is the nature of the rhetorical question not to expect a response since it presumes the answer to be indisputable. Here there are two aspects of the questions that are indisputable. First is the aspect of God's respond to sin. The issue is whether God should ignore or turn a blind eye to wealth gained by means of wickedness or acquit (זכה) those with dishonest weights and measures (מאזני רשע, 'unjust scales', and כיס אבני מרמה 'bag of deceitful stones'). Both of these are unfavorable to Yahweh:

> Diverse weights and diverse measures are both alike an abomination to the Lord (Prov. 20.10; cf. 20.23).

> A false balance is an abomination to the Lord, but an accurate weight is his delight (Prov. 11.1).

> You shall not have in your bag two kinds of weights, large and small... A full and just measure with you shall have...that your days may be prolonged in the land which the Lord your God gives you. For all who do such things, all who act dishonestly, are an abomination to the Lord your God (Deut. 25.13-16; cf. Lev. 19.36).

The significance of this question reaches back to the first part of the dispute in chs. 1–3 in which the sins and evil of Jerusalem are punished. In Amos 8.5-10 those who oppress the poor by means of deceitful weights are told that God will not forget but will punish them. The first aspect, then, is that without a doubt God will punish those who practice such deceit. The second aspect is that it is indisputable that the practice is happening. With the bag to conceal the weights, the merchants use the large or small stone according to the profit they desire. The consequence is that people are being cheated. Verse 12 expands on the deceitful practices by addressing the city concerning the violence of the rich and the general deceitfulness of the population.

II.B.1.a.2)b) *Announcement of judgment (6.13-16).*
This section is conceptually dependent on the preceding unit (6.10-12). Through this dependence on the impending judgment is presented as the consequence of sin.

II.B.1.a.2)b)(1) *Judgment (6.13).* The announcement of judgment is indicated by the use of וגם־אני. The general statement of judgment is that Yahweh has already began to punish the city by making it desolate.

It concludes with a purpose clause (v. 13b) 'because of your sins' (עַל־חַטֹּאתֶךָ)—that is, the use of deceitful weights and measures.

II.B.1.a.2)b)(2) *Expansion of the judgment (6.14-16)*. While the state of the impending judgment is relatively brief, its brevity is complemented by an expansion whose function is to verify the validity of the judgment.

II.B.1.a.2)b)(2)(a) *Specification (6.14-15)*. The judgment is expanded to further specify the nature of the desolation. The economic basis and its significance for the wellbeing of the city is what was being compromised by the deceitful weights and measures. In the same way, the judgment will focus on the economic basis of the city's livelihood. The futility of the efforts of self-preservation will be evident in the fact of a famine, the futility of farming, and the lack of resources even with the attempts to store them away. For example, the curse in Deut. 28.25-68, esp. 30-31, 38-40 befalls those who do not obey the voice of the Lord:

> You shall plant vineyards and dress them, but you shall neither drink of the wine nor gather the grapes, for the worms shall eat them. You shall have olive trees throughout all your territory, but you shall not anoint yourself with the oil, for the olives shall drop off (Deut. 28.39-40).

The punishment is also directed against those who oppress the poor in the book of Amos (cf. Hos. 4.10; Zeph. 1.13; Hag. 1.6).

> Therefore because you trample upon the poor
> and take from him exactions of wheat,
> you have built houses of hewn stone,
> but you shall not dwell in them;
> you have planted pleasant vineyards,
> but you shall not drink their wine (Amos 5.11).

According to Mays, these curses are not intended to depict the specifics of a situation but to depict how the blessings have become curses.[105]

II.B.1.a.2)b)(2)(b) *Rationale (6.16)*. Verse 16 is a further expansion of the announcement of judgment that reiterates the reason for the judgment and the correspondence between sin and punishment. The sins of the city are compared to the statutes of Omri (cf. 2 Kgs 10.18; 21.3, 25-26). The judgment will be desolation; and this desolate status will be the object of derision and scorn (cf. 2 Chron. 29.8; Jer. 19.8).

---

105. Mays, *Micah*, p. 148.

II.B.1.b. *Response to judgment—woe oracle (אַלְלַי לִי) (7.1-6).*
This unit is the conceptual counterpart to others including 1.8-16 and
2.12-13. Each of these units functions within the conceptuality of the
larger units. Here (7.1-6) the response is signaled by the 1st person
address.

II.B.1.b.1) *Introduction (7.1aα₁).* The woe oracle functions as a lament
concerning the desolation depicted in the preceding judgment speech. It
opens with the typical formula (אַלְלַי) in v. 1 and continues on to v. 6.
The object of the lament is designated לִי and presumably refers to the
city (cf. Job 10.15).[106] This woe oracle does not function in the same
way as that in 2.1-5. There it announces judgment specifying the nature
of the sins to which the judgment is targeted. Here the oracle does not
announce judgment but depicts the response to the judgment. As such
the first part of the oracle (7.1a-5) gives an account of the desolation.

II.B.1.b.2) *Account of the desolation (7.1aα₂-6).* The content of the
lament is illustrated by the desolation that ensues from the judgment.
Through its language, this unit demonstrates the encompassing nature
of the desolation and sets the stage for an admonition.

II.B.1.b.2)a) *Nature of the desolation (7.1aα₂-4).* The community's
lamentable circumstances could not be more embedded in its relationship to Yahweh. The nature of the desolation is that it is inescapable
and its source unexpected.

II.B.1.b.2)a)(1) *Personal (7.1aα₂-b).* In 7.1 the language of the 6.14-16
is employed, thus repeating the imagery of desolation and famine by
the depiction of the empty fields (after the harvest) and the lack of food.
Furthermore, assuming the custom of leaving scraps for the poor (cf.
Lev. 19.9-10; 23.22; Deut. 24.19-22; Ruth 2.3, 7, 15-19), the simile
may illustrate a situation wherein the speaker comes to the field after
the harvest to find the remains. Extreme hunger is the result if there are
no leftovers, and this is the cause of further distress (cf. Isa. 24.13; Jer.
49.9).[107] So with respect to the announcement of judgment, 7.1 recasts
the desolation of the judgment as the basis of the lament—desolation
that threatens existence.

II.B.1.b.2)a)(2) *Community (7.2-4).* The account of the desolation continues with a depiction of the situation in the larger community. There

106. Thus Mays, *Micah*, pp. 150-51; Smith, *Micah, Zephaniah*; contra Renaud,
La Formation; Wolff, *Micah*, p. 204, believes that the speaker is the prophet.
107. Wolff, *Micah*, p. 204.

is an absence of the 'faithful' (חסיד)—those who practice חסד in devotion to God (cf. Pss. 12.2; 31.24), and the 'upright' (ישר; cf. 6.8). The חסידים 'live in an atmosphere of חסד which creates trust'.[108] The ישר is upright in heart and practices fairness and justice with others (Pss. 11.7; 19.9; 33.4; 37.14, 37; 111.8; 119.137).[109] The community over which the speaker laments is characterized by the absence of these two groups and is instead full of persons who destroy each other (vis-à-vis 6.8). They are devoted to doing evil (cf. 2.1; 3.1; 6.10-12).

II.B.1.b.2)b) *Admonition concerning the desolation (7.5-6)*. The following admonition is the result of the experience of the atmosphere of evil. It is an admonition to distrust even one's closest relative. The scope of the desolation encompasses the livelihood of the city, its leaders and people in such a way that each does evil against the other—for example, mother against daughter and father against son. In contrast to chs. 4–5 where the enemy of Israel was seen as the nations, here the enemy of Israel is introduced as being within Israel (7.6). The articulation of this perspective makes explicit what chs. 2–3 have already implied in their depiction of leaders and others in power who oppress the less powerful members of the community.

II.B.2. *Future: prospect of hope (7.7-20)*
The contrast with the preceding unit is signaled by ואני. Some have argued that the waw-adversative never begins a lament and in this case is to be taken as the concluding statement of the unit 7.1-7.[110] However, the unit indicated by the particle is not independent of what precedes. It is a logical continuation of 7.1-6 inasmuch as it presents a further response to the judgment announced. As such, it presents a contrast between the response of utter despair at the desolation and a basis for hope. The unit culminates with an expression of confidence in God, adoring God for God's compassion and forgiveness of sin.

II.B.2.a. *Introduction (7.7)*. Verse 7 functions as an introduction to the unit. Its language is a typical expression of hope—'I will wait (יחל) for the God of my salvation'. Typically, the waiting is a time of outcry and

---

108. Hans-Joachim Kraus, *Theology of the Psalms* (trans. Keith Crim; Minneapolis: Augsburg, 1986), p. 157.

109. Kraus, *Theology of the Psalms*, p. 157.

110. Thus Mays, *Micah*, pp. 152-53, who attributes v. 7 to a redactional seam that connects vv. 8-20 to vv. 1-6.

prayer, not a time of silent passivity or apathy toward the desolation. It is born out of belief in God and its very nature is defined by trust in God and the certainty that God will help.[111] The hope in this unit is initiated by the speaker as compared to 2.12-13 and chs. 4–5 where it is introduced by God as a possible response to God's promise to resolve the distress of the present.

II.B.2.b. *Bases for hope (7.8-20)*
Israel's hope is founded both in its realities (7.8-17) and in the character of God that manifests itself in forgiveness for Israel's remnant (7.18-20). II.B.2.b.1) *Israel's realities (7.8-17).* How does one hope when circumstances seen to compel fear, distrust and despair? As a unit chapters 4-5 indicates that hope may be grounded in adversities that are the reason for hop. Her in 7.8-17 the confidence to hope is born out of Israel accepting its role in its present adversities.
I.B.2.b.1)a) *Basic expression of hope (Israel) (7.8-10).* With confidence, the speaker (presumably the city as the community) addresses its enemy (אֹיֶבֶת; cf. Pss. 13.2, 4; 41.11).[112] The speaker presupposes desolation and admonishes the enemy not to rejoice. The reason is the confidence that God will deliver the city; but in that confidence is also the expression of an awareness of and acknowledgment of sin (חָטָא; cf. Mic. 6.13; Pss. 41.4; 51.4). Notably, the confidence does not come from a claim of innocence. Here, as in 6.10, the issue arises as to God's response to sin. Does God overlook the sin and thus deliver the city? Or does God punish the city for its sin but reserve the option of later delivering it? The latter seems to be the perspective of the text (cf. 7.18-20). The God who judges is the God who saves and delivers. It is the confidence that there is a larger context to the judgment (cf. Isa. 57.15; Ezek. 33.11; cf. Jer. 1–4).[113]

Verse 10 comments on the expression of confidence in God's deliverance. The enemy (אֹיַבְתִּי), unnamed as in many of the Psalms, will see the deliverance and be overcome with shame because the enemy gloated and taunted the city (Joel 2.17; Pss. 42.3, 10; 79.10).[114] The picture is

111. Kraus, *Theology of the Psalms*, pp. 158-59.
112. See Kraus, *Theology of the Psalms*, pp. 125-26, for a discussion of the types of enemies referred to in the Psalms.
113. Wolff, *Micah*, p. 221.
114. Mays, *Micah*, pp. 159-60.

of an ongoing situation in which the desolation of the city was met with derision and taunting (cf. 6.16). Reconstructed from the text, the taunt seems to have been that God has abandoned the city (v. 10a). The fundamental idea is that God's presence is contrary to the desolation that is upon the city (cf. 3.11). The deliverance will therefore cause the enemy to be ashamed and the city will in turn gloat over its enemy.

II.B.2.b.1)b) *Affirmation of hope (Yahweh) (7.11-13)*. The 2nd person account addressing the city would suggest the speaker to be either the prophet or Yahweh. Thus far in this unit the speakers have been the city and Yahweh. Here it is likely that the speaker is again Yahweh addressing the city. First, Yahweh announces a time when the walls of the city will be built (יום לבנות גדריך, v. 11a). That day (יום ההוא, v. 11b) is further characterized as a time of expansion. Also it will be a time (יום הוא, v. 12aα) when the city will be central to the nations who will come to it (Zion) from all directions (v. 12aβ+b; cf. 4.1-5). The reason is different from that stated in 4.2-5. Here the nations will come because they are experiencing desolation (v. 13a) brought about by their own devices and the punishment that followed (v. 13b).

II.B.2.b.1)c) *Call to Yahweh (7.14-17)*. The speaker calls out to Yahweh acknowledging Yahweh's particular relationship to Israel. The requests to Yahweh (7.14-15) are then made on the basis of the relationship and the expected results (7.16-17).

II.B.2.b.1)c)(1) *The requests (7.14-15)*. In v. 14 the second person account addressed to Yahweh petitions Yahweh for guidance. Yahweh is addressed as shepherd and the people as 'flock of his possession', thus suggesting a relationship of dependence (Pss. 28.9; 74.1; 80.2). Yahweh is petitioned to perform the duties of the shepherd to lead (cf. 2.12-13), to protect and to feed. The need for protection is indicated in the depiction of the people being alone in a forest (cf. 4.10). The petition concerning provision of food picks up the language of the desolation of the city of which famine was characteristic (6.14-15). [115]

Verse 15 picks up the temporal indicator כימי used in v. 14 (כימי עולם). According to Wolff, v. 15 is addressed to Yahweh by the people who petitions Yahweh to show the miraculous works he did when he came out of Egypt.[116] Mays shares Wolff's argument but also proposes that the phrase מארץ מצרים 'from the land of Egypt' was added to

---

115. Mays, *Micah*, pp. 164-65.
116. Wolff, *Micah*, p. 227.

clarify the reference; and that the reference should be to the conquest.[117] The people are requesting that Yahweh shows some of his miraculous acts (cf. 6.3-4; Exod. 3.20; Judg. 6.13; Pss 78; 105; 106; 107). This request is not motivated by Israel's lack of confidence in God, but by its concern to make a good showing before its enemies who have taunted Israel because of its distress (7.10).

II.B.2.b.1)c)(2) *Desired effect (7.16-17)*. The focus here is on the nations. Israel hopes that the nations will see Yahweh's actions on behalf of Israel and be ashamed. Their shame would come because of the nations' presupposition that Yahweh has abandoned Israel. The rest of the unit depicts the behaviors typically associated with shame and humiliation.[118] Finally, the nations will be afraid because of Yahweh. This unit, along with vv. 8-10, reflects a concern that the deliverance of Yahweh and Yahweh's work on behalf of Israel be recognized by the nations. The underlying idea is that the fate of Yahweh's people is a direct reflection on Yahweh.

II.B.2.b.2) *God's character—song of praise (7.18-20)*. The conclusion of the unit is a hymn concerning the character of Yahweh. It locates the basis of hope in Yahweh's character, namely, the incomparable nature of Yahweh (cf. Exod. 15.11; Jer. 10.7; Ps. 89.9). There are passages that attest the incomparable nature of Yahweh to be his glory and power (Ps. 89.7-18), his marvelous deeds (Pss. 71.19; 77.14) and those deeds on behalf of the poor (Pss. 35.10; 113.5-7).[119] Here, however, the incomparable nature being referred to is Yahweh's response to sin (cf. 6.10). Yahweh is depicted as forgiving sin נשׂא עון (vis-à-vis Nah. 1.3). Basic to the understanding of the expression is the ritual of the day of atonement when the scapegoat carries away the transgression of all the people.[120] The second depiction is that of passing over (עבר) the crime (פשׁע) of the remnant of his possession (לשׁארית נחלתו; cf. 2.12-13; 4.6-7; 5.6-7).

The declaration of Yahweh's response to sin is then qualified with respect to the remnant. Unlike 2 Kgs 21.14 where the remnant of Yahweh's inheritance will be given to the enemy—signaling the end of its existence—here the remnant will be pardoned. Wolff contends that

---

117. Mays, *Micah*, p. 165.
118. Cf. 3.7 above for a discussion of the concept of shame.
119. Wolff, *Micah*, p. 229, Mays, *Micah*, p. 167.
120. Knierim, *Die Hauptbegriffe für Sünde*, pp. 119, 237-38.

that means a revocation of the judgment of chs. 1–3, 6.9-16.[121] However, this hardly seems to be the case. The pardon is for the sins of the remnant of his possession. This does not suggest that the nation from which the remnant came is pardoned. Presumably they are already punished.

Verse 18 further indicates that not only does Yahweh forgive sin, but that he does not remain in anger forever. The anger of Yahweh is only for a time (cf. Pss. 30.6; 103.9; Isa. 57.16; Jer. 3.12). Verse 18 does not suggest the duration of Yahweh's anger—long or short time. The כי-clause provides the motivation for Yahweh's forgiveness of sin—that Yahweh delights in חסד (cf. 6.8). God does not reluctantly forgive but does so with delight, willingly, without coercion. This suggests that God's forgiveness is not viewed as an obligation nor given because of the faithfulness of the recipients. It is not a matter of whether or not they deserve forgiveness. God's forgiveness is indicative of his devotion to חסד. According to Sakenfeld, this חסד is characterized by freedom, constituted by the nature of the relationship between the one giving חסד and the one receiving it. She cites Gen. 19.19 as an example. What is distinct about this type of חסד is that the one requesting it—whether or not deserving of it—has no other means of obtaining it.[122]

The second part of the hymn (vv. 19-20) further expresses the confidence that God will 'do away' with the sin of the people. In the third person (יכבש) it is said that Yahweh will tread (as in the sense of extinguishing) the transgression (עון) under his foot. He will cast all the sins (חטאות) into the depths of the sea. Perhaps the use of three different terms for sin is indicative both of the pervasiveness of Israel's sin and of the thoroughness of Yahweh's forgiveness to cover them. The declaration of the final part of the hymn is the confidence that Yahweh acts on behalf of Jacob as he has done in the past. This suggests both a relationship in which חסד happens as well as some responsibility on the part of Yahweh to do חסד. Thus, Sakenfeld discusses the responsibility of Yahweh to do חסד for Joseph (Gen. 39.21-22). She argues that while it is deserved, it is freely given.[123] It is in this sense that the חסד of Yahweh is spoken of in this text—that is, the responsibility created by the covenant relationship.

---

121. Wolff, *Micah*, pp. 229-30.
122. Sakenfeld, *Meaning of Ḥesed*, pp. 96-97.
123. Sakenfeld, *Meaning of Ḥesed*, pp. 102-103.

Thus, in the dispute concerning Israel, the final word is that the remnant will be forgiven but the nation will be judged for its sins. So Israel will not be exempt from judgment; but in that judgment there is hope for forgiveness constituted in Israel's relationship with God.

Conclusion

This analysis of the text is built on the proposal that there are different levels of coherence signaled by the structural levels (namely, macro- and micro-structural). In this analysis it is apparent that there is a relative degree of coherence of the individual units and the levels that they constitute. As such the coherence of ch. 3, due to the typical form of the judgment speeches, is more salient than that of chs. 1–3.

To further clarify what is meant by levels of coherence, several observations are noteworthy at this juncture. A 'level' may be a unit of text. Levels may also signify aspects of the texts such as the intra- and inter-textual aspects. Here level of coherence refers to the unit while recognizing that the unit consists of infra-, intra- and contextual aspects. It is further recognized that the intertextual aspects are present in the unit inasmuch as the unit exists in relationship to other texts. First, the salience of the levels of coherence as indicated by the structural elements is relative to the salience of their indicators. As such, when the cohesion of a unit is questionable so is its coherence. Furthermore, the conceptuality of that unit is also obscured by any ambiguity of the structural indicators. This is noted for example with 2.12-13. The unit itself exhibits a coherence centered on restoration of the remnant. However, its position amid prophecies of judgment contributes to the challenge of discerning the coherence of the entire unit of which it is a part. Hence, it is not just ch. 2 that is called into question by the placement of 2.12-13 but also ch. 3 and chs. 1–5.

Second, the coherence of the book of Micah is indicated by several complementary aspects including: (a) conceptual aspects (that is, the focus on sin throughout the book, the depiction of judgment as a just response to sin, as well as the announcement of promise and its relationship to judgment and hope); (b) structural aspects that signal the cohesion of the text (that is, syntactical and grammatical elements, and generic elements such as the summons at the beginning of the major units and the presence of a judgment speech and a lament in each part of the book). (See Table 3 in Chapter 3.)

Third, the coherence on the micro-structural levels is also indicated conceptually and structurally. However, the presence of connective particles (as in the judgment speeches) is typical of the indicators on this level (לכן, 2.3; 3.6, 12; אז, 3.4; וגם־אני, 6.13; על־זאת, 1.8). Other examples include the temporal transitions in chs. 4–5 (והיה באחרית הימים, 4.1; ביום ההוא, 4.6; 5.9; עתה, 4.9, 14; ועתה, 4.11).

Finally, the coherence of the whole cannot be determined by the observation of only parts of that whole. Potentially, a partial analysis yields only a partial picture. Accordingly, in order to talk about the coherence of the whole it is necessary to consider the whole, regardless of the apparent clarity of the coherence of its various parts. That clarity may have more to do with the salience of a few features than with the interrelationship of all features within the whole.

The final part of the task that remains is the discerning of the inter-relationship of the concepts identified through the above analysis of the text. This is the task that is pursued in Chapter 6.

Part III

DISCERNING CONCEPTUALITY

Chapter 6

CONCEPTS AND CONCEPTUALITY

Introduction

As a means of demonstrating the literary integrity/cohesion of the text, an analysis of its structure is presented above in Chapter 3. It was proposed that structure is a manifestation of cohesion. It was further proposed that while the structure is an indicator and essential aspect of coherence, it is not the totality of that coherence. The unit-by-unit analysis in Chapters 4 and 5 addresses the question of the extent of coherence with respect to both the structural indicators and the conceptual elements of the units at the various structural levels. While these two aspects of the task of discerning coherence were presented separately, their simultaneity is suggested by their intricate interrelationship. In turn, this interrelationship demands that consideration be given to the extent of their concurrence in the conceptual coherence of the whole.

Therefore, as a means of discerning their interrelationship within the conceptuality of the whole, the task of Chapter 6 is to analyze the conceptual elements identified in the text. It is proposed that the interrelationship of the indicators within the text and their conceptual presuppositions are essential for understanding the conceptuality and thus the conceptual coherence of the text. This analysis is necessitated by the fact that the conceptuality of a text both defines and is defined by its conceptual elements. Therefore, this chapter will examine the contextual aspects of the book of Micah and specifically the extent to which these and other intertextual aspects contribute to the understanding of its conceptual framework. The identification of the conceptual coherence is dependent on the reconstruction of the conceptual framework—out of which the conceptuality of the present text emerges.

One of the main propositions of the concept-critical method is that texts are multi-conceptual units whose concepts are not all operative on the same level. Furthermore, inherent to each concept are conceptual presuppositions that are generative of the concepts[1] and their various contextual and intertextual nuances. The book of Micah as demonstrated above consists of several concepts variously indicated in the text, including: justice, sin, judgment, responsibility, hope, forgiveness. Of these concepts, four are discussed as the main concepts of the book of Micah, namely, justice, sin, judgment and hope. The other two, responsibility and forgiveness, are discussed as inextricable aspects to the conceptual framework of the main concepts.

Justice

By its numerous appearances in the book of Micah the concept of justice must be given consideration to determine its significance in the conceptual coherence of the text. This is in no way to argue that quantity and salience of the indicators of a concept are the criteria for determining their significance to the conceptuality of a text. One cannot deny, however, that regardless of the degree of a concept's significance to the conceptuality of the whole, the salience of its indicators heightens attention to it more readily than the obscurity its indicators. Consequently, the danger of using only quantity and/or the typicality of indicators is overlooking important aspects of the conceptuality of the text and therefore misconstruing its conceptual coherence.[2]

1. *Aspects in the Text*
The concept of justice is signaled by semantic indicators—מִשְׁפָּט (3.1, 8, 9b; 6.8)—and other aspects of the text. The text, however, does not talk about justice in the abstract. The clues to the concept of justice are found, for example, in the accusations in ch. 3—for example, the leaders hate good and love evil. In its literary context, this functions as an explication of what justice is not (cf. 3.1). More specifically, it suggests a method of discerning the specifics of 'justice' in ch. 3. This method is comparative—for example, it examines the antonyms for information about a particular concept.

In the book of Micah, there are several indicators of the concept of

---

1.   Knierim, 'The Interpretation of the Old Testament', pp. 87-88. He discusses the pre-understanding of texts specifically with reference to the concept of justice.

2.   See Chapter 2 above.

justice. These may be classified as primary and secondary indicators.[3] Primary indictors are both direct and indirect.[4] The direct indicators are terms that are used to convey the concept of justice (e.g. מִשְׁפָּט, 3.1b, 8, 9; 6.8). These indicators may also be synonyms. In this category, the synonym may be both contextual or semantic. The contextual synonyms are those used as synthetically parallel expressions but otherwise do not denote the concept. The semantic synonyms are those whose etymology denotes the same or a similar idea (יָשָׁר, טוֹב).[5]

To the category of primary indirect indicators belong the antithetical parallel expressions. These may also be contextual or semantic (e.g. רעה/רע, אָוֶן [2.1, 3]; עֹשֶׁק [2.2]; עוֹלָה/עוּל [3.10]). In the case of 2.1-4, the context does not explicitly classify the condemned behaviors as acts of injustice or by explicit terminology for 'sin'. The context makes these suggestions.

If the statement in 1.5 is seen as a programmatic statement of what chs. 2 and 3 are explicating, then it may be argued that, in this context, a relationship between injustice and 'sin' is at least suggested. The question becomes whether 'sin'—as identified by its various terms and their particular nuances—is synonymous with injustice as indicated here and elsewhere by the overlap of the terms.[6] A thorough examination of the nature of the relationship of sin and injustice would have to answer several questions, including: Are all sins acts of injustice? Are all acts of injustice sin? What are criteria by which to assess the nature of the relationship? It is suggested that 'sin'—as indicated by terms such as פֶּשַׁע—may be deemed as antithesis to justice, insofar as it is a deliberate violation of moral and ethical standards. Certainly, in the context of ch. 3 it is suggested that there is such a relationship of sin and injustice. The behavior of the leaders, considered as acts of injustice (3.1-3), is identified as the 'sin' that the prophet has been empow-

3.   See Knierim, *Text and Concept*, pp. 65-66, 82-83, for his identification of 'direct' and 'indirect' signals in his discussion of the text's unity. His lack of definition makes his use of these designations ambiguous.

4.   Note that the discussion of the indicators applies generally to the task of identifying a concept within a text. That it is discussed here with regard to the concept of justice is an organizational matter.

5.   Others include צֶדֶק/צְדָקָה, אֱמוּנָה, אֱמֶת, and so on.

6.   Knierim, 'Hamartiology', pp. 425-28; see *idem*, *Die Hauptbegriffe für Sünde*, for a detailed discussion of the terms, the distinctive nuances of each and the possibility of their synonymous meaning: חָטָא (pp. 19-22); פֶּשַׁע (pp. 113-15); and עָוֺן (pp. 185-88).

ered to declare (3.8; cf. 1.5). Thus, while all acts of injustice are sin, not all sins may be considered acts of injustice.

The relationship of sin and injustice may be further supported by the observation of other secondary indicators. Note that 'secondary' is used here with the sense of mode—explicit (primary) vs. implicit (secondary). Here 'secondary' does not refer to origin—original (primary) vs. redactional (secondary)—nor to quantity. Furthermore, that one indicator is secondary while the other is primary does not necessarily suggest the relative importance of the concept to the whole nor the extent of its presence within that whole. The secondary indicators do not employ the particular semantic associated with the concept, but exhibit the characteristic or identifiable elements of the concept. Even further, they allude to the conceptual presuppositions that gave rise to the articulation of the concept.

This category of secondary indicators may include metaphorical language used to describe a feature typical of a concept. For example, in 3.2-3 violence as a typical feature of oppression is described in the metaphorical language of cannibalism. In this instance, the metaphorical language is indicative of the antithesis of justice—injustice. Justice is seen to be contrary to the practices of those characterized in ch. 3. Likewise, in 3.9-11, the leaders are accused of abhorring justice. The antithetical expression provides the specification of this accusation, namely, the mistreatment of the people, taking of bribes and fostering a false sense of security. Typical of all these unjust behaviors is their destruction of the wellbeing of people and the community.

In the first part of the book of Micah, all these aspects focus on the community. The issue of justice in this respect has to do with the way that the people are treated by their leaders. Notably, however, it is not just how people are treated that is brought into focus, but specifically how those with power and responsibility to execute justice use that responsibility. The importance of this observation for understanding the book of Micah lies in the cause–effect scheme that is suggested by the association of injustice (cause) with judgment (effect) in 2.1-5, 3.1-12 and 6.9-16.

With regard to the aspects of justice in the text, it is further observed that in the context of 6.1-8 there is a hint that justice is placed in contrast to sacrifices. In this respect, justice is also interpersonal. As the requirement of God, the practice of justice is indicated in connection with the love of חסד. By inference, justice rather than abundance of

sacrifices is what is required. Within that context, however, the requirement of justice is articulated in the form of an instruction. The people
of Israel may have misunderstood what is required, and in this misunderstanding apparently accused God of placing the burden of abundance
of sacrifices on Israel. In the text, no mention is made of situations that
exemplify the need for justice. It is from the contextual and intertextual
frameworks that one may deduce that nature of the requirement. No
mention is made of the marginalized nor of the leaders. While it may be
rightly suggested that the demand to practice justice is for all of Israel,
it is also noteworthy that the requirement of justice is usually placed on
those who have the power to execute it (e.g. 3.1). Thus, it should not be
discounted that in both chs. 3 and 6 the concern for justice has in view
those marginalized by their lack of power and resources to take care of
themselves. The interpersonal aspect has to do with the community
aspect. Justice or injustice practiced by the leaders of the community
affects the whole community to some degree.

2. Conceptual Framework

The above discussion of the textual aspects has focused on justice as
related to the interpersonal aspects. It is suggested, based on the observation of the indicators, that what constitutes justice in the perspectives
of the text may be discerned by comparison to what the text condemns
as injustice or sin. On the basis of these same indicators, it is further
suggested that what is said in the text is a representation of a larger
conceptual framework. It is in awareness of this conceptual framework
that some questions concerning justice arise. This awareness makes it
possible to achieve a clearer understanding of the place of the concept
of justice in the larger conceptuality of the book of Micah.

First is the question concerning the nature of the behaviors characterized as injustice. These behaviors are the cause of the destruction
of the wellbeing of the people and for this reason may be condemned.
However, on the same principle that a behavior or course of action
threatens the wellbeing of a person, people, or nation, how are the
actions depicted in 4.11-13 and 5.7-9 to be assessed? In the first of
these instances, the assembled nations are said to be acting on behalf of
God to fulfill God's plans. It is said that Israel will be used to destroy
these nations for God's glory. To what extent is this justice? Is it justice
in that it is an execution of God's plan? Or is it justice in that the assembled nations were enemies of Israel and are therefore destroyed for their

aggression against Israel? This possibility finds support throughout the Old Testament.[7] In Isa. 10.5-19 Assyria, used by God against Israel, is then punished. The former question suggests that justice is constituted not by the nature of the act and its effect on all peoples but by the actor. If God is actor then that which is executed, regardless of the effects on the wellbeing of the community, is somehow construed as justice. The larger scope of this aspect of justice, however, is that Israel's and the nations' fate are a part of God's plan toward the establishment of God's reign. This is suggested by the immediate context of chs. 4–5. It is also suggested as the reason for Israel's triumph over the nations among whom it lived in exile (5.6-8).

Second, questions also arise concerning the just nature of the judgment to be brought against Israel. Wherein lies the justice of the judgment? At this point the nature of the judgment as compared to injustice will be addressed. Other aspects such as the justice of the extent of the judgment will be considered below in the discussion of judgment.

On the question of the justice of the judgment—that is, as compared to the nature of injustice—the following is observed. On the one hand, the destruction of the wellbeing of the people and the community is condemned and subject to punishment. On the other hand, the wellbeing of the community is threatened and even destroyed by God's deliberate acts of judgment. The text itself notes this in the depiction of God's actions as 'devising evil' (2.3), the destruction of Jerusalem (3.12) and the desolation of the populace of Jerusalem (6.13-14). In the latter instance, God is depicted as bringing about large-scale desolation in the form of famine and the futile efforts to achieve wellbeing. In this particular instance, the deceitful practices of those in positions to administer the economic and commercial aspects of Jerusalem are the focus of the concern. The actions are depicted as the deliberate misuse of weights and measures, as well as deception and violence. That those who encountered these injustices were adversely affected by them is without question. Yet the judgment results in further desolation of the people and is, in nature or at least in effect, comparable to the sins that it addresses. To what extent is this judgment an extension of injustice? Is this judgment and any that duplicates the effects and circumstances

7. Knierim, 'The Interpretation of the Old Testament', p. 100, cites Deut. 32.34-43; Isa. 10.5-19 and Isa. 36–39 as examples of justice against the nations for oppressing Israel.

of injustice 'just' by nature of being the means of judgment? Is the basic criterion for justice, the preservation of wellbeing, applicable only to human actions? Can judgment be just as a response to sin but be unjust in its effects? By what criteria is judgment in the book of Micah to be regarded as constitutive of justice?[8]

The depiction of judgment using the characteristic features of the condemned injustice is part of the larger Old Testament ethos. In this context, justice lies not in the nature of the circumstances that constitute it, but within its very nature as the divine response to sin.

Although it is an essential concept to the book of Micah, the conceptual framework suggests that justice is variously construed. The questions that arise in relation to the book of Micah are therefore typical of the intertextual aspects of the concept. Nonetheless, it is noted that justice in the book of Micah has two distinct yet inseparable spheres: human–human sphere and the divine–human sphere (see Figure 2 below). To the first category belong human acts of justice, injustice and sin. To the second belong God's justice and judgment in response to injustice and sin. These spheres intersect at various points, including the point of judgment—inasmuch as judgment is addressed to injustice and sin. Likewise, the spheres diverge in two ways. (a) The criteria for assessing justice in the two spheres are relative. This relativity allows for the same effects of an action to be construed as both justice and injustice depending on the source of the behavior. (b) God's judgment in response to sin is only a manifestation of the totality of God's justice and involvement in human history. The understanding of justice in the book of Micah is therefore to be considered within its relationship to sin, judgment and hope and not apart from these.

The following figure illustrates the interrelationship of the spheres of justice, showing the point of intersection as well as the aspects that are distinctive to each sphere. It also shows that judgment does not necessarily address all the aspects of injustice/sin. Furthermore, there are aspects of both the divine and humans spheres that are outside the area of their intersection. What this means it that there may be aspects of these that are not explained by this simple representation. Among these are the suffering of the innocent, natural disasters, forgiveness, promise and repentance.

---

8. Cf. Jacob Milgrom, 'Israel's Sanctuary: The Priestly "Picture of Dorian Gray"', *RB* 83 (1976), pp. 390-99 (397), for a discussion of the destroyer (מַשְׁחִית) as the agent of God's collective retribution.

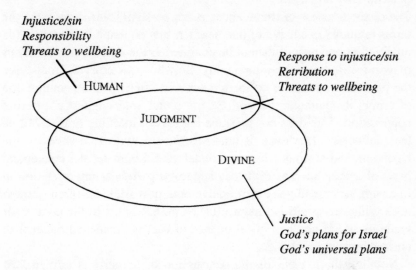

Figure 2. *Spheres of Justices as Indicated by the Conceptual Framework of the Concept.*

Sin

1. *Aspects in the Text*

a. *Terminology*

As with the concept of justice, the concept of sin in the book of Micah is signaled by various indicators. Semantically three of the typical terms for sin occur in the book of Micah: פשׁע, 'to commit a breach' (1.5, 13; 3.8; 6.7; 7.18); חטא, 'to err' (1.5, 13; 3.8; 6.7, 13; 7.9, 19); עוף/עוה, 'to incur guilt' (7.18).[9] The concept is also indicated by semantic synonyms: רעה/רע, און (2.1, 3); עשׁק (2.2); עולה/עול (3.10). (These are the same indicators of the concept of injustice as discussed above so the discussion will not be repeated.) All these are used within the text to indicate the behaviors that are condemned. In these instances, the distinctive nuances of the terms seem less significant to the argument of the text than the depiction of the behaviors that are qualified by these terms.

---

9. Knierim, 'Hamartiology', pp. 425-28; *idem, Die Hauptbegriffe für Sünde,* pp. 19-112 (חטא), pp. 113-84 (פשׁע), pp. 185-229 (עוף/עוה); cf. K. Koch, 'חטא', in *TDOT,* IV, pp. 309-19; Robin C. Cover, 'Sin, Sinner', in *ABD,* VI, pp. 31-40.

b. *Distinctive nuances*

The distinctiveness of the nuances is not so significant as to make the terms mutually exclusive of one another, that is, that a behavior that is qualified as one nuance cannot be qualified as the other. Different terms may in fact indicate the same reality. So while the term פשע may have the particular nuance of deliberate act, and often with the connotation of crime, its synthetic use with חטא, 'to err', may suggest a different connotation. This does not presume the loss of meaning or that פשע is less deliberate. However, it qualifies the use with references to the behaviors and attitudes that are condemned. Likewise, the conceptual basis of a term such as חטא may suggest a particular interpretation in line with the typical nuance of inadvertent, unwillful acts often (though not exclusively) cultic in nature (cf. Num. 6.9-11).[10] In the context of the book of Micah, the typical nuance of חטא is broadened rather than tapered by is use with פשע.

Notably, the reason for the destruction of Samaria is termed פשע (1.5). The destruction of Samarian images and idols may be interpreted to mean the condemnation of cultic practices. Yet פשע typically denotes 'crime'.[11] The uses of the terminology for sin indicate that in the perspective of the text פשע and חטא are subject to the same consequence—judgment. They are used to depict the same types of behaviors, none of which are inadvertent. Likewise, to whatever extent פשע denotes 'international crime', in this context that denotation is noticeably absent. Instead, פשע and חטא are used of condemned behaviors in Israel. The condemned behaviors are deliberate, violent, and deceitful. As such, both פשע and חטא connote acts that are deliberately committed in violation of moral and/or cultic standards.

2. *Conceptual framework*

a. *Nature of sin*

External—social dimension. The uses of the terms indicate a reference to social realities (2.1-5; 3.1-12; 6.9-16). The behaviors being punished

10. Jacob Milgrom, 'The Concept of Ma'al in the Bible and the Ancient Near East', *JAOS* 96 (1976), pp. 236-47. Cultic sins were no less subject to punishment than willful and immoral acts (cf. Lev. 7.20-21; 19.5-8). Cf. Cover, 'Sin, Sinner', p. 34.

11. Knierim, 'Hamartiology', pp. 425-28; *idem, Die Hauptbegriffe für Sünde,* pp. 113-84.

are attributed to leaders within the community (the heads of Jacob, the prophets, the priests and generally those in authority and with some measure of power). Thus, to some extent the sins depicted all refer to some abuse of the leadership responsibility. This abuse in itself, however, has far-reaching consequences for the community, not simply to be seen in the punishment addressed to the sin. The consequences have to do with the threat to the wellbeing and existence of that community. In this way, the consequences are not as far removed from sin as is suggested by those who link them only to the judgment brought against sin. Yet the text does not explicitly concern itself with specifying the immediate consequences of sin on the community. These are surmised from the nature of the behaviors depicted and the judgment announced.

Furthermore, the focus on the leaders in the text may indicate a preconception of the nature of the sin depicted. The ones who commit the sin are a significant part of the extent of the consequences of the sins. This means that the leaders' action have a broader scope of influence and as such affect the community to a different degree than the sins of a marginalized person. This is not to justify the nature of sin as being more or less significant depending on the sinner. However, it is to suggest that there are degrees of sin—lesser and greater sins.[12] It is also to suggest that the broader the scope of the influence of the sinner, the broader the scope of the consequences of the sin. In this perspective, the sins of the leaders (as depicted in ch. 3) are the measure of the justice and wellbeing of the community.

Internal—mental dimension. Sin as depicted in the text is the abuse of power, and therefore a social phenomenon related to responsibility within the community. Nonetheless, it is not entirely an outward, behavioral phenomenon. It is as much an inward as an outward condition insofar as the behaviors are preceded by inward thoughts, plans, emotions, and so on. This is evident in 2.1 which states that the accused plot to do evil and then do evil in the morning. Similarly, the correspondence of mind and behavior is signaled in all three judgment speeches in ch. 3. In 3.1b love and hate (internal) are manifested in violence (external). In 3.5-8 there seems to be a presupposition on the part of the prophets (internal) that Yahweh will give vision regardless of their behaviors (external). When proven wrong, the prophets feel ashamed.

12. Knierim, 'Hamartiology', pp. 432-33, 448.

Also in these verses the feeling of shame is manifested in the behavior of covering the lips. In 3.9-12 the abhorrence of justice (internal) is exemplified by violence and exploitation (external). Likewise, the belief in the unconditional security of Zion (internal) results in sinful practices (external) since there is no fear of the consequences.[13]

The internal state in these instances provided the precondition to the behaviors judged as sin. However, is the precondition itself 'sin'? For example, in 2.1-5 the plotting of evil is qualified by the doing of evil. But is the plotting itself sin or is sin only the behavior? As part of the accusation of the leaders in 3.2, 'the hating of good and loving of evil' is connected to the ravaging of the people. In this instance, the connection does not indicate sequential occurrences as in 2.1-5 The dependence of the parts of the accusation is seen in the qualification of the first (3.2a) by the second (3.2b). Thus, the loving of evil is qualified by the acts of injustice. As such, the internal state is the starting point of the behavior, and the behavior in this sense is the extension of the internal state. In the conceptuality of the book of Micah, the internal and external are paired together as sin. Their pairing is indicative of the deliberate nature of the sin and hence the justifiable nature of the judgment.

b. *Consequences of sin*

The passages in the book of Micah represent sin as part of an act–consequence pattern. As such the concept of sin functions as a justification for judgment. The consequences to the community are both immediate and long term. The immediate consequences are the effects on the wellbeing of the community. While these may also be long-term, typically, the long-term effects are God's response of judgment and the circumstances it perpetuates.

Judgment. The nature of the judgment in these instances is directly related to the nature of the sin. However, its proportionality at times is not characteristic of the relationship of sin and judgment. As with corporate retribution, the sin of the group results in the punishment of the entire nation.

The punishment of sin by God suggests that God is somehow affected by sin. However, the nature of the influence of sin on God is open to

---

13. See Knierim, 'Hamartiology', pp. 433-34, on the discussion of the correspondence of mind-behavior.

discussion. God's response suggests—in however broad a sense—that sin is sin against God (cf. 7.9). Such a broad statement leaves much room for the delineation of the specific ways that sin may be construed as sin against God.

With regard to the means of removing the consequences of sin, 6.6-7 refers to the sacrificial system as an option. However, this reference is not made as an instruction in how to approach sin. The immediate context is that of questioning the extent to which sacrifices are required by God. Sacrifices in this respect are not being advocated, but elsewhere in the Old Testament the cultic ritual is an acceptable means of dealing with sin.[14]

The concept of sacrifice in the book of Micah is depicted as that which constituted the weariness of Israel. As a concept, it is represented by direct indicators עלות, עגלים בני שנה, אילים, נחלי־שמן and בכור. Sacrifices are represented as Israel's way of currying Yahweh's favor, and restoring relationship. Thus, the concept in 6.1-8 does not represent the governing concept to which all others are supportive. The infra-textual and inter-textual aspects of the concept indicate that it is a point of Israel's confusion. This confusion is not due to the malevolence of Israel and a lack of understanding but to a confusion inherent in the very system itself.

Sacrifices are not in and of themselves bad or repudiated by the prophets. What is repudiated is the practice of sacrificing while practicing injustice. Yet the irony of the repudiation is that sacrifices are the means of obtaining forgiveness for injustices. There is therefore more to the repudiation than the concurrent practicing of sacrifices and injustice. The neglect of loyalty to God and an empty performance of sacrifices seem to be at issue—that is, a performance without penitence for the sins committed.[15] Another aspect is also present, namely, God's desire for sacrifices. Thus, the response of Israel in 6.6-7—does God want sacrifices?—is neither absurd no facetious but possibly a genuine expression of an underlying misconception. One has to repent of one's sins in order to receive forgiveness. One cannot remain unrepentant and

14. Jacob Milgrom, *Studies in Cultic Theology and Terminology* (SJLA, 36; Leiden: E.J. Brill, 1983), pp. 47-74; Knierim, *Text and Concept*, pp. 40-45.

15. Jacob Milgrom, *Cult and Conscience: The Asham and the Priestly Doctrine of Repentance* (Leiden: E.J. Brill, 1976), pp. 117-18.

continue in the practice of injustice without experiencing the consequences. This is the essence of the critique of Israel's sacrifices and the basis of judgment.

Forgiveness. Yahweh sometimes responds to sin with forgiveness (7.18-20). However, such forgiveness does not replace the immediate consequences of sin on the community nor deny the existence of those consequences. In 7.18 the forgiveness or the 'taking away of guilt' is specifically tied to the remnant. This is not to deny that God forgives more than the remnant. What the text of the book of Micah presumes is that judgment has already been implemented. This is suggested in use of the term 'remnant' which presupposes a remaining entity. The text clearly does not speak of a removal of the judgment. In this perspective, forgiveness and judgment are two responses to sin, each particular to its time but not necessarily exclusive of the other. People may suffer as a result of their sin and later be forgiven for the sin (Ps. 107.17-18; 1 Kgs 8.44-51). This is the perspective of the book of Micah. Such an interpretation both respects the sin–judgment scheme and explains hope and forgiveness. In this interpretation, hope does not contradict or replace judgment, but is as much a response of God to sin as is judgment. Forgiveness is not a consequence of sin in the sense of cause and effect. Forgiveness has to do with God's mercy and as such is not justified by the nature or extent of the sin (cf. Exod. 33.19) or by a guarantee to those who sin.[16]

Judgment

1. *Aspects in the Text*

As a concept, judgment is implicit and operative in the form and argumentation of the text.[17] Judgment is presented as a consequence of sin in each of the judgment speeches (3.1-4, 5-8, 9-12; 6.9-16), and the woe oracle in 2.1-5 and in 1.5-7. This pattern of correspondence is signaled by secondary indicators (אז, 3.4; לכן, 2.3; 3.6, 12; וגם־אני, 6.13) that connect the accusation with the announcement of judgment. The connection further indicates the dependence of the judgment on sin—a dependence that justifies the judgment. This correspondence is presented in Table 4 below.

16. See Section D below for further discussion.
17. See the compositional analysis presented in Chapter 3 above.

Table 4. *Indicators of the Correspondence of Sin and Judgment*

Accusation of Sin	Logical Connection	Judgment
1.5	ו	1.6-7
2.1-2	לכן	2.3-4
3.1-3	אז	3.4
3.5	לכן	3.6
3.9-11	לכן	3.12
6.10-12	וגם־אני	6.13-16

As in the judgment speeches in ch. 3, 6.9-16 and 2.1-5, the nature of the correspondence between sin and judgment may vary.[18] According to P.D. Miller, there are several types of correspondence.[19] In 2.1-2 the correspondence of sin and judgment is signaled by the use of the same language in both the accusation and the announcement of judgment— 'devise evil'. Likewise, in 2.1-4, the oppressors are accused of plotting evil and executing this evil. They seize the land from those to whom it had been entrusted. The punishment is that the land will be taken from Israel and redistributed as restitution for the sin, and without Israel's participation in the process (2.4-5). Another way that the correspondence is shown is that the effects of the sin become the effects of the judgment. In 3.1-4 the leaders will be left helpless in their time of distress just as their injustice had left helpless those for whom they were responsible. Likewise, in 6.9-16 the effect of the exploitative use of weights and measures is that some are left in need, having been cheated out of the resources they sought. The punishment is the destruction of the basis of the economy and livelihood of the community. Consequently, all will be needy and desolate as a result of the famine and the futility of their efforts to acquire the resources they seek.

18. Westermann, *Basic Forms*, pp. 118-25.
19. Miller, *Sin and Judgment*. These categories are: (a) General correspondence which is natural, legal movement from offense to retribution where the punishment reflects the crime. Some talionic principles are present in this type of correspondence. (b) Talionic correspondence as found in: Exod. 21.23-24; Lev. 24.19-20; Deut. 19.21; Hab. 2.15-17; Joel 4.4-13. In some instances the language of the accusation is used in the announcement of the judgment: Deut. 32.21; Mic. 2.1-5; 3.1-4; Hos. 4.4-6; Jer. 30.16; Isa. 33.1. (c) Correspondence of means—the means of the sin is the means of the punishment, e.g. Deut. 25.11; Amos 7.16-17; Hos. 10.1-3, 13-15; Mic. 3.5. Note that Miller does not consider Mic. 3.9-11. Cf. also Westermann, *Basic Forms*, p. 160, for the correspondence of accusation and judgment speech 1 Sam. 15.23; 2 Sam. 12.7-12.

In 3.5-8 the prophets abused their means of authorization and thus misled the people. The corresponding judgment is dissolving of the prophetic role by means of removing the source of authorization. Finally, out of their false security, the leaders in 3.9-12 build a city by exploiting their offices and the people. The corresponding judgment is the destruction of the city and hence the leaders' false sense of security.

2. *Conceptual framework*

a. *Justice and judgment*

As signaled by the correspondence between sin and judgment, the judgments are presupposed to be 'just'. Judgment in this perspective is not arbitrary in either timing, effect or intent. In all of the instances (1.5-7; 2.1-5; 3.1-12; 6.9-16), the 'justice' of the judgment consists of its correspondence to the sins committed—that is, retributive judgment (7.9) (see the discussion above).

Competing perspectives. In 2.6-11 and 3.11 the text itself signals that there are competing perspectives to the justice of judgment. However, 2.12-13, 4.1–5.14 and 7.18-20 are not considered here as indicative of perspectives in tension with the idea of just judgment. In the extant form of the book of Micah these, as discussed above, are regarded as indicators of the fate of Israel beyond the circumstances of judgment, not in replacement of those circumstances.[20]

On the other hand, Mic. 2.6-11 as a unit indicates—in its form, content and placement—a point of view that is in tension with the dominant perspective of just judgment. Basic to the competing perspective is the presupposition that its advocates are exempt from judgment. This is suggested in the command to the prophet not to preach of disaster (2.6). The incredulity of the proclamation is cited as the reason for the command. This presupposition, however, is not based on a protestation of innocence. Notably, there is no denial of the accusation. The presupposition is based on belief about God.

---

20. Note that the prophecies of hope are not regarded here as competing perspectives. Throughout the history of research, there have been many who have construed these passages as indicators of the contradiction of the announcement of judgment. See my discussion in Chapter 1 for further information. Also see the various references in Chapter 4 in the sections dealing with 2.12-13 and chs. 4.1–5.14.

The disputation speech's recount of the opponents seems to presume that judgment is antithetical to the character of God. The tension is between the belief about God on the one hand, and the reality of judgment on the other. First, the reconstructed perspective is that God is patient. Since judgment is a sign of impatience, it cannot be validly seen as an act of God, that is, because 'God is patient, low to anger, abounding in steadfast love' (Exod. 34.6; Neh. 9.17). Yet, in the opponents' perspective, the further qualifications to the character of God—as not keeping his anger forever and punishing the guilty—are left aside (cf. Exod. 34.7; Nah. 1.3).

Another aspect of the competing perspective is seen in 3.11. The leaders espoused the belief that God's presence is the safeguard against disaster. Here as in 2.6-11 there is no denial of the accusation. Within its context, 3.11 is part of the accusation and illustrates the beliefs of those who are being accused. The perspective is that whether or not the people have sinned, the determinant of judgment is God's presence, the guarantee of safety and wellbeing.

The competing perspective to just judgment is also based on the recollection of the nature of God's saving acts. This is an argument of historical precedence. In the past God has acted to save his people. The proclamation of judgment presumes that God in this instance will punish rather than save. Therefore, the proclamation must be invalid. Judgment is not a part of God's saving acts. Such is the reconstructed argument of the competing perspective (2.7). This, however, is not the governing perspective in the book of Micah. As indicated by the relationship of the perspective to others in the text, its presence illustrates the challenges to the judgment.[21]

The extent of judgment. While the justice of judgment is apparent from the perspective of its addressing particular sins, its justice may not be as apparent with respect to the people affected by the judgment. It is understandable that those who have sinned are punished and that the judgment is focused on them. But is there justice in the inclusion of all in the judgment brought about by the sins of the few? The text does not concern itself with the justice of the judgment in terms of its effects on the oppressed.

21. See Chapter 4 above for a discussion of the exegetical basis of this argument.

In 1.5-7 the nations in their entirety are identified as the reason for the judgment. No particular groups are named. In 2.1-2 the accused are not addressed by title, but are identified by their abuse of their power. They use their power to dispossess the people of their 'land' and in this way they reduce the people to poverty and a marginalized existence. These people, however, along with the oppressors, become the subject (עמי) of inescapable judgment. Chapter 3 also depicts the compounded distress of the ravaged masses who together with their oppressors experience punishment. This is also the case in 6.9-16 where all are desolate because of the sin of a portion of the population.

Viewed from this perspective the judgments do not show justice for those ravaged by the injustices of the leaders—that is, as justice is seen in liberation theology and in the classic utilitarian sense. However, from the prophetic and Pentateuchal perspectives of the concerns for the disadvantaged which hold that the oppressors are judged for failing to do justice, the judgments of chs. 2 and 3 constitute justice.[22]

The justice of the judgment may not necessarily be its corrective quality but its punitive quality. It is not that the oppressed are relieved of oppression and its circumstances; but that the oppressors are made to experience that to which they have subjected others. That the disadvantaged are punished with the oppressors is an issue that continues to challenge anyone who attempts to deal with the full ramification of the book of Micah in theologies of justice and of liberation. Most immediately, the concern is for how these aspects fit into the conceptuality of the book of Micah. It is proposed that the justice of judgment is to be regarded as an aspect of the interrelationship of sin and judgment. However, to see the effects and extent of judgment as justice for the people is much to ask.

Thus, concept-critical analysis regards this tension in the text as one of its concerns. However, the analysis recognizes that while this is a tension with respect to the universal and inter-textual aspects of the concept of retributive judgment, that tension is minimal in the coherence of the extant text of the book of Micah.

---

22. This concept resembles the 'contract response' theory proposed by John Rawls, *A Theory of Justice* (Cambridge, MA: Harvard University Press, 1971), pp. 318-19. One of his central arguments is the 'difference principles'. This includes the principal that economic and social inequalities are to be regarded in such a way that the least advantaged have the greatest benefits possible under these conditions. Cf. Weinfeld, *Social Justice*; Hamilton, *Social Justice and Deuteronomy*.

b. *Agents of judgment*

The agents of sin and injustice are humans (the oppressor, the leaders of Israel, the deceitful merchants), and the judgment is brought about by the divine agent. This is not to say that God does not use humans as a means of achieving judgment. There are several instances in the book of Micah where God is shown to use human agents to fulfill God's plans for the future (e.g. 4.10, 11, 13). In 4.11-15 the nations assembled against Israel are portrayed as being unaware of their role as instruments of Yahweh's plans. However, the attention to humans as agents of Yahweh's plans does not constitute the dominant concept of the book of Micah. In chs. 1–3 there is no explicit indication of human agents as instruments of judgment.

c. *Responsibility and judgment*

That judgment is dependent on the presence of sin, presupposes that the people who sinned had some responsibility for their actions. Chapters 2–3 and 6.9-12 further presuppose that the accused were 'authorized' in some way and are therefore subject to accountability. In ch. 3, the concept of responsibility is signaled by various semantic expressions חזה, כהן, נביא, קצין, ראש) the titles ,(3.1b) הלוא לכם לדעת את־המשפט, קסם) and their specific responsibilities (3.1, 5, 7, 9, 11; cf. 2.2). Furthermore, the charges indicate that judgment is aimed at those who have failed in their responsibilities.[23]

In 3.5, it is not that 'a person' is proclaiming 'peace' that constitutes the sin, but that 'prophets' with the responsibility to lead the people mislead them by capriciously making proclamations of 'peace'. Likewise, the responsibilities of the leaders in 3.11 mean that they are prohibited from accepting bribes and to accept bribes constitutes abuse of their responsibilities. Therefore, the nature of the responsibility partly determines the sin.

In 2.1-5 the nature of the responsibility of the accused is to allow the people to remain in possession of their land—or at least not to seize it unlawfully. It was also their responsibility not to oppress the people. Thus, the identification of the role responsibility of the accused functions as a part of the justification of their punishment.

This aspect of responsibility and judgment is further indicated in 6.1-16. Here, the nature of the responsibility is seen in the designation of a

---

23. Petersen, *Roles of Israel's Prophets*, pp. 10-12, 14-15, 51-52.

relationship. God has a dispute with his people. As discussed above, 6.1-8 delineate the nature of the dispute. Verse 8 in particular signals the responsibility of those who are confronted. If, as is proposed, the unit 6.1-8 serves as an introduction and basis for the articulation of the judgment on the city (6.9-16), then it could be further suggested that the justification for the judgment in 6.13-16 is two-fold. First, the accused have sinned. Second, they know and are reminded of their responsibility. Therefore, their sins, as the other sins cited in the book of Micah, are not inadvertent sins. Theirs are acts committed in opposition to the dictates of expected behavior—behavior prescribed if not required by the very nature of their responsibilities.

The entire scheme of sin and judgment is based, generally speaking, on the responsibility to that which sustains the wellbeing of others. In this respect, the responsibility assumed in the judgment is that assumed in the qualification of an act as sin.

d. *Goals of judgment*

Immediate. Judgment as a correspondence to or direct consequence of sin would presumably deal with the sin committed. Instead, in ch. 3 the direct focus of the judgment is the wrongdoers and indirectly the wrongs they committed. The text does not set in focus the wronged or the rationale for how the judgment would correct the wrongs. As a matter of fact, the judgments themselves seem to leave the wronged as devastated if not more devastated than before (cf. 3.5-8, 9-12).

The collective retribution for the sins of a group brings into focus the question of the goal of judgment. It is implied in the above analysis of the book of Micah that the judgment is punitive rather corrective. Yet, the intertextual evidence suggests that judgment is not inevitably punitive. For example, in Isa. 1.27 the goal is the purification of the city. Toward that goal the wicked are punished and the righteous are restored. In ch. 3 there is no talk of restoration or relief for the 'righteus/innocent', although such restoration is contextually indicated (e.g. 2.12-13; 4.1–5.14). Even in these instances, the restoration is not necessarily of the 'righteous', but of a remnant, to whatever extent the latter is constituted by the 'righteous'. On the whole, however, the judgments in the book of Micah are punitive.

Although 3.8 seems to allude to such a replacement, the judgments do not, for example, seek to replace the prophets who are misleading the people. Inasmuch as the disadvantaged are not the concern of the judgment, understanding the judgments in ch. 3 as a means to justice is often misconstrued. However, it is not surprising that the disadvantaged are not the focus since the governing concept of the text seems to be the judgment on the nation—the nation whose fate is being threatened by the crimes and sins of its leaders. Only by implication are the disadvantaged brought into focus as those against whom the crimes and sins of the leaders were committed.

Future. The immediacy of judgment has first to do with the presence of the situation to which it is a response. Judgment does not come in anticipation of what Israel may do in the future. In this respect, the perspective of chs. 1–3 and 6.9-16 is that judgment is grounded in the present—the present being the chronological result of past acts. Thus, the future aspects of judgment are the extensions of the circumstances that are perpetuated by judgment from which the judgment extends beyond the implementation of those circumstances. Thus, for example, judgment against Israel for the unlawful seizure of the land is the removal of Israel from the land and the redistribution of the land (2.4-5). As suggested by the sequencing of the events, this judgment extends into the future beyond the time of its initial execution. The redistribution of the land presupposes the implementation of judgment. Next, that there will be no representative of the people during this process suggests a breach in the relationship between God and the people.

Likewise, the destruction of Jerusalem announced in 3.12 extends into the future inasmuch as the destruction, when it happens, is not instantaneously reversed. Its effects and temporal extent are not specified. However, the execution itself is an indicator of the future though it alone does not determine the extent and longevity of the future circumstances.

The question concerning the future aspect of the judgment is seen in the book of Micah in both its organization and its substantive aspects. First, in 1.9 it is said the 'wound' of Samaria is incurable, suggesting that the future holds no cure and will be like the present—there is no hope for Samaria. In this respect, the future may be depicted as 'determined'. The question raised in the text concerning Jerusalem, to whose gate the 'wound' of Samaria has reached, is whether its future has already been determined to be one of judgment.

The widened perspective of the text with respect to the extension of the judgment into the future is achieved in several ways, including the oracles of hope and the location of the present distress in the larger context of promise for the future. Notably, in these texts (1.6-7; 2.1-5; 3.1-12; 6.9-16), judgment is not presented or alluded to as necessitated by a larger plan. Only in connection with chs. 4–5 and 7.7-20 is there any indication that the circumstances of judgment may be a part of a larger plan. Even so, it is not the judgment itself that is given this perspective, but the desolation out of which hope arises. As such, 4.9-13 does not allude to Israel's sin as the cause of the exile to Babylon. In this instance, the exile is seen as preliminary to deliverance and as such necessitated by it. In ch. 2, sin is the cause of the exile; but while the promise of the restoration of a remnant is present, its connection to the judgment is consequential. It is in 7.9 that the connection between sin–judgment and the larger historical context of God's deliverance is most clearly evident.

As seen in 4.9-13 and 7.8-17, the location of the present distress in the larger context of history may not resignify the reality of the present as being less devastating than it is. On the contrary, it shows that the devastation has a limited longevity. Thus, that which is judgment in the present may be followed by blessing, deliverance, and so on, in the future. This is the fundamental aspect of hope signaled in the book of Micah.

Hope

1. *Aspects in the Text*
While the typical vocabulary for hope is limited to a few passages, the concept is indicated throughout the book of Micah (יחל, 1.12; ארב, 7.2; צפה, 7.7; cf. 2.12-13; 4.1–5.14; 7.8-17).[24] The primary indicators, יחל, 'to wait', and צפה, 'to look at' (7.7), express a course of action—to wait for someone or something.[25] In 7.7 the object of hope is Yahweh. The hope is portrayed as being born out of the reality—past and present. The following text, 7.8-17, further establishes the basis of the hope. Hope is the confidence in God's deliverance. Most notably, however, this is not a hope that is blind to the reality of judgment or at least

24. Knierim, 'Hope in the Old Testament', in *Task of Old Testament Theology*, pp. 246-48, for discussion of the word field for hope in the Old Testament.

25. Knierim, 'Hope in the Old Testament', pp. 248-49. He cites numerous examples including: Job 7.2; Pss. 69.4; 25.5; 37.5; Amos 5.25.

the reality of one's circumstances. The perspective of hope recognizes sin and the fact that deliverance will come after the sin has been addressed.

Other indicators of hope include the passages concerning the remnant (שארית, 2.12-13; 4.6-7; 5.6-8; 7.18-20).[26] Hope is indicated in these passages secondarily in the sense defined above in this chapter. The remnant is an indicator of hope to the extent that it signals the limited extent of the judgment and the survivors of this judgment. However, the remnant is not always a sign of hope but is also a sign of doom (cf. Chapter 4 §I.B.2.b.1). That there is a remnant further suggests that the fate of Israel lies beyond the present judgment. The hope is then connected to God's promises to create, preserve, gather and forgive a remnant. In these, hope is from God inasmuch as it is born out of God's promises to bring about a specific future. Fundamentally, however, apart from any specific promise, hope is in essence from God 'in that humans have the fundamental chance, right, and freedom to hope which no power in this world can take away from them'.[27]

Notably, the passages that indicate the hope of Israel do not indicate the hope apart from judgment. In all these passages, the present reality of judgment is a logical if not a chronological presupposition. What is indicated with respect to hope is that it is not exclusive of distress. In 4.9-10, the promised deliverance is to come during the time when the people are captive in Babylon. Israel is promised victory over her enemies, but first the enemies are assembled against Israel (4.11-13). From the perspective of the text, the reality of the captivity and threats from the nations may themselves be regarded as hope; these circumstances are the antecedents of the deliverance and victory. These demonstrate the tension between the present distress (captivity) and the anticipated future (deliverance). As such, hope does not necessarily mean the anticipation of good.[28] Whether that which is hoped for is a means to an end or the end itself, hope itself may be the anticipation of evil, distress

26. Cuffey, 'Coherence of Micah', pp. 247-48, sees the place of the promises to the remnant as decisive to the organization of Micah. Cf. Cohen, 'שאר', pp. 894-95, notes that in most cases שארית refers to survivors out of Israel. There are also instances of reference to an eschatological remnant (Zech. 8.6, 11, 12). Cf. Hasel, *The Remnant*; Jenni, 'Remnant'.

27. Knierim, 'Hope in the Old Testament', p. 253.

28. Knierim, 'Hope in the Old Testament', p. 250.

and judgment.[29] What this means, then, is that hope is not defined by the quality of that which is hoped for, but is itself neutral to it. That which is hoped for, however, is defined by the realities in which hope arises. So, with respect to 4.10-13 the distress of captivity is part of the reality that is hoped for if only as a precursor to the actualization of the deliverance.

Such is also the case with the promise to restore a remnant. That the remnant will be gathered already presupposes that the people are scattered. The actualization of the promise presupposes the reality of the past (the scattering) and of the present (the devastation). Hope, then, is not depicted as utopia. Its very inception may lie in the reality of devastation and suffering. Hope in these instances has to do with the actualization of the promise in history—a promise whose actualization presupposes the tension between its present and the reality that will be replaced by its actualization in the future. Knierim describes this tension in his definition of hope:

> the words for hope show an attitude in which living beings, foremost humans, are in their respective situations intensely stretching out forward, looking forward, and focusing in anticipation for and in dependence on something or someone to arrive, to happen, or to be achieved. That attitude presupposes an uncertainty or a tension between the present state and the state hoped for, between the known present and the unknown future, and between the state of desire and the state of satisfaction in its fulfillment.[30]

Yet, hope is dependent on awareness of the relevance of the promise, while the awareness itself lies in reality. Thus the promise (whatever its content) does not become hope apart from its relevance to the present and significance for the future. In the contrasting realities—those actualized in the present devastation vs. those depicted in the promise—hope is generated insofar as it is the anticipation of a change from one reality to another. Still, hope itself is realistic. It does not assume that the actualization of the promise is devoid of circumstances that are themselves different from those depicted in the promise. Consequently,

---

29. J.G. McConville, *Judgment and Promise: An Interpretation of the Book of Jeremiah* (Winona Lake, IN: Eisenbrauns, 1993), p. 44. He proposes that in Jer. 1–24 there is 'a closing down of hope for a repentance which might avert the disaster of exile, then to offer a new kind of hope, which, however, is deferred until judgment has been experienced'.

30. McConville, *Judgment and Promise*, p. 247; cf. pp. 259-60.

hope may be constituted by judgment insofar as the presence of judgment is depicted as an antecedent to the actualization of the promise. In this respect, hope and judgment may be two aspects of the same historical reality.[31]

Along with this characteristic of the hope perspective in the book of Micah, there is hope concerning the remote future. This particular articulation of hope is addressed to the fate of Zion and is presented within the conceptual framework of the Zion tradition. The hope is that Yahweh will restore Zion. The language of the text, however, 'in the latter days', suggests that this is not a promise that will be fully actualized in the present or the immediate future. Thus, the pairing of this hope with the expression of the more immediate aspects of actualized promise may validate the promise and its actualization. This attention to the present and the promised salvation from its circumstances are indicative of realistic hope. This is not in any way to espouse the perspective that hope is merely that time will correct devastation. The basis of hope is not in the healing effect of time, but in the active involvement of God in the history of Israel to preserve Israel's existence.

Hope, specifically human hope, is compelled by the possibility for change. Still the existence of hope is not dependent on its own validity. One may in fact hope for something that is impossible—impossible within the time frame in which it is hoped for; impossible for the one who is hoping; or impossible as a reality, that is, that which is hoped for does not exist and most probable will never exist. In the present text, the hope is compelled by the validity of the promise and the awareness of its relevance to the present and significance for the future; but the validity of the hope depends, in this instance, on the source of the promise. In 4.1-5, the promise is that Zion will be exalted. The source of the promise is Yahweh (כי־פי יהוה צבאות דבר) and its actualization is guaranteed by Yahweh. The promise itself contains God's hope for the future inasmuch as it seeks to create that future. Thus, that which is hoped for is possible as a reality with respect to those who hope for it.

Nonetheless, Israel's hope itself does not create the possibility for actualizing that for which Israel hopes. But the possibility itself may inspire hope. If the promise is not accepted as valid, hope may not ensue from it. Validity has to do with the realistic possibility of

31. Cf. McConville, *Judgment and Promise*, pp. 43-44.

actualizing the promise by the one making the promise. Hope then is only as valid as the promise (explicit or implicit) upon which it is built. Still, hope as a phenomenon exists apart from promise and may be the antithesis of promise in its speculation about the future.

2. *Conceptual Framework*

There are at least two interrelated aspects that characterize hope as realistic: the source of the hope and the possibility to actualize that for which one hopes. Hope may be born in good or bad circumstances. As such, the source of hope may be the distress of the ones who hope (7.7). The distress signals that something lies beyond the present. Because they are aware of a possible existence beyond the present distress, the reality of the distress may lead some to hope for change, that is, for deliverance. The foundation of hope is that there is something to be anticipated that is not yet actualized (cf. 7.7).

In other situations, such as 1.9 and 2.3-4, the hope is seen as unrealistic. Thus the incurable wound of Samaria indicates that hope for escape from judgment is futile. The judgment is inevitable. Likewise, in 2.3-4 judgment is announced and qualified as inevitable in the sense that there is no escape from it. The hope for escape may therefore be unrealistic. In this case, hope in its speculation about the future is sandwiched between promise and judgment.

The second aspect of realistic hope has to do with the nature of promise. Hope may arise from a source outside of the distress, as in a promise announced to those in distress (2.12-13; 4.1–5.14). In these instances, the hope is constituted in the promise of God. The promise itself is validated by its source. Thus, the hope for the actualization of the promises is realistic as indicated by formulas such as נאם־יהוה in passages such as 4.6a and 5.9 (cf. 4.4).

Hope may also be constituted in the awareness of the character of God. Such is the case in 7.18-20. The hope is that God will forgive the sin of the remnant. While this is not a promise announced to the distressed (cf. 2.12-13; 4.1–5.14) the possibility of its actualization, as seen by the speaker, is the character of God (7.18-20). Furthermore, that possibility is strengthened by God's relationship to Israel.

The concept of hope in this respect addresses itself to the question prompted in 1.9. Is the fate of Israel comparable to that of Samaria? Is there any hope for Israel? The book of Micah indicates that there is hope for Israel constituted in the mercy of God to forgive and preserve a remnant. This hope is not that judgment will not come, but that judgment will not be the final state of Israel's existence.

The relationship of judgment and hope therefore incorporates several aspects. First, the relationship is suggested in the mutual relevance of judgment and hope to the past, present and future circumstances. Both presuppose the possibility for change. Judgment creates the present circumstances by addressing the past. This is not to suggest that all devastations are created by God's judgment. Certainly, devastations may also result from the practice of injustices against which judgment is brought. Devastations may also be unexplained, for example, the suffering of the innocent. However, with respect to the book of Micah, devastations result from God's judgment and are addressed by it. In both these instances, hope is the anticipation of a change in the present circumstances in light of the past and toward the future.

Second, the relationship of judgment and hope suggests itself in their existence as aspects of the same reality. As such, the presence of judgment may be indicative of the realistic nature of hope. This is seen in the anticipation of a future the actualization of which is dependent on the execution of judgment. The promise of restoration, deliverance and power in 4.1–5.14 all assume that the present state is not characterized by that which is anticipated. The promise as such, while pointing to a future, also points to the distress as an inevitable part of actualizing that future. Thus, the very promise that compels hope, defines the realistic nature of this particular hope as the presence of distress. So the actualization of that which is hoped for is dependent upon the actualization of the distress. How is one to subdue one's captors if one has not been captured? How will one triumph in exile if one is not in exile?

Third, the relationship of judgment and hope is further constituted by their source—they are both from God and are both manifested in human reality. In the book of Micah, as elsewhere, judgment is depicted as God's response to sin (2.3; 3.4, 6, 12; 6.9). Yet, while sin is inherent in human nature, judgment is not. Judgment is God's action, but more accurately God's action in response to sin. Hope, in the book of Micah is inspired by God's promises and in this respect it is from God. Also, it is from God in that as God's creation, humans are given the capacity to hope. Furthermore, human hope, whether or not it is realistic, is possible as long as the natural human mental and physical capacities exist. Hope is most often associated with adversity as the circumstances in which it develops, and happiness and wellbeing is what it anticipates.

Can there be hope apart from adversity? Certainly, there is nothing to say that hope is impossible apart from adversity. Even those in prosperity hope for something. However, in the conceptual framework of the book of Micah, hope presupposes adversity and in this respect (not to speak for all situations) hope and judgment are mutually dependent in their relationship to the same realities, their source, and their presupposition of a type dynamism. They are in no way mutually exclusive nor are they inevitable to each other.

Conclusion

Consideration of the various concepts in the book of Micah in light of their textual aspects and conceptual framework has shown the overlap of these concepts. In these relationships, however, it is apparent that all concepts do not make the same degree of contribution to the conceptuality of the book of Micah. However, the presence of each is decisive to that conceptuality. Thus, for example, the concepts of justice, sin and judgment are all present and operative toward the coherence of chs. 1–3 and 6.9-16. These are not as present or operative in the same way in chs. 4–5, 6.1-8 and 7.7-20. By observing the quantitative presence of judgment and its interrelated concepts, it may appear that the conceptuality of the book of Micah is solely the judgment on Israel. However, the quantitative aspect of the concept may not be directly indicative of its place in the conceptuality of the book of Micah.

The identification of the conceptual coherence of the book of Micah calls for the identification of the conceptuality that is generative of the book of Micah as a whole and its constitutive concepts. Are they present to support the conceptuality of God's justice, the justice of God's judgment on the leaders of Israel, the sin of Israel, the responsibilities of Israel's leaders, the hope for Israel, and so on? All these conceptual aspects are present. Justice is operative in the text as that which is violated and is the sin that is to be punished. Responsibility is that which is abused and is that which constitutes the measure of the infractions—that is, the injustice, the sin. Judgment is present as God's response to Israel's sin. Hope is indicated by the promised restoration of Zion and the remnant and by the prospect for God's forgiveness of the remnant.

What then constitutes the conceptuality of the book of Micah? Is it judgment or hope? The fact of the matter is that it is both. The conceptuality as seen through the preceding discussion is more than the distinctive concepts and their conceptual frameworks. Yet the conceptuality that constitutes the coherence is non-existent without the distinctive parts. It is proposed that the conceptuality of the book of Micah concerns the fate of Israel. Israel's fate is affected by Israel's sin on the one hand and God's response to that sin on the other. The reality is that Israel has sinned and is judged for its sin. Thus Israel's existence is threatened by the judgment. The final word, however, is not the judgment, but the hope that beyond the judgment lies a future in which the existence of Israel is a reality (see discussion above). The 'fate' of Israel is shaped by Israel's relationship with God and by the dynamics of that relationship (see *Addendum* in Chapter 3). Within the dynamics of that relationship, the sin–judgment and promise–hope dynamics are to be understood as the conceptual framework of God's justice in judgment and God's mercy in preserving and forgiving Israel.

Chapter 7

SYNTHESIS AND CONCLUSION

Synthesis

1. *Concerning the Final Form of the Book of Micah*

Using the concept-critical method, the present study has attempted to discern the coherence of the book of Micah. It is proposed that the final form of the book of Micah exhibits a conceptual coherence which is discernible through its structure. It is further proposed that this structure is the result of a deliberate organization by the redactors in their effort to contemporize the book of Micah for their audiences. As such, the final form of the book of Micah reflects the concerns and conceptual framework of the final redactors. Thus, even the older materials in the book of Micah are reconceptualized with reference to the redactors' concerns and the conceptual framework that is generative of the concerns. The choice of these materials is itself indicative of the redactors' understanding of the materials and their usefulness in achieving their purposes.

Insofar as the final form is purposeful, there are elements within it that are used to achieve the purposes of the redactors. These elements are both textual and substantive—conceptual. The textual elements are those of structure and vocabulary that are employed simply because structure and vocabulary are essential to all texts. Textual elements are also the units formed by the smaller elements such as the judgment speech, the disputation, the woe oracle. Each has a distinct generic form, but the particular purpose of its use is determined by the concerns of the redactors. Thus, the substantive or conceptual elements in conjunction to the textual elements are the indicators of the purpose of the final text.

Fundamental to the task of discerning the coherence of the book of Micah is understanding its conceptuality, for this is the generative aspect of the coherence—the coherence itself is a manifestation of the conceptuality. The task of discerning the coherence of the book of Micah involves the awareness of the structural indicators and hence the literary integrity and cohesion of the whole. Yet this task both presupposes the understanding of the conceptuality of the book of Micah and is necessitated by that understanding.

2. *Summary of the Present Study*

The task of discerning the coherence of the book of Micah proceeded along the following lines. First, Chapter 1 reviewed previous research looking specifically at the structure proposed by the scholars and their criteria used in determining coherence. There it was noted that only within the last thirty years has the question of the coherence of the book of Micah come to the fore as a question pursued in its own right. Prior to that, it was usually assumed that the book of Micah, as a composite entity, lacks coherence. There was little denial that parts of the book of Micah exhibit a type of coherence. The denial was that the diverse origins of the materials and the complex redactional processes had produced something other than an incoherent mass characterized by numerous inconsistencies.[1]

Studies on the coherence of the book of Micah assumed that coherence is constituted by more than the origin of the materials (see Table 1 in Chapter 1 above). However, with the emergence of these studies came different sets of problems. These concerned the definition of 'coherence'. For the first twenty years after the introduction of the question of the coherence of the book of Micah (as a concern in its own right), coherence was associated mainly with literary integrity/cohesion.[2] It was therefore dismissed by some as literary and without concern for the theological aspects of the text. However, during this time

---

1. Note that similar trends were taking place in studies on the books of Hosea and Isaiah, namely, efforts to explain the inconsistencies in the text. See Gale A. Yee, *Composition and Tradition in the Book of Hosea: A Redactional Investigation* (SBLDS, 102; Atlanta: Scholars Press, 1987), pp. 1-25, for a discussion of the theories of Hosean composition. Yee notes that the nineteenth-century discussion centered on questions of the authenticity of the material. The first quarter of the twentieth century was characterized by the literary discussion, while the second quarter focused on form-critical questions. During the 1980s rhetorical critical concerns took center stage. Earlier studies on Isaiah include: Bernhard Duhm, *Das Buch Jesaia* (Göttingen: Vandenhoeck & Ruprecht, 5th edn, 1968); Thomas K. Cheyne, *Introduction to the Book of Isaiah* (London: A. & C. Black, 1895).

2. Hagstrom, *The Coherence*.

there were those who attempted to understand the theological concerns of the book of Micah its coherence.[3]

Chapter 2 of this study addressed this problem of a definition of coherence. It is proposed that coherence is inherently conceptual and discernible through the structure and conceptual interconnectedness of the units of a work. It is defined as the interrelationship of the parts of a work to create an overall logical unity. This interrelationship is constituted by the conceptuality of the work. The conceptuality itself is generative of and discernible in the text's structure and the other literary and substantive features that together define the text's literary and conceptual integrity. Conceptual coherence is the product of its constitutive units insofar as the units lend to and are constitutive of the whole.

While the concern of Chapter 2 is the book of Micah, the theoretical observations may have value for studies whose intent is to discern the coherence of other books. These studies would also have to define what they mean by coherence, and evaluate studies such as this one in light of the proposed definition of coherence.

Chapter 3 of this study presented a structural analysis of the book of Micah based on the proposal that its structure is an indicator of its coherence. It noted that the macro-structure consists of two parts: chs. 1–5 and 6–7. These parts are both concerned with the fate of Israel and deal with this concern by means of a dispute.[4] Other units are introduced by a dispute in which Yahweh's judgment of Israel is depicted as a part of but not the totality of Israel's fate. While Israel is the subject of both disputes, the particular aspect of Israel is not the same in each of the two parts.

In chs. 1–5, the perspective is universal in that all the peoples of the earth are summoned. Israel is first brought into focus as one of the nations summoned by Yahweh (1.2). Throughout the unit, the focus is modified in such a way that Israel's leaders are depicted as the source of Israel's sin, and Jerusalem is the focal point of the judgment (3.12) and hope of Israel (4.1-5). In this unit hope is signaled by God's announcement of promises (2.12-13; 4.1–5.14). These promises, however, do not invalidate the judgment, or in any way presume the judgment to be unjust. The promises presuppose judgment or at least adverse

3. Mays, *Micah*; *idem*, 'Theological Purpose'; Cuffey, 'Coherence of Micah'.
4. See the *Addendum* in Chapter 3 above for the definition of fate as used in this study.

circumstances that will be overcome as the promises are actualized.

The unit consists of an introduction (1.2-16); a section of judgment (2.1–3.12) and a section on hope (4.1–5.14). The introduction raises the question concerning the fate of Israel as compared to Samaria, while the two other units provide the response. The coherence of the constitutive units are variously indicated, it being more salient in some than in others. Yet, the coherence of the larger units, as seen in the discussion, may be obscured by the more salient features of their constitutive parts.

Chapters 6–7 as a unit is particularistic in focus as indicated by the unit's introduction (6.1-8) and conclusion (7.18-20), as well as the various allusions to the covenant relationship (6.3-5; 7.20). In this unit, hope is brought into focus as a longing on the part of those experiencing the desolation of judgment. The hope is articulated primarily with an outward focus. The concern is for how Israel's devastation will be perceived by the nations. The element of promise is introduced in the form of an affirmation of the hope of the city (7.11-13). Notably, the hope expresses a confidence based on God's character.

With regard to the coherence of the two parts, these are observed in their shared concern about Israel's fate. The condemnation of Israel's sin through judgment in both sections is depicted as a just response. The responses of deliverance, restoration and forgiveness, when placed beside the judgment, introduce the concept of God's mercy. Thus the text's coherence, seen through the discussion of the various units in Chapters 4 and 5 of this study and the concepts and their framework in Chapter 6 (also of this study), is generated by the conceptuality of Yahweh's justice and mercy as significant determinants of Israel's fate. This accounts for the presence of the judgment and hope sections and makes sense of the introductions in each unit.

3. *Concerning Coherence*

This study shows that coherence is exhibited at various levels of the text in such a way that a small unit may exhibit coherence that is more discernible than a larger unit of which it is a part (see Chapter 3 above). It is the nature of coherence to be relative to the specific structure of its material and to the larger conceptual framework that is the source of its manifestation. Coherence itself is only part of the conceptual framework, and may be reflective of that framework only to the extent that the indicators left by the redactors are discernible. Thus, the discernibility of coherence depends as much on the clarity of the indicators as on the ability of the interpreter to perceive and interpret them within the confines of the text (see Chapters 4 and 5).

The indicators may be anything from the use of specific vocabulary to the sequencing of generic forms to create parallel units (see Chapter 3 Delimitation of the Text. The task of discerning the coherence is to determine the relative importance of the indicators and the interrelationship of the units marked off by these indicators (see Chapter 3 Micro-structure). This involves criteria not limited to quantity or typicality of the indicators (see Chapter 2).

Due to factors of subjectivity inherent in the interpretative process and specifically in the study of coherence, the indicators—no matter their quantity or clarity—may still be misconstrued. What one interpreter may regard as significant may be downplayed by another. The danger is also to presume a coherence that the text itself does not confirm. Such a danger is increased with the increased size of the corpus of material and the increased variations in the content of the material.

Thus, for example, the coherence of a prophetic book is sought on the basis of its structural integrity and conceptual continuity. In cases such as the book of Isaiah, where the text itself reflects clear divisions of material that may be attributed to different historical times, the coherence is not readily apparent. Yet the question of its coherence is raised by virtue of the juxtaposition of the parts. Coherence in this instance may be exhibited in various degrees in various parts of the book. However, the coherence of the book of Isaiah, as compared to the book of Micah, may be quite different. Coherence in this respect is not a monolithic entity. Yet it is this aspect of coherence that constitutes its greatest challenge, for it has in essence to do with the nature of the entity itself.

As with the book of Micah or Isaiah, the coherence of the Book of the Twelve will long be a debated issue. It confronts the challenges noted in this study, namely, discerning the structure of the final form, assessing the relative importance of the constitutive parts in the conceptuality of the whole, and allowing for the possibility of revision of one's proposal with the insights gained at all points of the analysis.

Coherence is the extension of the conceptuality of the text which in turn is the product generated by the conceptual framework of the redactor/author. The extent to which coherence is present and discernible is already determined by the text. What is left to be determine is the extent to which it is discerned.

Conclusion

One implication of this study is that coherence, insofar as it is the product of purposeful redaction, is to some degree present in all works. This implies that the challenges of discerning coherence are inherent in the text. As argued above, the older materials in a book are reconceptualized in light of the redactors' purposes and concerns. Therefore, it cannot be assumed that a text is to be construed in the same way in all its occurrences. Similarly, the occurrences of technical vocabulary may need to be examined in light of their infra-textual, contextual and inter-textual aspects. This calls for a more critical assessment of the text in its particular context. Likewise, it calls for a degree of caution against the tendency to reduce the text to selected elements in order to see coherence. While it is proposed that there is a degree of coherence in every literary work, it is also proposed that there are degrees of discernibility determined to a great extent by the work itself. Coherence does not mean the absence of competing and/or contradicting perspectives. It may incorporate these perspectives. However, the incorporation of these already presupposes a new perspective in which the diverse ones coexist.

Another implication of the study of coherence is that it touches the same concerns as theological construction. The task of discerning coherence is reflective of the task of theology. First, both tasks necessitate the discerning of the conceptual presuppositions of their constitutive elements. At this point, the tasks do not presume that every text is generated by the same conceptuality, nor do they presume the same degree of discernibility of conceptuality for all texts. Second, both tasks entail a systematization of the data according to the indicators in the text. Consequently, allowance is made for revision of insights as one part of the task is evaluated by the other.

This discussion suggests several other studies. First, that the concerns of this study be extended to the other prophetic books. Since all prophetic books are not composite in the same way or to the same extent, it would be necessary to evaluate the theoretical basis of this study in order to determine the extent to which it applies to the other prophetic books. The main questions to be answered would be: To what extent does a prophetic book exhibit conceptual coherence? By what criteria is the coherence of the whole to be determined?

Second, it suggests possibilities for dialogue with those seeking to discern the unity of the Book of the Twelve. To what extent does the prophetic corpus exhibit coherence? How does the coherence of the individual books compare with that of the whole? Is the coherence of the prophetic corpus to be assessed on the same basis as that of the Book of the Twelve and the individual prophetic books? Some of these questions have already been addressed in studies on the Book of the Twelve.[5] Thus Nogalski critiques House for overdrawing the phenomenon of theme. He argues that the result is that House's arguments are circular. The same may be said of Nogalski who is so committed to the 'catchword' phenomenon that he is willing to explain away any apparent exceptions. For example, with respect to Micah 1 and Jonah he argues that a stronger connection appears between Micah and Obadiah and that Jonah may have been inserted into an already established unit.[6] Perhaps too much weight is laid on the catchword phenomenon and not enough on what it represents. While the catchwords are important to the unity, these are not employed simply to signal literary relationship. The choice of these words may have to do with the purposes for which the books were actualized in their final from.

Finally, this study suggests that its questions are appropriate for all parts of the Old Testament. However, it must be determined whether the criteria for determining coherence are the same for all genres of literature or whether the criteria are particular to the various genres. Also because of the nature of the interrelationship of its parts, the question of the coherence of the Old Testament would demand further clarification of the definition and methodology of discerning coherence. Having said this, it is evident that the task of discerning coherence as pursued here is a small part of the task that confronts Old Testament exegesis and theology.

5.   Paul House, *The Unity of the Twelve* (JSOTSup, 77; Sheffield: JSOT Press, 1990); Nogalski, *Literary Precursors*, focuses on the catchword phenomenon as the key to understanding the unity of the Book of the Twelve.

6.   Nogalski, *Literary Precursors*, p. 13.

APPENDIX

Author's Translation and Text-Critical Notes[1]

The extant text is the primary concern of this study. It is recognized, however, that there are some variants particularly between the MT and LXX.[2] In some instances, these variants may indicate a difference of conceptuality between the two versions. This study is not intended to be an exhaustive analysis or comparison of each variant and the conceptual coherence of each version. Though presently deferred, however, certainly the tasks of discerning the coherence of the LXX and the comparison of the MT and LXX are noteworthy.

Text criticism, in this instance, is used primarily to analyze these variants and to arrive at a responsible reading of the text. At various points in its examination of the variants, the present discussion begins inquiry into the difference of conceptualities between the MT and LXX. This inquiry is limited since the main purpose of this appendix is to provide the translation of the book of Micah upon which the present discussion is based.

Chapter 1

1. *Translation*

1 ᵃThe word of Yahwehᵃ, which came to Micah the Moreshite,
   in the days of Jotham, Ahaz, Hezekiah, kings of Judah,
   which he saw concerning Samaria and Jerusalem:

1.   The text-critical notes are designated by the chapter and verse where they occur in the MT along with letter(s) in the translation to indicate the particular variant, for example, 1.2a or 1.5a-a. The reader should be aware that the letter designations are not intended to correspond to those of the MT; therefore the reader is advised to refer to the present accompanying translation.

2.   Joseph Ziegler, *Doudecim Prophetae* (Septuaginta: Vetus Testamentum Graecum; Göttingen: Vandenhoeck & Ruprecht, 2nd edn, 1967 [1943]), XIII; see Emanuel Tov, *The Greek Minor Prophet Scrolls From Nahal Hever (8Hev XIIgr)* (DJD, 8; Oxford: Clarendon Press, 1990), for Mic. 1.1–5.6.

2   Listen peoples, all of you!
    Pay attention, earth and you who dwell in her!
    that the Lord Yahweh[a] will be a witness against you,
    the Lord from his holy temple.

3   For behold Yahweh is going forth from his place;
    he descends and treads upon the high places of the earth.

4   Then the mountains will melt beneath him
    and the valleys will split
    like wax before the fire,
    like water poured down a slope.

5   All this is because of the crime of Jacob,
    because of the sins[a] of the house of Israel.
    What[b] is the crime of Jacob?
    Is it not Samaria?
    [c]And what are the high places of Judah?
    Are they not Jerusalem?[c]

6   So I will make Samaria into the ruins of the field—
    for planting vineyard.
    And I will hurl her stones into the valley;
    and her foundations I will lay bare.

7   All her images will be destroyed;
    all her wages[a] will be burned in the fire;
    all her idols I make into waste.
    For from the wages of a prostitute she collected [them],
    and to the wages of a prostitute they will be returned.

8   Concerning this I will lament and wail;
    I will walk around barefoot and naked.
    I will lament like jackals and wail like ostriches.

9   For her wounds[a] are incurable;
    indeed it has come to Judah.
    It has reached the gate of my people, to Jerusalem.

10 In Gath, do not proclaim.
    Do not weep at all.
    In Beth-le-aphrah roll yourself in the dust.

11 Pass on, inhabitants of Shaphir, naked, ashamed.
    The inhabitants of Zaanan will not go out;
    the lamentation of Beth-ha-ezel
    takes away from you its standing place.

12 For the inhabitants of Maroth wait for good;
    because evil has come down from Yahweh
    to the gate of Jerusalem.

13 Harness the steeds to the chariots, inhabitants of Lachish;
    [a]it is the beginning of sin for the daughter of Zion;
    for in you the crimes of Israel[a] are found.

14 Therefore, you will give parting gifts to Moresheth-gath;
   the houses of Achzib are disappointing to the kings of Israel.

15 Again the heir comes to you, inhabitants of Mareshah,
   the glory of Israel comes to Adullam.

16 Make yourself bald and shave
   on account of the children of your delight.
   Make yourself as bald as a vulture;
   for they will go away from you into exile.

2. *Text-Critical Notes*

1.1a-a   MT   דבר־יהוה אשר היה
          LXX   καὶ ἐγένετο λόγος κυρίου

The MT uses the relative clause (אשר היה) to qualify and further specify
the subject—דבר־יהוה. The LXX uses a declarative sentence to indicate
that 'word of the Lord' came.

1.2a   MT   ויהי אדני יהוה
       LXX   κύριος
       1QpMic יהוה אדני יהיה

While the expression used in the MT is more frequent than that of
1QpMic, the latter is exclusive to hymns (e.g. Pss. 68.21; 109.21).[3]

1.5a   MT   ובחטאות
       LXX   καὶ διὰ ἁμαρτίαν

It has been suggested that the sing. בחטאת is an attempt to alleviate the
difficulty of the text. However, the plur. form fits with the parallel
expression in v. 5bβ—במות יהודה. It is also the more difficult of the two
readings in parallel with the sing. פשע (cf. 1.13 where the situation is
reversed—פשע is plur. while חטאת is sing.) The LXX assumes the sing.
ובחטאת.

1.5b   MT   מי
       LXX   τίς
       1QpMic מה

The MT's use of the pronoun may be translated 'who' or possibly
'what'. The interrogative pronoun itself does not indicate by its occurrence the sense in which it is to be understood. Admittedly, the presence of the names Samaria and Jerusalem may suggest that the interrogative pronoun is meant to (a) identify and classify or (b) inquire

3.   Waltke, 'Micah', pp. 617-18.

about a condition or something. The former would be expressed by 'who'. The latter sense is better expressed in English as 'what'.[4] The LXX and 1QpMic clarify the use of מי, and thus facilitates the reading by their use of τίς and מה;[5] however, context supports the MT.[6]

1.5c-c	MT	ומי־במות יהודה הלוא ירושלם
	LXX	ἡ ἁμαρτία

For discussion of מי see 1.5b above. In place of במות, the LXX has its typical word for sin—ἁμαρτία. This represents an interpretation of the text, clarifying the referent of the noun, high places (במות). It also facilitates the parallel חטאת/פשע. However, the parallel is also present in the MT in as much as the high places are used as a metonymy for sin.

1.7a	MT	וכל־אתנניה...

It has been suggested that this reading resulted from a transposition of the word from the following line. Therefore, on the basis of maintaining a parallel with וכל־פסיליה at the beginning of 1.7, the text is often emended to read אשריה.[7] Such an emendation, however, is unnecessary. The term אתנן 'hire' (Isa. 23.17, 18) occurs with the specific 'connotation' of wages of a prostitute (אתנן זונה—Deut. 23.19).

1.9a	MT	מכותיה
	LXX	ἡ πληγὴ αὐτῆς

The plur. of the MT stands alongside the sing. verbs in v. 9—אנושה, באה, נגע. The plur. of the LXX may be explained as an attempt to facilitate the reading in light of the sing. verbs. However, it is not necessary to explain this plur. noun (מכותיה) as an error resulting from the

---

4. Waltke and O'Connor, *Syntax*, 18.2d states that 'most occurrences of מי refer to persons in a straightforward way, but some are not so clear. When a thing is closely associated with the person or is pregnant with the idea of a person, or where persons are understood and implied, מי may be used. For example, "What is your name?" can be expressed by מי שמך, because the name is conceived of as a surrogate for the person. Because the inquiry however, is about something or condition etc., English idiom requires other interrogatives, "what, how, where, etc".' Cf. GKC §37; Gen. 33.8; Mic. 1.5.

5. Those who substitute מה for מי include: Mays, *Micah*, p. 41; Allen, *The Books*, p. 266.

6. Waltke, 'Micah', p. 618; Wolff, *Micah*, p. 42.

7. Mays, *Micah*, p. 46.

recollection of the plur. nouns in vv. 6-7—יסדיה, אבניה, פסיליה, אתנניה, עצביה—or as a collective, referring to פשע and חטאת. The subject of the sing. verb may be plur. in instances where that subject is preceded by that verb.[8]

1.13a-a MT	ראשית חטאת היא לבת־ציון כי־בך נמצאו פשעי ישראל
RSV	you were the beginning of sin to the daughter of Zion
NRSV	it was the beginning of sin to daughter Zion

The sing. form היא and the plur. נמצאו may have lead to translations such as that of the RSV. However, the plur. נמצאו refers to the crimes (פשעי) and the pronoun היא refers to רכב.

Chapter 2

1. *Translation*

1   Woe to those who devise injustice
    and do evil on their beds.
    When morning dawns they perform it;
    for it is in the power of their hand.

2   They covet fields and seize [them],
    houses and take them.
    They oppress a man and his house,
    a man and his inheritance.

3   Therefore, thus says Yahweh:
    Behold I am devising evil against this family
    from which you cannot remove your necks
    nor will you walk upright;
    for this is an evil time.

4   In that day, one will take up a taunt against you;
    he will lament a lamentation saying:
    'We are utterly ruined,
    the possession of my people is changed[a].
    How he takes what is mine![b]
    To make restitution[c] for our fields,
    he divides [them]'.

5   Therefore no one will be there for you casting a line by lots
    in the assembly of Yahweh.

8.   R. Williams, *Hebrew Syntax: An Outline* (Toronto: University of Toronto Press, 2nd edn, 1976), §228. Notably, the verb in these instances is usually 3rd masc. sing. with an inanimate subject.

6   'Do not preach', they preach.
    'You shall not preach these things;
    disgrace will not overtake us'.

7   Is it said,[a] house of Jacob?
    Is the Spirit of Yahweh impatient?
    Are these his deeds?
    Do not my words[b] do well with the one who lives right?

8   But lately my people[a] arise[b] as an enemy.
    [c]From the front of a cloak you strip its glory[c],
    from those who pass by in confidence, averse to war.

9   You drive away the women of my people
    from their[a] pleasant houses;
    from their[a] children you take away
    my glory forever.

10 Arise and go,
    for this is no resting place.
    Because of uncleanness you shall be destroyed
    by ruinous destruction.

11 If a man goes about in the spirit
    and deceived with lies—
    'I will preach to you about wine and beer'—
    he would be the preacher of this people.

12 I will surely assembly all of you Jacob;
    I will gather the remnant of Israel.
    I will unite them like a flock in the fold,
    like a herd in the midst of the pasture.
    And they shall be in commotion because of man.

13 The breaker shall go up before him.
    They shall pass through the gate and go out by it.
    Their king shall pass through before them,
    Yahweh in front of them.

2. *Text-Critical Notes*

2.4a   MT   ימיר
       LXX   κατεμετρήθη ἐν σχοινίῳ

The LXX probably assumes ימד (the niph. impf. of the verb מדד, 'to measure') and adds the indirect object. Wolff and others adopt this reading while omitting the indirect object.[9] The MT reads ימיר (hiph. impf. from the verb מור, 'to change').[10]

9.   Wolff, *Micah*, p. 70; cf. Mays, *Micah*, p. 60; Vuilleumier, 'Michée', pp. 27-28.
10.   Allen, *The Books*, p. 292; Waltke, 'Micah', p. 640;

2.4b MT אֵיךְ יָמִישׁ לִי
LXX καὶ οὐκ ἦν ὁ κωλύσων αὐτὸν

The LXX, translating as 'there is none to hinder him', qualifies the previous condition.[11] The MT represents the content of the taunt taken up against the people. This reading is to be understood in conjunction with what follows.

2.4c MT לְשׁוֹבֵב

The MT reading לְשׁוֹבֵב suggests the adjectival from of שׁוֹב[12] used as a substantive—'apostate'. In Jer. 31.22 the phrase הַבַּת הַשּׁוֹבֵבָה is used of Israel's faithlessness.[13] The question raised by this option concerns the identity of those being referred to. There is the possibility that the reference is to the faithless in Israel, that is, those who have rebelled against Yahweh. But how does this fit the context? The context does not support a reading in which the land is divided among those who are being judged for seizing the land.

The apparatus suggests the reading לְשׁוֹבֵינוּ, 'our captors' (from שָׁבָה), a suggestion followed by the RSV: 'Among our captors he divides our fields'. This interpretation presupposes the pronouncement of judgment in v. 3 and clarifies the apparent difficulty. It presents a situation in which the land that was given to Israel is now being divided among the captors of Israel. While this interpretation may fit the context, the text itself may resist the interpretation insofar as the textual basis of the interpretation is an emendation.

Another possibility is that the MT is an inf. cstr. as in Isa. 49.5:

> And now the Lord says:
> who formed me from the womb to be his servant
> to bring Jacob back to him...

In this sense, the verb functions as a complementary infinitive of the preceding verb, that is, to 'make restitution'.[14] The interpretation, in this

11. Mays, *Micah*, p. 60.
12. Waltke, 'Micah', p. 640.
13. Waltke, 'Micah', p. 640. He considers this occurrence to be similar to Jer. 49.4. He interprets this occurrence as a reference to the Assyrians. Grammatically the ל may indicate the indirect object of the following verb. Cf. Allen, *The Books*, p. 285.
14. Dominique Barthélemy, *Critique Textuelle de l'Ancien Testament* (Orbis Biblicus et Orientalis, 50.3; Göttingen: Vandenhoeck & Ruprecht, 1992), p. 731; Wolff, *Micah*, p. 70.

instance, is that Yahweh is making restitution for the fields by dividing them. The understanding is that the land which has already been divided is again divided though not necessarily as was previously done. Also, in this interpretation, the emphasis is on the fact of dividing land that was already divided, and not on the persons who will be given the land as a result of the distribution. What therefore comes into focus is the reason for the division of the land—to make restitution.

> 2.7a   MT   הָאָמוּר
>   LXX   ὁ λέγων...

The passive part. of אמר is considered unusual,[15] and has been interpreted in several ways. One way is proposed in the apparatus, that is, הֶאָרוּר (qal pass. part.)—'is it cursed?' This reading has been adapted by various scholars including Wolff.[16] According to the latter rendering, the question is whether or not the house of Jacob is cursed. I propose to follow the MT—'Is it said...'—with the particular nuance of ascertaining the truth of the claims presupposed in the following questions.

> 2.7b   MT   דברי ייטיבו
>   LXX   οἱ λόγοι αὐτοῦ εἰσιν καλοὶ

The LXX assumes דבריו in place of the MT reading.[17] The LXX reading conforms this part of the verse with the preceding references to Yahweh, namely, מעלליו and רוח יהוה. It has been suggested that the MT indicates a change of speaker from the opponents back to the prophet. Waltke proposes that the 1st person pron. suff. refers to Yahweh and not to the false prophets.[18] This possibility should be considered though not solely on the basis of the interpretation of this part of the verse.[19]

---

15. BDB, p. 55, proposes that the MT 'it is grammatically indefensible' and should be read as an infin. abs. plus inter. part., הֶאָמוֹר.

16. *Micah*, pp. 68, 70; cf. Vuilleumier, 'Michée', p. 31.

17. Mays, *Micah*, p. 66, proposes that the MT is a result of confusing the speakers. He follows the LXX at this point. Cf. Vuilleumier, 'Michée', p. 31.

18. Waltke, 'Micah', p. 645; contra Willis, 'Micah 2.6-8', pp. 77-78, who argues that these are the words of the false prophets.

19. Wolff, *Micah*, p. 70.

2.8a	MT	וְאֶתְמוּל עַמִּי
	LXX	καὶ ἔμπροσθεν ὁ λαός μου εἰς ἔχθραν ἀντέστη
	NRSV	But you rise up against my people as an enemy

The difficulty of v. 8 is the understanding of the conceptuality of the verse, particularly the identity of the speaker. The MT has been emended in various ways usually as follows: וְאַתֶּם עַל־עַמִּי, 'but you against my people...'[20] Like the LXX, in which the people are not the enemy, this emendation assumes that עַמִּי is not the enemy, that is, the object rather than the subject of the verb יְקוֹמֵם. This is assumed on the basis of v. 9 in which עַמִּי is the object of oppression.[21] On the basis of this emendation, it may be assumed that the antecedent of the 1st person pron. suff. is Yahweh, in which case Yahweh is the speaker. In light of the characteristic of the text and the presence of the elements typical of the disputation speech, it is more plausible that the speaker in this verse is the prophet. As such the antecedent of the pron. suff. would be the prophet (cf. 3.2). One challenge to the latter interpretation is that in Micah, when used in reference to the prophet, עַמִּי usually is portrayed as the object of oppression, as a sub-group in Israel. Nonetheless, it is not necessary to emend the text in order to present עַמִּי as the object against whom an enemy arises. The conceptuality of the text allows for the עַמִּי as enemy to the extent that עַמִּי refers to the people of Israel as a whole (cf. 2.3). Also, 2.11 suggests that the עַמִּי is not entirely faithful to Yahweh's message.

This emendation assumes that אֶתְמוּל arose as a dittography from מִמּוּל. However, an emendation of וְאֶתְמוּל עַמִּי is not necessary for an understanding of the terms. The word אֶתְמוּל may connote 'formerly, recently' (cf. 2 Sam. 15.20; Isa. 30.33). The LXX has this nuance in its rendering of the phrase.

2.8b   MT   יְקוֹמֵם

The verb יְקוֹמֵם is also emended to קָמִים or תְּקוֹמְמוּ.[22] Wolff proposes that the piel (contra poel) may be the original reading with אַתֶּם as the original subject. He therefore translates the verse as follows: 'Against

20. Thus Mays, *Micah*, p. 67; Wolff, *Micah*, p. 70; Allen, *The Books*, p. 292; cf. Vuilleumier, 'Michée', p. 31, וְאַתֶּם עַל־עַמִּי לְעָמִּי לְאוֹיֵב תְּקוֹמְמוּ; Wellhausen, *Die Kleinen Propheten*, p. 138. Cf. Barthélemy, *CTAT*, p. 734, for further discussion.

21. Allen, *Micah*, p. 293.

22. Wolff, *Micah*, p. 70; J. Wellhausen, *Die Kleinen Propheten* (Berlin: W. de Gruyter, 1963), p. 138.

my people you come forth as enemies'.[23] This emendation is also unnecessary.

2.8c-c   MT   ממול שלמה אדר

The term ממול in the MT has been emended by scholars as follows: מעל שלם האדרת, 'you strip the cloak from the peaceful'.[24] Those who emend the text argue that without such an emendation, ממול שלמה cannot fit into its present context. The emendation makes the final ה of שלמה the article of the following word, thus האדר. It also assumes that as a result of haplography, the final ת of אדרת was lost. Here the MT is retain on the grounds that it represents the more difficult reading and also a reading from which others may have been derived.

2.9a   MT   תעוניה...עלליה
         LXX   ἡγούμενοι λαοῦ μου ἀπορριφήσονται ἐκ τῶν οἰκιῶν
                 τρυφῆς αὐτῶν

The LXX refers to the leaders of the people who are evicted from their houses; and thus uses the masc. plur. article. The MT, however, refers to the women (נשי), thus fem. plur. pron. suff. are expected (תעוניהן, עלליהן). Instead, fem. sing. suff. are present (תעוניה, עלליה).

Chapter 3

1. *Translation*

1 And I said:
   Listen you heads of Jacob,
   and leaders of the house of Israel.
   Is it not your responsibility to know justice,

2 who hate good and love evil,
   who strip their skin off of them,
   and their flesh from off their bones;

3 and who devour the flesh of my people,
   strip their skin off of them,
   break their bones,
   and chop them as into a pot,
   like meat into a caldron?

23. Wolff, *Micah*, pp. 70-71; BDB, p. 878; Vuilleumier, 'Michée', p. 31; Mays, *Micah*, p. 67.
24. Mays, *Micah*, p. 67; Wolff, *Micah*, p. 71; cf. Wellhausen, *Die Kleinen Propheten*, p. 138, מעל שלמים.

4 Then they will cry out to Yahweh;
 but he will not answer them.
 Instead he will hide his face from them in that time,
 because they have done evil deeds.

5 Thus says Yahweh concerning the prophets
 who lead my people astray,
 who bite with their teeth and proclaim 'peace';
 but whoever does not give according to their demand,
 against him they sanctify war.

6 Therefore it will be night to you without vision,
 darkness will be to you without divination.
 And the sun will go down upon the prophets,
 the day will darken upon them.

7 Then the seers will be ashamed,
 the diviners will be disgraced;
 and they will cover their lips,
 because there is no answer from God.

8 But as for me, I am filled with power—
 with the spirit of Yahweh—
 with justice and courage,
 to proclaim to Jacob his crime
 and to Israel his sin.

9 Listen to this you heads of the house of Jacob,
 leaders of the house of Israel;
 who abhor justice,
 and pervert all that is right;

10 who build Zion with blood,
 and Jerusalem with wickedness.

11 Her heads give judgment for a bribe,
 her priests teach for a price:
 and her prophets divine for money.
 Yet they rely on Yahweh saying:
 'Is not Yahweh in our midst?
 Evil will not come against us'.

12 Therefore because of you,
 Zion will be plowed as a field,
 Jerusalem will become a heap of ruins,
 and the temple mount will be a forest.

Chapter 4

1. *Translation*

1 And it will happen in the latter days,
 the mountain of the house of Yahweh will be established

as the head of the mountains.
It will be lifted up above the hills,
and peoples will stream to it.

2   And many nations will come
and they will say:
'Come let us go up to the mountain of Yahweh,
and to the house of the God of Jacob;
that he will teach us his way,
and that we may walk in his path'.
For from Zion instruction goes forth,
and the word of Yahweh from Jerusalem.

3   He will judge between many peoples;
he will adjudicate between numerous distant nations;
and they will beat their swords into plowshares,
their spears into pruning hooks.
Nation will not take up sword against nation,
and they will no longer learn warfare.

4   Each man will sit under his vine,
under his fig tree and there will be none to terrify.
For the mouth of Yahweh Sabaoth has spoken.

5   For all the people walk,
every man in the name of his god;
but we will walk in the name of Yahweh our God,
for ever and ever.

6   In that day, declares Yahweh:
I will assemble the lame,
and those whom I have scattered
and those whom I have afflicted.

7   And I will make the lame into a remnant,
and the wounded into a mighty nation.
Then Yahweh will rule over them on Mount Zion,
from now and forever.

8   And you, O tower of the flock,
hill of the daughter of Zion—
unto you shall come the dominion of the former days,
the kingdom of the daughter of Jerusalem.

9   But now you——
Why do you cry out loud?
Is there no king in you?
Or has your counselor perished
that anguish grips you like a woman in labor?

10   Writhe and howl, daughter of Zion like a woman in labor;
for now you will go out from the city
and dwell in the field.
You shall go to Babylon,

there you will be delivered;

there Yahweh will redeem you from the hand of your enemies.

11 But now many nations are assembled against you saying:

'Let her be desecrated and let our eyes gloat over Zion'.

12 But they do not know the plans of Yahweh;

and they do not understand his thoughts—

that he gathers them like sheaves to the threshing floor.

13 Arise and thresh, daughter of Zion;

for I will make your horn into iron,

and your hooks into bronze;

that you may trample many peoples,

and devote their gains to Yahweh,

their strength to the Lord of the whole earth.

14 Now gash yourself, daughter of the troops;

a siege is set up against us.

With a rod they strike the cheek of the judge of Israel.

Chapter 5

1. *Translation*

1 But you Bethlehem Ephrathah,

who are small among the tribes of Judah.

From you [one] will come forth for me to be a ruler in Israel;

and his origins are from of old, from former days.

2 Therefore he will give them up until the time

when she who is in labor has given birth.

Then the rest of his brothers will return

to the children of Israel.

3 And he will stand and shepherd

in the strength of Yahweh,

in the majesty of the name of Yahweh, his God.

And they will endure, for now he will become great

to the ends of the earth.

4 And this will be peace.

When Assyria comes into our land

and when it treads upon our fortress;

then we will set up against him seven shepherds

and eight chiefs.

5 And they will shepherd the land of Assyria with a sword,

and the land of Nimrod with an unsheathed sword;

and he will deliver from Assyria

when it comes to our land

and when he treads our territory.

6   And the remnant of Jacob will be in the midst of many peoples,
    like dew from Yahweh,
    like showers upon the plants,
    which does not tarry for man
    nor wait for the sons of man.

7   Then the remnant of Jacob will be among the nations
    in the midst of many peoples,
    as a lion among the beasts of the forest,
    as a young lion among the sheep,
    which tramples when it passes
    and tears down but there is no deliverer.

8   You will raise your hand against your adversary;
    and all your enemies will be cut off.

9   And in that day, declares Yahweh:
    I will cut off your horses from your midst;
    and I will destroy your chariots.

10 I will cut off the cities of your land;
    and I will demolish all your fortresses.

11 Then I will cut off the sorcerers from your hand;
    and you will have no soothsayers.

12 And I will cut off your images;
    and your pillars from your midst;
    so that you will no longer bow down to the work of your hands.

13 And I will up root your Asherim from your midst;
    and I will destroy your cities.

14 And I will take vengeance in anger and wrath
    on the nations who have not heeded.

Chapter 6

1. *Translation*

1   Hear what[a] Yahweh says:
    Arise! Plead before[b] the mountains;
    and let the hills hear your voice.

2   Hear mountains[a] Yahweh's controversy,
    and you enduring foundations[b] of the earth;
    for Yahweh has a controversy with his people,
    with Israel he contends.

3   My people, what have I done to you,
    and how have I wearied you?[a]
    Testify against me!

4   For I brought you up from the land of Egypt,
    from the house of slavery I redeemed you;
    and I sent before you Moses, Aaron, and Miriam.[a]

5   My people,
      remember what Balak, [a]king of Moab,[a] plotted;[b]
      and what Balaam, [a]son of Beor,[a] answered him;
      [c]...from Shittim to Gilgal;
      in order to know the saving acts[d] of Yahweh.

6   With what shall I come before Yahweh
      and bow down before God on high?
      Shall I come before him with burnt offerings,
      with calves a year old?

7   Would Yahweh be pleased with a thousand rams,
      with tens of thousands rivers of oil?[a]
      Shall I give my firstborn for my crimes,
      the fruit of my body for the sin of my soul?

8   It has been told[a] to you, man, what is good.
      And what does Yahweh demand from you
      except to do justice, love *hesed*
      and to walk humbly[b] with your God.

9   The voice of Yahweh calls to the city—
      [a]And it is wisdom to fear your name.[a]
      Hear [b]O tribe and assembly of the city[b]—

10 Can I forget[a] the house of the wicked, treasures of wickedness,
      and the accursed ephah?

11 Shall I acquit[a] him [who trades] with wicked balances
      and with a bag of deceitful stones?—

12 whose rich are full of violence
      and whose inhabitants speak falsehood,
      and their tongue is deceitful in their mouths.

13 But I have surely begun to smite you
      to make you desolate because of your sins—

14 You will eat and not be satisfied;
      and your hunger[a] will be inside you;
      and you will put away[b] but not save;
      and what you save I will give to the sword.

15 You will plant but will not reap.
      You will tread olives but you will not anoint yourself with oil;
      [you will have] new wine but will not drink wine.

16 For you have kept the statues of Omri,
      and all the deeds of the house of Ahab;
      and you live according to their counsels—
      In order that I will give you up to destruction,
      your inhabitants to hissing;
      and you will endure the scorn of my people.

2. Text-Critical Notes

> 6.1a   MT   אֵת אֲשֶׁר־יהוה אמר...
>
>   LXX   ...λόγον κυρίου· κύριος ἓιπεν
>
>   LXX^B ...λόγον· κύριος κύριος ἓιπεν
>
>   LXX^A ....λόγον κυρίου ἅ ὁ κύριος ἓιπεν

Kennicott Ms adds הדבר (Hear the word which Yahweh says)

The LXX versions represent attempts to clarify the relative clause אֵת
אֲשֶׁר which functions as object of the main clause. The Kennicott Ms by
adding הדבר, makes the object explicit, and the relative clause thus
modifies the object. Modern scholars address this variant in at least two
ways: (a) following the MT 'what Yahweh says',[25] and (b) following the
Kennicott Ms 'hear the word which Yahweh says'.[26]

> 6.1b   MT   ריב אֶת־הֶהרים
>
>   LXX   κρίθητι πρὸς τὰ ὄρη

The multivalency is due to both conceptual and textual difficulties and
most likely not an orthographical error. The MT ריב אֶת־הֶהרים is
multivalent and specifically the translation of the particle אֵת.[27] At issue
is the role played by the mountains—accused, witness, or judges. The
LXX perceives this multivalency and attempts to clarify the role of the
mountains by use of the preposition προς. In doing so, the LXX makes
clear that the mountains are not the accused but the witnesses. Wellhausen, in following the LXX, suggests the emendation אֶל, 'before', the
mountains.[28] The emendation represents a harmonization with v. 2 in
which the mountains are called upon as witnesses. While this emendation has been adopted by many scholars,[29] others see no need for

---

25. Renaud, *La Formation*, p. 289; Ewald, *Commentary on the Prophets*,
p. 326; Procksch, *Die kleinen prophetischen Schriften*, p. 19; Allen, *The Books*,
p. 363; Mays, *Micah*, p. 127; Vuilleumier, 'Michée', p.70; Wellhausen, *Die Kleinen
Propheten*, p. 25; Waltke, 'Micah', pp. 724, 726; Hillers, *Micah*, p. 75; Wolff,
Micah, p. 164.

26. Smith, *Micah, Zephaniah*, pp. 118-19; cf.Willis, 'Structure, Setting', p. 338,
who further emends the text to clarify the addressee (the prophet) thus reading:
'Hear now the word which Yahweh is speaking to me'.

27. J.A. Sanders, 'A Multivalent Text: Psalm 151.3-4 Revisited', *HAR* 8 (1984),
pp. 167-84, note especially the idea of the hermeneutic of 'readings'.

28. Wellhausen, *Die Kleinen Propheten*, p. 146.

29. Vuilleumier, 'Michée', p. 70; Ewald, *Commentary on the Prophets*, p. 326;

it.[30] Still others see the mountains, who have witnessed the whole of Israel's history, as being called upon to be judge.[31] Another proposal is to render the particle את as an adversative 'against', in which case the mountains are the accused.[32] Wolff argues that in 6.1b the mountains as the accused are used as metaphors for the nations (Ezek. 6.3; 36.4, 6; cf. Nah. 1.5).[33] He further argues that v. 1b is a redactional element by which the redactor fostered a connection with the preceding unit and specifically with 4.13; 5.7. In this line of argument, Israel is the plaintiff. Wolff, in order to account for the different roles of ההרים, then contends that v. 2 is the original beginning of ch. 6. Even he, however, recognizes that his interpretation is highly disputable. Wolff's suggestion is not to be discounted but retained on the basis of the occurrence of the verb-preposition combination with the adversative meaning.

Notably the emendation to אל, following the LXX, is unnecessary since את can have the meaning 'before'.[34] Limburg notes that, in each of its occurrences, the construction ריב את has the meaning of 'to make an accusation against' (Num. 20.13; Judg. 8.11; Isa. 45.9; 50.8; Jer. 2.9; Neh. 5.7; 13.11, 17).[35] The difference in Mic. 6.1 is that 'the value of the preposition is clearly "before" as in Gen. 20.16; Isa. 30.8'.[36]

6.2a	MT	שמעו הרים
	LXX	ἀκούσατε, λαοί
	LXX[B]	ἀκούσατε, ὄρη
	LXX[A]	ἀκούσατε, βουνοί

The LXX reading λαοί seems to be a harmonization with 1.2—שמעו עמים כלם—where the focus is the peoples, that is, the nations vis-à-vis Israel. With this reading the parallelism between 6.2aα and 6.2aβ is

Keil and Delitzsch, *The Twelve Minor Prophets*, pp. 492-93; Procksch, *Die kleinen prophetischen Schriften*, p. 119; Hillers, *Micah*, p. 75; Allen, *The Books*, p. 362; Mays, *Micah*, pp. 127-28; Waltke, 'Micah', p. 727.

30. Willis, 'Structure, Setting', pp. 335-36.
31. Smith, *Micah, Zephaniah*, pp. 118-20.
32. Renaud, *La Formation*, pp. 289-91; Wolff, *Micah*, pp. 172-73.
33. Wolff, *Micah*, p. 169.
34. BDB, p. 86.
35. Limburg, 'The Root ריב', pp. 296, 301.
36. Limburg, 'The Root ריב', p. 296.

destroyed unless v. 2aβ is otherwise rendered. LXX[B] [37] retains the parallelism between v. 2aα and v. 2aβ and with that the concept of the mountains as witnesses.

6.2b   MT   והאתנים מסדי ארץ
        LXX   καὶ αἱ φάραγγες θεμέλια τῆς γῆς

The textual variant is due to attempts to deal with the conceptuality of the text. Scholars have suggested the reading והאזינו in place of והאתנים. This would create parallel clauses each with its own verb—that is, שמעו and אזן (cf. Hos. 5.1; Isa. 1.2, 10; Deut. 32.1). This parallelism is observed in Mic. 1.2a+b, namely, שמע plus עמים parallel to הקשבי plus ארץ. In the MT the term האתנים is the modifier of מסדי ארץ. In this instance, the phrase is governed by the verb שמעו in v. 2aα in such a way that the verb governs parallel nouns: הרים and האתנים מסדי ארץ. The 'summons to hear' therefore has one addressee, 'the mountains' (collectively), qualified as the enduring foundations of the earth.

Wellhausen proposes reading והאזינו in parallel with שמעו.[38] This reading has been adopted by many including Willis and Smith.[39] Wolff explains the variant as a copying error—that is, haplography—where the scribe omitted the verb והאזינו because of its orthographical similarity to האתנים.[40] Accordingly, he argues that the MT probably followed a *Vorlage* in which האתנים functioned as an object of the verb והאזינו.

Another explanation was offered by Haupt who argues for והאזינו as the original reading that was corrupted in the transmission process. After discounting the LXX reading as merely a guess, he constructs his argument on the basis of various conjectural emendations.[41] The mem (מ) of the word האתנים is due to dittography with the mem (מ) of מסדי; metathesis of זי resulted in יז which was subsequently confused thus yielding ה, because of similarity of ז and ה in the old script. In this case Haupt reads: והאזינו מסדי ארץ.[42]

---

37. Lancelot C.L. Brenton, *The Septuagint with Apocrypha* (Peabody, MA: Hendrickson, 4th edn, 1992), p. 1101.

38. Wellhausen, *Die Kleinen Propheten*, p. 146.

39. Willis, 'Structure, Setting', p. 339; Smith, *Micah, Zephaniah*, p. 119.

40. Wolff, *Micah*, p. 164.

41. Haupt, 'Critical Notes on Micah', p. 220.

42. Haupt, 'Critical Notes on Micah', p. 248. Cf. Smith, *Micah, Zephaniah*, p. 119, who shares this explanation for the MT reading; Mays, *Micah*, p. 128, also argues that the final mem (מ) of the MT reading האתנים is due to dittography.

Here it is argued that the MT reading be adopted on the following basis. (a) The adjective derived from יתן 'permanent, enduring' is well attested (Gen. 49.24; Exod. 14.27; Job 12.19; 33.19; 1 Kgs 8.2). Specifically in association with נחל (Amos 5.24), and נהר (Ps. 74.15, cf. גוי, Jer. 5.15) it is used to characterize enduring natural elements. (b) Grammatically the occurrences of the adjective before the noun may indicate emphasis[43] (cf. Jon. 2.7[6][44] 'roots' of the mountains). From this perspective, the order of construction would be intelligible.[45] (c) The emendation is highly conjectural and is probably a harmonization if not a recollection of similar formulations. For example:

> Give ear, O heavens, and I will speak:
> let the earth hear the words of my mouth (Deut. 32.1; cf. 4.26).

> Hear O heavens, and listen O earth (Isa. 1.2).

> Hear this O priest!
> Give ear O house of Israel (Hos. 5.1).

6.3   MT   עמי מה־עשיתי לך
        LXX   ἢ τί ἐλύπησά σε ἢ τί παρηνώχλησά σοι;

The LXX reading is probably a recollection of other texts wherein the concept of being wearied often occurs in parallel expressions:

> Your new moons and your appointed festivals my soul hates;
> they have become a burden to me,
> I am weary of bearing them (Isa. 1.14).

and

> Surely now God has worn me out;
> he has made desolate all my company (Job 16.7).

6.4   MT   את־משה אהרן ומרים:
        LXX   καὶ Ααρων καὶ Μαριαμ

The LXX reading supports the MT. However, it has been proposed that עמי of v. 5 be emended to עמו and transposed to the end of v. 4 thus reading: 'I send Moses before you, Aaron and Miriam with him'.[46] This

---

43. Waltke and O'Connor, *Syntax*, §12.2.

44. This text has its own difficulty. The apparatus suggests a transposition of the terms such that the adjective would follow the noun.

45. Contra Wolff, *Micah*, p. 164.

46. Lindblom, *Micha literarisch untersucht*, p. 99; Mays, *Micah*, p. 128; Allen, *The Books*, p. 364.

conjecture is the result of the perception of Aaron's and Miriam's roles as subordinate to Moses'.[47] The three appear together only in the name list in Num. 26.59 (cf. 1 Chron. 5.29 [Eng. 6.3]). Elsewhere only Moses and Aaron are mentioned (Exod. 7.1; Ps. 105.26). In the former text Aaron's roles is subordinated to that of Moses.[48] In Num. 12.1-16 where Aaron's and Miriam's jealousy of Moses is reported, the narrative itself portrays Aaron and Miriam as being aware of their subordination. However, it is possible that the text of Micah reflects a different tradition about the roles of the siblings as Israel's leaders than Num. 12.1-16, where the presumption of Miriam to assert equality with Moses is punished by God. Arguments for the equal status of the three are usually based on all three being referred to as prophets: Aaron and Miriam in Exod. 15.20 and Moses (implicitly) in Hos. 12.13.[49]

6.5a-a   MT   מלך מראב and בן־בעור

It has been argued that the appositives to Balak and Balaam be deleted.[50] This deletion is suggested on the grounds that the appositives 'overload the meter' and are added on analogy with Numbers 22.[51] Another suggestion is that בן־בעור is a misreading of בעברך. On that basis, it has been suggested that מלך מואב be deleted and that בן־בעור be transposed to the beginning of the following phrase where a verb appears to be missing.[52] Wolff argues against this emendation on the grounds of probable chronological sequence—that is, '[it is] difficult to image as are the consequences of such a construction, namely, that only after these corruptions crept in, the phrase "the king of Moab" was inserted into the text'.[53] He therefore proposes that as a result of haplography of ב(י)ן בעור (defectively written), the phrase at the beginning of v. 5b was lost in the final phrase of v. 5a.[54] Wolff's argument is plausible in that the omission of a verb is evidenced by the resulting

---

47. While Allen, *The Books*, p. 364, for example, favors the emendation he denies that it is motivated by a perception of the subordinate roles of Aaron and Miriam.

48. Willis, 'Structure, Setting', p. 340.

49. Vuilleumier, 'Michée', p. 71.

50. Smith, *Micah, Zephaniah*, p. 119; Lindblom, *Micha literarisch untersucht*, p. 99; Vuilleumier, 'Michée', pp. 71-72.

51. Mays, *Micah*, p. 128.

52. Vuilleumier, 'Michée', p. 72.

53. Wolff, *Micah*, p. 165.

54. Wolff, *Micah*, p. 165.

sentence fragment. Second, the reconstruction of בין־בעור from בן־בעור does not require conjectural emendations that resist the logic of the plausible chronological emergence of the reading. Furthermore, the reconstruction also completes the reference to the saving acts—that is, passage from Shittim to Gilgal.

Others suggest transposition of זכר־נא to v. 5b thus reading זכר־נא מן־השטים.[55] While this creates a parallel structure it does not resolve the lack of verb to govern the preposition מן. There are a range of suggestions concerning the verb/phrase to be supplied at the beginning of v. 5b. Haupt argues for a gloss: 'Remember how your fathers were marvelously helped'.[56] Willis proposes: 'Remember what happened...'[57] Lindblom argues for 'and what I did...'[58] Ewald suggests that the sentence fragment in the MT is to be deleted on account of it being 'a marginal observation intended to serve as a reference to the last portion of the Pentateuch where the history of Bileam might be found, comp Num. 25.1; 31.8; Josh. 4.20'.[59] The difficulty with Ewald's argument is that it changes the conceptuality of the text. Thus, rather than the text including the entrance into the Promised Land, it stops right outside the land. The extent to which one adheres to this tradition of God redeeming Israel, leading them up to but not into the land, is the extent to which Ewald's argument will find support. How plausible would be Yahweh if indeed Yahweh's works are portrayed in such as way as to suggest that even the deliverance—whose goal is entrance into the land—was aborted by Yahweh. (See the discussion of 6.5c below.)

6.5b   LXX   κατὰ σοῦ

This gloss, which provides a complement to the verb and thus clarification of the allusion, is unnecessary since in the Balak–Balaam account there is no ambiguity as to whose demise Balak sought. The LXX clarification may also be a device of intensification to emphasize that the recipients of God's benevolence are the same as those addressed by the vocative.

6.5c   LXX   ἀπὸ τῶν σχοίνων

55. Smith, *Micah, Zephaniah*, p. 119.
56. Haupt, 'Critical Notes on Micah', p. 248.
57. Willis, 'Structure, Setting', p. 340.
58. Lindblom, *Micha literarisch untersucht*, p. 100.
59. Ewald, *Commentary on the Prophets*, p. 351.

It has been suggested that the LXX had in mind the Sea of Reeds.[60] But no further suggestion is offered as to the nature of the reminiscence. The plausibility of this account would have to note the LXX reading in Exod. 15.22—ἀπὸ φαλάσσης ἐρυφρᾶς—but v. 5 is not reminiscent of Exod. 15.22 in terms of vocabulary. The other possibility is a conceptual reminiscence. A summarization of God's saving acts from the Sea of Reeds to Gilgal encompassing all the events in between. The MT does not allow such a translation or conceptuality. The NRSV rendering 'and happened from Shittim to Gilgal' suggests that the Balak–Balaam incident is one of many incidents.

The LXX's conceptuality would indicate the journey's beginning from Egypt to the journey's end—the first stopping place in the Promise Land—with both beginning and end marked by a miraculous crossing (Exod. 14.21-31; Josh. 2.10-14; 3.1-17). The strongest support for the explanation of the LXX reading is:

> Those twelve stones…Joshua set up in Gilgal…
> For the Lord your God dried up the waters of the Jordan for you until you crossed over, as the Lord your God did to the Reed Sea, which he dried up for us until we crossed over,
> so that all the peoples of the earth may know that he hand of the Lord is mighty, and so that you may fear the Lord your God forever' (Josh. 4.20a, 23-24).

Here the setting up of the twelve stones at Gilgal is done in light of God's miraculous acts on behalf of Israel as made poignant by the 'crossing'.

Also in support of the LXX reading is v. 5b 'that you may know…', which is analogous to Josh. 4.24. The present writer suggests that the LXX had a different conceptuality that account for its reading. Rather than signifying the last phase of the journey, it depicts the departure and arrival into the Promised Land—signifying the stages—Exodus and guidance through the wilderness, and a remembrance of the whole. Thus למען governs the immediately preceding phrase which itself is a concise statement of the whole.

6.5d   MT   צדקות יהוה

In light of the 1st person style of vv. 3-5 it has been suggested that יהוה צדקות be emended to צדקותי.[61] The explanation offered is that the final

---

60. Wolff, *Micah*, p. 165.
61. Lindblom, *Micha literarisch untersucht*, p. 99; Mays, *Micah*, p. 128.

ʼ (yod) was mistaken for an abbreviation of יהוה.[62] Others, in one way or another, explain the phrase as a normative 3rd person style of the circumlocution.[63] The 3rd person may be accounted for by a change in speaker.

Willis supports the MT on the basis of the prophet as speaker.[64] It is possible that the prophet is speaker and that there is a switch from 1st to 3rd person. However, Willis gives no clarification as to when this switch occurred: at the beginning of v. 5 such that the מעי is used like in 3.3-5—the prophet identifying with the people, or just in v. 5bβ such that prophet is calling the people to remembrance.

The present writer retains the MT on the basis of the various attestations in the Old Testament (e.g. Judg. 5.11). Other examples include:

> Now therefore take your stand, so that I may enter into judgment with you before the Lord, and I will declare to you all the saving deeds of the Lord that he performed for you and your ancestors (1 Sam. 12.7)

and

> O Lord, in view of all your righteous acts, let your anger and wrath, we pray, turn away from your city Jerusalem, your holy mountain… (Dan. 9.16; cf. Ps. 103.6).[65]

6.7a	LXX	χειμάρρων
	LXX^B	χιμαρων
	LXX^A	ἀρνῶν

Though some assume that variants in the Greek versions are solely orthographical errors,[66] the variants may be a conceptual difference facilitated by an orthographical similarity of two terms: χειμάρρων and χιμαρων. Conceptually LXX^{A+B} read 'fat goats' and 'fat sheep', respectively, creating a parallel with אלפי אילים of v. 7aα. These readings suggest an increase in the specified sacrifice from a thousand to tens of thousands. These is no difference in the type of sacrifice—animal to

62. Contra Wolff, *Micah*, p. 165.

63. Hillers, *Micah*, p. 76 (cf. Lam. 2.20, 22; 3.35-36, 66; Amos 4.11); Renaud, *La Formation*, p. 296, sees it as part of the rapid switch from God and messenger attested in prophetic literature.

64. Willis, 'Structure, Setting', p. 341.

65. Wolff, *Micah*, p. 165, argues for the retention of the MT; however, he is mistaken in his claim that Judg. 5.11, 1 Sam. 12.7 and Ps. 103.6 are Yahweh speeches.

66. Wolff, *Micah*, p. 165; Hillers, *Micah*, p. 76.

libation—according to the MT reading. In the LXX, therefore, the enumeration is from lesser to greater quantity of burnt offerings. Thus, the difference in conceptuality is one of the range of types of sacrifice and their quantitative significance (MT) versus the quantitative significance of one type of sacrifice (LXX). The qualitative issue is not to be stressed for only the best was offered as sacrifice. What is more likely—that is, to support the claim that Israel has been wearied—is an emphasis on quantity. In other instances where Israel is wearied, it is the quantity of the sacrifice that is indicated as the reason for the resulting weariness. (See Chapter 5 above.)

6.8   MT   הגיד
       LXX   εἰ ἀνηγγέλη σοι

The LXX (aroist passive) interprets הגיד (hiph. perf. 3rd person masc. sing.) in the passive sense. Wellhausen reads הֻגַּד (hoph.) seeking to follow the LXX.[67] This emendation is unnecessary since the 3rd person masc. sing. may be used with the passive sense.

The MT of vv. 9-10 poses major difficulties. While some omit parts of the text,[68] others have proposed a rearrangement of the text such that v. 12 comes directly after v. 9a.[69] Others have opted to interpret the verses in their present order while explaining the textual difficulties.[70]

6.9a   MT   ותושיה יראה שמך
        LXX   καὶ σώσει φοβουμένους τὸ ὄνομα αὐτοῦ

The LXX assumes והושיע יראי שמו. 'And he will deliver those who fear his name'. It assumes ישע, 'to help, deliver', and ירא, 'to fear'. The LXX also uses a 3rd person pronoun αὐτοῦ presupposing the 3rd person pron. suff., שמו. Thus while the MT assumes a 2nd person address—possibly a prayer[71]—the LXX assumes a continuation of the 3rd person account.

---

67. Wellhausen, *Die Kleinen Propheten*, p. 147.

68. Eor example, Smith, *Micah, Zephaniah*, p. 131, assumes that v. 9b is a gloss and therefore omits it.

69. Willis, 'Structure, Setting', pp. 132-33, 343-44; Vuilleumier, 'Michée', pp. 75-76. Cf. Mays, *Micah*, pp. 143-44, who favors various emendation in order to sense of the text. He places v. 12 after v. 9b and omits v. 10aα.

70. Allen, *The Books*, p. 375; Wolff, *Micah*, p. 185.

71. Willis, 'Structure, Setting', p. 134, categorizes v. 9a as a 'liturgical parenthesis' expressed in confidence by the worshipping community in affirmation of Yahweh. Cf. Vuilleumier, 'Michée', p. 75.

The LXX further indicates that Yahweh's deliverance of the people is dependent on their response to Yahweh. The use of והושיע may be its attempt to clarify the text due a perceived ambiguity resulting from the term's uses and etymology. In the MT ותושיה has various nuances including: 'help, deliverance, wisdom, wealth, and security' (cf. Prov. 2.7; 3.21; 8.14; Job 6.13; Isa. 28.29).[72] Thus, v. 9a may indicate the nature of 'wisdom' by means of the predicate nominative—namely, to fear the name of Yahweh is wisdom. Here, as in v. 8, what is indicated is that a regard for Yahweh is suggested or even necessary. Wolff suggests that the MT is the infinitive form of ירא.[73] However, Waltke cites Deut. 33.9 in translating ראה as 'to regard'.[74]

6.9b	MT	ומי יעדה
	LXX	καὶ τίς κοσμήσει πόλιν

It is generally agreed that the MT is unintelligible.[75] The LXX reading presupposes ומי יעדה עיר. This reading takes the first word of v. 10, עוד—as the last word of v. 9b. It further presupposes a misreading of י for ו and ר for ד. On this basis the text has been emended in light of the LXX. Most follow Wellhausen in reading ומועד העיר.[76] The latter reading provides a parallel with לעיר of v. 9a.[77]

6.10	MT	האש
	LXX	μὴ πῦρ

The LXX presupposes הָאֵשׁ, 'Is there not fire?'. The apparatus proposes האשה or האשׁא. The first option האשה, 'to forget', derives from the root

72. Wolff, *Micah*, pp. 186, 191. As a basis for his argument he points to the use of the term as a synonym for עצה in Prov. 8.14 and Isa. 28.29. He further argues that the term be translated 'wisdom' in light of its similarity to wisdom tradition and to the wording in various petitions (Mal. 3.30; Pss. 61.6; 102.16; 111.10a; 112.1).

73. Wolff, *Micah*, p. 186; Wellhausen, *Die kleinen Propheten*, p. 147; cf. Smith, *Micah, Zephaniah*, p. 130; Willis, 'Structure, Setting', p. 343.

74. Waltke, 'Micah', p. 737.

75. Waltke, 'Micah'; Wellhausen, *Die kleinen Propheten*, p. 148; Wolff, *Micah*, p. 186.

76. Lindblom, *Micha literarisch untersucht*, p. 116; Smith, *Micah, Zephaniah*, p. 130; Vuilleumier, 'Michée', p. 75; Willis, 'Structure, Setting', p. 344; Waltke, 'Micah', p. 737.

77. Waltke, 'Micah', pp. 737-38 for further discussion.

נשׂה.[78] This emendation adds a final ה to the MT in order to facilitate a parallel with the verb in v. 11, האזכה. The first ה is then taken as an interrogative. The difficulty or rarity of אשׂ plus interrogative is the grounds upon which the emendation is often made. The second option האשׂא, 'to forgive', derives from the root נשׂא, 'to lift, carry'.[79]

6.11	MT	...האזכה
	LXX	δικαιωθήσεται ἐν ζυγῷ ἄνομος
	RSV	Shall I acquit the man with wicked scales?

The LXX reading translates 'shall the wicked be justified...?' According to Waltke, the MT, 'If I forget...', is from the root זכך/זכה, 'to be clean, innocent'. There are a variety of suggestions including: הַאֲזֻכֶּה, following the Vulgate '*justificabo*',[80] הַאֲזֻכֶּה or הַאֲזֻכֵּהוּ.[81]

| 6.14a | MT | וישׁחך |
| | LXX | καὶ σκοτάσει ἐν σοί |

The difficulty of the reading lies in the etymology of the word. Accordingly, Wolff argues that the LXX reading (= יֶחְשַׁךְ) 'and darkness will be in you' is due to a misreading resulting from metathesis of ה and שׂ. On the grounds that it does not follow the typical form of the futility curse as seen in the rest of vv. 14 and 15, he further argues that v. 14aβ is an interpolation.[82] Quite apart from the form of v. 14aβ, is the difficulty in translating the MT reading. Thus several proposals have been made including: 'dysentery'.[83] In light of the immediate context (תאכל ולא תשׂבע), this *hapax legomenon* may be translated as 'hunger'.[84]

78. Wellhausen, *Die kleinen Propheten*, p. 148; Waltke, 'Micah', p. 738; Willis, 'Structure, Setting', p. 345; Smith, *Micah, Zephaniah*, p. 130.

79. Vuilleumier, 'Michée', p. 76; Lindblom, *Micha literarisch untersucht*, p. 116.

80. Vuilleumier, 'Michée', p. 76; Wellhausen, *Die kleinen Propheten*, p. 148; Lindblom, *Micha literarisch untersucht*, p. 116

81. Smith, *Micah, Zephaniah*, p. 130.

82. Wolff, *Micah*, pp. 187-88; the form to which he refers is the main clause consisting of two verbs plus ולא (cf. vv. 14aα, 14bα, 15a, 15b).

83. Waltke, 'Micah', p. 741; contrast Wolff, *Micah*, pp. 187, 196, who translates the term as 'hunger.'

84. Cf. Renaud, *La Formation*, pp. 331-32 for a discussion of the various emendations.

6.14b MT   וְתַסֵּג

      LXX   ἐκνεύσει

      NRSV   you put away

      RSV   you will store up

The root is presummably סוג with the nuance of removing something secretly, that is, to put away (cf., regarding the boundary stone/marker, Hos. 5.10; Deut. 19.14).[85]

Chapter 7

1. *Translation*

1 Woe is me.
    For I have become as a gatherer of summer fruit,
    as a gleaner of the vintage;
    there is no cluster to eat
    no ripe fig as my soul desires.

2 The faithful has perished from the land;
    and there is no upright person among men.
    All of them lie in wait for blood,
    each hunts his brother to death.

3 [Their] hands are upon evil to do it well—
    the official makes demands;
    the judge [demands] a bribe;
    the great one speaks the desire of his soul
    and twists it.

4 The best of them is like a brier,
    the most upright like a thorn hedge.
    The day[a] of your watchman, of your visitation, has come;
    now their confusion[b] will come.

5 Do not believe the neighbor.
    Do not trust a friend.
    from her who lies in your bosom,
    guard the doors of your mouth.

6 For a son treats his father as a fool;
    a daughter rises up against her mother;
    a daughter-in-law against her mother-in-law;
    a man's enemies are the men of his own house.

7 But I will watch for Yahweh.
    I will wait for the God of my deliverance,
    my God will hear me.

---

85. Wolff, *Micah*, pp. 187, 196; Waltke, 'Micah', p. 741.

8   Do not rejoice over me, my enemy.
    When I fallen, I will rise;
    when I sit in darkness,
    Yahweh is my light.
9   I will endure Yahweh's wrath—
    because I have sinned against him—
    until he pleads my case and executes justice for me.
    And he will bring me to the light;
    I will see his deliverance.
10 Then my enemy will see,
    and shame will cover her.
    The one who says to me:
    'Where is Yahweh your God?'
    My eyes will stare at her,
    now she is trampled like dust in the street.
11 A day to build your walls,
    that day when your border will be extended;
12 a day when even to you will come [peoples]
    from Assyria and the cities of Egypt,
    and from Egypt to the Euphrates,
    from sea to sea and from mountain to mountain.
13 And the earth will become desolate
    because of her inhabitants,
    from the fruit of her deeds.
14 Shepherd your people with your staff,
    the flock of your possession;
    who lie abandoned in the forest,
    in the midst of the orchard.
    May they find pasture in Bashan and Gilead
    as in the ancient days.
15 As in the days of your going forth from the land of Egypt,
    let us see wonders.
16 May the nations see and be ashamed for all of their might.
    May they place their hand over their mouth.
    May their ears become deaf.
17 May they lick the dust like a serpent,
    like those who creep on the ground.
    And may they come shaking from their strongholds.
    Before Yahweh, our God, may they come trembling.
    May they fear because of you.
18 Who is God like you?
    Who takes away transgression;
    and who overlooks the crime of the remnant of his inheritance?
    He will not keep his anger forever;
    for he delights in *ḥesed*.

19 He will again have compassion on us.
    He will trample our transgressions under foot.
    He will cast into the depths of the sea all their sins.[a]
20 May you give faithfulness to Jacob,
    ḥesed to Abraham,
    as you have swore to our fathers from the days of old.

2. *Text-Critical Notes*

7.4a   MT   יום
        LXX   οὐαὶ οὐαί

Many have followed the LXX and thus propose הוי in place of יום.[86]

7.4b   MT   מבוכתם

In Isa. 22.5 יום מהומה ומבוסה ומבוכה...is used as the qualifier of the
day, the subject of which is Yahweh. In Mic. 7.4 the 3rd masc. plur.
pron. suff. appears to have as its antecedent the groups mentioned in
7.4a—'the best of and the most upright of them'. These suffixes themselves may perhaps refer back to the 7.3. The occurrence of the 3rd
person pron. suff. breaks the sequence of the 2nd person pron. suff. in
7.4bα whose occurrences are unclear in this context.

7.19a   MT   חטאותם
        LXX   τὰς ἁμαρτίας ἡμῶν

The 3rd person pron. suff. in the MT is a switch from the 1st person
pron. suff. in the preceding clause. On the basis of this observation the
LXX reading may be explained as an attempt to clarify the antecedent of
the suff. and in so doing to resolve the difficulty created by the presence
of the 1st and 3rd person pron. suff. While the MT is the more difficult
reading, it represents the style of the writing in switching pronouns.

86. See Barthélemy, *Critique Textuelle*, p. 777, for the references and annota-
tion of the authors who follow the reading LXX.

BIBLIOGRAPHY

Adamaik, R., *Justice in the Old Testament: The Evolution of Divine Retribution in the Historiography of the Wilderness Generation* (Cleveland, OH: John T. Zubal, 2nd edn, 1985).

Albertz, R., 'צעק', in *THAT*, II, p. 573.

Alden, R.L., 'קסם', in *TWOT*, II, p. 805.

Allen, L.C., *The Books of Joel, Obadiah, Jonah and Micah* (NICOT; Grand Rapids: Eerdmans, 1976).

Anderson, G.W., 'A Study of Micah 6.1-8', *SJT* 4.2 (1951), pp. 191-97.

Balentine, S.E, *The Hidden God* (Oxford: Oxford University Press, 1983).

Barlett, J.B., 'The Use of the Word ראש as a Title in the Old Testament', *VT* 19 (1969), pp. 1-10.

Barthélemy, D., *Critique Textuelle de l'Ancien Testament* (OBO, 50.3; Göttingen: Vandenhoeck & Ruprecht, 1992).

Barthélemy, D., and J.T. Milik, *Qumran Cave 1* (DJD, 1; Oxford: Clarendon Press, 1955).

Bechtel, L.M., 'Shame as a Sanction of Social Control in Biblical Israel: Judicial, Political and Social Shaming', *JSOT* 49 (1991), pp. 47-76.

Beckson, K., and A. Ganz, *Literary Terms: A Dictionary* (New York: Farrar, Straus & Giroux, 1975).

Bennett, M., *The Book of Micah* (Grand Rapids: Baker Book House, 1968).

Beyerlin, W., *Die Kulttraditionen Israels in der Verkündigung des Propheten Micha* (Göttingen: Vandenhoeck & Ruprecht, 1959).

Bleek, F., *Eineitung in day Alte Testament* (ed. J. Wellhausen; Berlin: Georg Reimer, 4th edn, 1878).

Bovati, P., *Re-Establishing Justice: Legal Terms, Concepts and Procedures in the Hebrew Bible* (trans. M. Smith; JSOTSup, 105; Sheffield: JSOT Press, 1994).

Bowling, A., 'לאה', in *TWOT*, I, p. 464.

Brenton, L.C.L., *The Septuagint with Apocrypha* (Peabody, MA: Hendrickson, 4th edn, 1992).

Brown, M.L., ' "Is it Not?" or "Indeed!" ': *HL* in Northwest Semitic', *MAARAV* 4.2 (1987), pp. 201-209.

Brown, R., 'Theme', in I.R. Makaryk (ed.), *Encyclopedia of Contemporary Literary Theory: Approaches, Scholars, Terms* (Toronto: University of Toronto Press, 1993), pp. 662-46.

Brown, S.J., *The World of Imagery: Metaphor and Kindred Imagery* (New York: Russel & Russel, 1966).

Buchanan, George W., 'The Old Testament Meaning of the Knowledge of Good and Evil', *JBL* 75 (1956), pp. 14-20.

Budde, K., 'Micha 2 und 3', *ZAW* 38 (1919–20), pp. 2-22.

Burkitt, F.C., 'Micah 6 and 7: A Northern Prophecy', *JBL* 45 (1926), pp. 159-61.

Buss, M.J., 'The Social Psychology of Prophecy', in J.A. Emerton (ed.), *Prophecy: Essays Presented to Georg Fohrer on his Sixty-fifth Birthday* (Berlin: W. de Gruyter, 1980).

Cheyne, T.K., *Micah: With Notes and Interpretation* (The Cambridge Bible for Schools and Colleges; Cambridge: Cambridge University Press, 1893).

—*Introduction to the Book of Isaiah* (London: A. & C. Black, 1895).

Childs, B.S., *The Book of Exodus* (OTL; Philadelphia: Westminster Press, 1974).

Clark, G.R., *The Word Ḥesed in the Hebrew Bible* (JSOTSup, 157; Sheffield: JSOT Press, 1993).

Clifford, R.J., 'The Use of Hôy in the Prophets', *CBQ* 28 (1966), pp. 458-64.

Clines, D.J.A., *The Theme of the Pentateuch* (JSOTSup, 10; Sheffield: JSOT Press, 1978).

Coats, G.W., 'Conquest Traditions in the Wilderness Theme', *JBL* 95 (1976), pp. 177-90.

Cohen, G., 'שָׁאַר', in *TWOT*, II, pp. 894-95.

Coppes, L.J., 'נחל', in *TWOT*, II, pp. 569-70.

—'קוּם', in *TWOT*, II, p. 793.

Cover, R.C., 'Sin, Sinner', in *ABD*, VI, pp. 31-40.

Croatto, J.S., *Biblical Hermeneutics: Towards a Theory of Reading as the Production of Meaning* (Maryknoll, NY: Orbis Books, 1987).

Cuffey, K.H., 'The Coherence of Micah: A Review of the Proposals and a New Interpretation' (unpublished PhD dissertation, Drew University, 1987).

Daniels, D.R., 'Is there a "Prophetic Lawsuit" Genre?', *ZAW* 99 (1987), pp. 339-60.

Deane, W.J., 'Micah', in H.D.M. Spence *et al.* (eds.), *The Pulpit Commentary* (New York: Funk & Wagnalis, 1950).

Deissler, A., 'Micha 6, 1-8: Der Rechtsstreit Jahwes mit Israel um das rechte Bundesverhältnis', *TTZ* 68 (1959), pp. 229-34.

Detweiler, R. (ed.) *Reader Response Approaches to Biblical and Secular Texts* (Semeia, 31; Atlanta: Scholars Press, 1985).

DeVries, S.J., *Yesterday, Today, and Tomorrow* (Grand Rapids: Eerdmans, 1975).

—*1 and 2 Chronicles* (FOTL, 11; Grand Rapids: Eerdmans, 1989).

—*From Old Revelation to New: A Tradition-Historical and Redaction-Critical Study of Temporal Transitions in Prophetic Prediction* (Grand Rapids: Eerdmans, 1995).

Dozemann, T.B., *God on the Mountain* (SBLMS, 37; Atlanta: Scholars Press, 1989).

Driver, S.R., *An Introduction to the Literature of the Old Testament* (New York: Meridian Library, 1956).

Duhm, B., *Das Buch Jesaia* (Göttingen: Vandenboeck & Ruprecht, 5th edn, 1968).

Durham, J.I., 'שָׁלוֹם and the Presence of God', in J. Durham *et al.* (eds.), *Proclamation and Presence: Old Testament Essays in Honor of Gwynne Henton Davie* (Macon, GA: Mercer University Press, corrected edn, 1983), pp. 272-93.

—*Exodus* (WBC, 3; Waco, TX: Word Books, 1987).

Eichrodt, W., *Theology of the Old Testament*, I (OTL; Philadelphia: Westminster Press, 1961).

Ewald, G.H., von, *Commentary on the Prophets of the Old Testament* (trans. J.F. Smith; 5 vols; London: Williams & Norgate, 1876).

Exum, J.C., and D.J.A. Clines, *The New Literary Criticism and the Hebrew Bible* (JSOTSup, 143; Sheffield: JSOT Press, 1993).

Feinberg, C.L., 'אָסַף', in *TWOT*, I, pp. 60-61.

Fishbane, M., *Biblical Interpretation in Ancient Israel* (Oxford: Clarendon Press, 1991).

Freedman, D.N., 'Discourse on Prophetic Discourse', in H.B. Huffmon (ed.), *The Quest for the Kingdom of God: Studies in Honor of George E. Mendenhall* (Winona Lake, IN: Eisenbrauns, 1983).

Gaster, T.H., 'Micah', in I. Landman (ed.), *The Universal Jewish Encyclopedia* (New York: Ktav, 1969), VII, p. 529.

Gerstenberger, E.S., 'The Woe-Oracles of the Prophets', *JBL* 81 (1962), pp. 249-63.

—*Psalm. Part 1: With an Introduction to Cultic Poetry* (FOTL, 14; Grand Rapids: Eerdmans, 1988).

Gilchrist, P.R., 'יכח', in *TWOT*, I, pp. 376-77.

—'ילל', in *TWOT*, I, pp. 868-69.

—'יסר', in *TWOT*, I, pp. 386-87.

Goldman, S., 'Micah', in A. Cohen (ed.), *The Twelve Prophets* (Bournemouth: Soncino, 1948), p. 153.

Glueck, N., *Ḥesed in the Bible* (trans. A. Gottschalk; Cincinnati: Hebrew Union College Press, 1967).

Graffy, A., *A Prophet Confronts his People* (AnBib, 104; Rome: Biblical Institute Press, 1984).

Gray, G.B., *Sacrifice in the Old Testament* (New York: Ktav, 1971).

Grogan, G.W., 'Isaiah', in F.E. Gaebelein (ed.), *The Expositor's Bible Commentary* (12 vols.; Grand Rapids: Zondervan, 1986), VI, pp. 3-354.

Groningen, G., van, 'קצין', in *TWOT*, II, p. 807.

Hagstrom, D., *The Coherence of the Book of Micah: A Literary Analysis* (SBLDS, 89; Atlanta: Scholars Press, 1988).

Halévy, J., 'Le Livre de Michée', *RevSém* 12 (1904), pp. 97-117, 193-214, 291-312.

Hamilton, J.M., *Social Justice and Deuteronomy: The Case of Deuteronomy 15* (SBLDS, 136; Atlanta: Scholars Press, 1992).

Hamilton, V.P., 'פשט', in *TWOT*, II, p. 741.

—'פעל', in *TWOT*, II, pp. 729-30.

—'שחד', in *TWOT*, II, p. 914.

Hammershaimb, E., *Some Aspects of Old Testament Prophecy from Isaiah to Malachi* (Kopenhagen: Rosenkilde & Bagger, 1966).

Harris, L.R., 'חסד', in *TWOT*, I, pp. 305-307.

Harvey, J., 'Le "rîb-pattern": requisitoire prophétique sur la rapture de l'alliance', *Bib* 43 (1962), pp. 172-96.

Hasel, G.F., *The Remnant* (Berrien Spring, MI: Andrews University Press, 1972).

Haupt, P., 'Critical Notes on Micah', *AJSL* 26 (1910), pp. 201-52.

—'The Book of Micah', *AJSL* 27 (1911), pp. 1-63.

Havice, H.K., 'Concern for the Widow and Fatherless in the Ancient Near East: A Case Study in Old Testament Ethics' (unpublished PhD dissertation, Yale University, 1978).

Hawthorn, J., *A Glossary of Contemporary Literary Theory* (New York: Edward Arnold, 1992).

Hillers, D.R., *Micah: A Commentary of the Book of the Prophet Micah* (Hermeneia; Philadelphia: Fortress Press, 1984).

—'Micah', in *ABD*, IV, pp. 807-810.

Hoonacker, A., van, *Les douze petits prophètes* (EBib; Paris: J. Gabalda, 1908).

House, P., *The Unity of the Twelve* (JSOTSup, 77; Sheffield: JSOT Press, 1990).

Huffmon, H.B., 'The Covenant Lawsuit in the Prophets', *JBL* 78 (1959), pp. 285-95.

Hyatt, J.P., 'On the Meaning and Origin of Micah 6.8', *ATR* 34.4 (1952), pp. 232-39.

Jenni, E., 'Remnant', in *IDB*, III, pp. 32-33.

Jeppesen, K., 'New Aspects of Micah Research', *JSOT* 8 (1978), pp. 3-32.

—'How the Book of Micah Lost its Integrity', *ST* 33 (1979), pp. 101-31.

Johnson, A.R., *The Cultic Prophet in Ancient Israel* (Cardiff: University of Wales Press, 1962).

Kaiser, W.C., 'עבד', in *TWOT*, II, pp. 639-41.

Kedar-Kopfstein, B., 'דם', in *TDOT*, III, p. 241.

Keil, C.F., and F. Delitzsch, *The Twelve Minor Prophets*, I (trans. J. Martin; Edinburgh: T. & T. Clark, 1885).

Knierim, R.P., 'Exodus 18 und die Neuordnung der mosaischen Gerichtsbarkeit', *ZAW* 73 (1961), pp. 158-59.

—*Die Hauptbegriffe für Sünde im Alten Testament* (Gütersloh: Gerd Mohn, 1965).

—'חטא', in *THAT*, I, pp. 541-49.

—'פשע', in *THAT*, II, pp. 488-95.

—'Old Testament Form Criticism Reconsidered', *Int* 27 (1973), pp. 435-68.

—'Customs, Judges, and Legislators in Ancient Israel', in Craig A. Evans and William F. Stinespring (eds.), *Early Jewish and Christian Exegesis* (Atlanta: Scholars Press, 1987), pp. 3-15.

—*Text and Concept in Leviticus 1.1-9: A Case in Exegetical Method* (Forschungen zum Alten Testament, 2; Tübingen: J.C.B. Mohr, 1992).

—*The Task of Old Testament Theology: Method and Cases* (Grand Rapids: Eerdmans, 1995).

—'Conceptual Aspects in Exodus 25:1-9', in *idem*, in *The Task of Old Testament Theology*, pp. 389-99.

—'Hope in the Old Testament', in *idem*, *The Task of Old Testament Theology*, pp. 244-68.

—'Revelation in the Old Testament', in *idem*, *The Task of Old Testament Theology*, pp. 416-67.

—'On the Contours of Old Testament and Biblical Hamartiology', in *idem*, *The Task of Old Testament Theology*, pp. 416-67.

—'Criticism of Literary Features, Form, Tradition, and Redaction', in D.A. Knight and G. Tucker (eds.), *The Hebrew Bible and its Modern Interpreters* (Chico, CA: Scholars Press, 1995), pp. 123-53.

Knight, G.A.F., *Deutero-Isaiah: A Theological Commentary on Isaiah 40–55* (New York: Abingdon Press, 1965).

Koch, K., 'חטא', in *TDOT*, IV, pp. 309-19.

Koch, R., *Die Sünde im Alten Testament* (Bern: Peter Lang, 1992).

Köhler, L., *Theologie des Alten Testaments* (Tübingen: J.C.B. Mohr, 1947).

Kosmala, H., 'גבורה', in *TDOT*, II, p. 369.

Kraus, H.-J., *Theology of the Psalms* (trans. K. Crim; Minneapolis: Augsburg, 1986).

Lescow, T., *Micha 6, 6-8: Studien zu Sprache, Form und Auslegung* (Stuttgart: Calwer Verlag, 1966).

—'Die dreistufige Tora Beobachtungen zu einer Form', *ZAW* 82 (1970), pp. 362-79.

—'Redaktionsgeschichtiche Analyse von Micha 1–5', *ZAW* 84 (1972), pp. 46-85.

—'Redaktionsgeschichtiche Analyse von Micha 6–7', *ZAW* 84 (1972), pp. 182-212.

Levine, B.A., *Leviticus* (JPS Torah Commentary; Philadelphia: Jewish Publication Society, 1989).

Limburg, J., 'The Root ריב and the Prophetic Lawsuit Speeches', *JBL* 88 (1969), pp. 291-304.

Lindblom, J., *Micha literarisch untersucht* (Acta Academiae Aboensis: Humaniora, 6.2; Äbo: Äbo Akademi, 1929).

—*Prophecy in Ancient Israel* (Philadelphia: Fortress Press, 1962).

Livingston, G.H., 'עול', in *TWOT*, II, p. 652.

—'און', in *TWOT*, I, pp. 23-24.

—'רעע', in *TWOT*, II, pp. 854-56.

Lofthouse, W.F., 'Ḥen and Ḥesed in the Old Testament', *ZAW* 51 (1933), pp. 29-35.

Long, B.O., *1 Kings: With an Introduction to Historical Literature* (FOTL, 9; Grand Rapids: Eerdmans, 1984).

Luker, L.M., 'Doom and Hope in Micah: The Redaction of the Oracles Attributed to an Eighth-Century Prophet' (unpublished PhD dissertation, Vanderbilt University, 1985).

Lux, R.C., 'An Exegetical Study of Micah 1.8-16' (unpublished PhD dissertation, University of Notre Dame, 1976).

Macholz, G., 'Zur Geschichte der Justizorganisation in Juda', *ZAW* 84 (1972), pp. 314-40.

Mann, T.W., *Divine Presence and Guidance in Israelite Traditions: The Typology of Exaltation* (Baltimore: The Johns Hopkins University Press, 1977).

Mariottini, C.F., 'The Problem of Social Oppression in the Eighth Century Prophets' (unpublished PhD dissertation, Southern Baptist Theological Seminary, 1983).

Marti, K., *Das Dodekapropheton* (KHAT, 13; Tübingen: J.C.B. Mohr, 1904).

Mays, J.L., *Amos* (OTL; Philadelphia: Westminster Press, 1969).

—*Micah: A Commentary* (OTL; Philadelphia: Westminster Press, 1976).

—'The Theological Purpose of the Book of Micah', in H. Donner *et al.* (eds), *Beiträge zur Alttestamentlichen Theologie* (Festschrift W. Zimmerli; Göttingen: Vandenhoeck & Ruprecht, 1977), pp. 276-87.

McConville, J.G., *Judgment and Promise: An Interpretation of the Book of Jeremiah* (Winona Lake, IN: Eisenbrauns, 1993).

Meier, S.M., *Speaking of Speaking: Marking Direct Discourse in the Hebrew Bible* (VTSup, 46; Leiden: E.J. Brill, 1992).

Milgrom, J., 'The Concept of MA'AL in the Bible and the Ancient Near East', *JAOS* 96 (1976), pp. 236-47.

—*Cult and Conscience: The Asham and the Priestly Doctrine of Repentance* (Leiden: E.J. Brill, 1976).

—'Israel's Sanctuary: The Priestly "Picture of Dorian Gray"', *RB* 83 (1976), pp. 390-99.

—*Studies in Cultic Theology and Terminology* (SJLA, 36; Leiden: E.J. Brill, 1983).

Miller, P.D., *Sin and Judgment in the Prophets: A Stylistic and Theological Analysis* (SBLMS, 27; Chico, CA: Scholars Press, 1982).

Miscall, P.D., 'The Concept of the Poor in the Old Testament' (unpublished PhD dissertation, Harvard University, 1972).

Morgan, D.F., *Between Text and Community: The Writings in Canonical Interpretation* (Minneapolis: Fortress Press, 1990).

Mosala, I.J., *Biblical Hermeneutics and Black Theology in South Africa* (Grand Rapids: Eerdmans, 1989).

Muilenburg, J., 'Form Criticism and Beyond', *JBL* 88 (1969), pp. 1-18.

Murray, D.F., 'The Rhetoric of Disputation: Re-Examination of a Prophetic Genre', *JSOT* 38 (1987), pp. 95-121.

Nielson, E., *Oral Tradition* (SBT; London: SCM Press, 1954).

Nielsen, K., *Yahweh as Prosecutor and Judge* (JSOTSup, 9; Sheffield: JSOT, 1978).

Nogalski, J., *Literary Precursors to the Book of the Twelve* (BZAW, 217; New York: W. de Gruyter, 1993).

North, C.R., *Isaiah 40–55* (London: SCM Press, 1956).

—*The Second Isaiah: Introduction, Translation and Commentary to Chapters 40–55* (Oxford: Clarendon Press, 1964).

Noth, M., *Exodus* (OTL; trans. J.S. Bowden; Philadelphia: Westminster Press, 1962).

—*Numbers* (Philadelphia: Westminster Press, 1968).

—*A History of Pentateuchal Traditions* (Scholars Press Reprints and Translations Series; trans. B.W. Anderson; Atlanta: Scholars Press, 1981).

Odell, M., 'The Inversion of Shame and Forgiveness in Ezekiel 16.59-63', *JSOT* 56 (1992), pp. 101-12.

Ollenburger, B.C., *Zion the City of the Great King: A Theological Symbol of the Jerusalem Cult* (JSOTSup, 41; Sheffield: JSOT Press, 1987).

Orelli, C., von, *The Twelve Minor Prophets* (Edinburgh: T. & T. Clark, 1897).

—'Micah', in *ISBE*, III, pp. 2046-47.

Osborn, A.R., 'The Nature of True Religion: Micah 6.1-8', *BR* 17 (1932), pp. 74-78.

Oswalt, J.N., 'גבר', in *TWOT*, I, pp. 148-49.

Oxford American Dictionary (New York: Oxford University Press, 1980).

Patterson, R.D., 'ספד', in *TWOT*, II, p. 630.

Pedersen, J., 'Honour and Shame', in *idem* (ed.), *Israel: Its Life and Culture* (4 vols.; London: Oxford University Press, 1962), II, pp. 213-44.

Perrine, L., *Literature: Structure, Sound and Sense* (New York: Harcourt Brace Jovanovich, 4th edn, 1983).

Petersen, D.L., 'A Thrice-Told Tale: Genre, Theme, and Motif', *BR* 18 (1973), pp. 30-43.

—*The Roles of Israel's Prophets* (JSOTSup, 17; Sheffield: JSOT Press, 1981).

Ploeg, J.P., van der, 'Les chefs du Peuple d'Israel et Leurs Titres', *RB* 57 (1950), pp. 40-61.

Procksch, O., *Die kleinen prophetischen Schriften vor dem Exil* (Stuttgart: Verlag der Vereinsbuchhandlung, 1910).

Rad, G., von, *Old Testament Theology* (2 vols.; San Francisco: Harper & Row, 1962), I.

—'The Promised Land and Yahweh in the Hexateuch', in *idem, The Problem of the Hexateuch and Other Essays* (trans. E.W.T. Dicken; New York: McGraw–Hill, 1966), pp. 79-83.

Ramsey, G.W., 'Speech-Forms in Hebrew Law and Prophetic Oracles', *JBL* 96 (1977), pp. 45-48.

Rawls, J., *A Theory of Justice* (Cambridge, MA: Harvard University Press, 1971).

Renaud, B., *Structure et Attaches littéraires de Michée IV–V* (Paris: J. Gabalda, 1964).

—*La Formation du Livre de Michée: Tradition et Actualisation* (Paris: J. Gabalda, 1977).

Rendtorff, R., *Leviticus* (BKAT, 3.1. Neukirchen–Vluyn: Neukirchener Verlag, 1985).

Robinson, G.L., *The Twelve Minor Prophets* (New York: George H. Doran, 1926).

Roche, M., de, 'Yahweh's Rîb Against Israel: A Reassessment of the So-Called "Prophetic Lawsuit" in the Pre-Exilic Prophets', *JBL* 102 (1983), pp. 563-74.

Rudolph, W., 'Zu Micha 1, 10-16', in J. Schreiner (ed.), *Wort, Lied und Gottesspruch* (Festschrift Joseph Zeigler; FzB, 2; Würzburg: Echter Verlag; Stuttgart: Katholisches Bibelwerk, 1972), pp. 233-38.

—*Micha, Habakuk, Zephanja* (KAT, 13.3; Gütersloh: Gütersloher Verlagshaus, 1975).

Sakenfeld, K., *Meaning of Ḥesed in the Hebrew Bible: A New Inquiry* (Missoula: Scholars Press, 1978).

—'Love (OT)', in *ABD*, IV, pp. 375-81.

Sanders, J.A., *Torah and Canon* (Philadelphia: Fortress Press, 1972).

—'Text and Canon: Concepts and Method', *JBL* 98 (1979), pp. 5-29.

—'A Multivalent Text: Psalm 151.3-4 Revisited', *HAR* 8 (1984), pp. 167-84.

—*Canon and Community* (Philadelphia: Fortress Press, 1984).

Schupphaus, J., 'גזל', in *TDOT*, I, pp. 456-58.

Seebass, H., 'בוש', in *TDOT*, II, p. 52.

—'פשע', in *ThWAT*, VI, p. 791.

Shaw, C.S., *The Speeches of Micah: A Rhetorical-Historical Analysis* (JSOTSup, 145; Sheffield: JSOT Press, 1993).

Smick, E.B., 'גזל', in *TWOT*, I, pp. 157-58.

Smith, J.M.P., *Micah, Zephaniah, Nahum, Habakkuk, Obadiah, and Joel* (ICC; Edinburgh: T. & T. Clark, 1911).

Smith, R.L., *Micah–Malachi* (WBC, 3; Waco, TX: Word Books, 1984).

Snaith, N.H., *The Distinctive Ideas of the Old Testament* (London: Epworth Press, 1944).

—'Sacrifice in the Old Testament', *VT* 7 (1957), pp. 300-17.

Solecki, S., 'Ideology', in I.R. Makaryk (ed.), *Encyclopedia of Contemporary Literary Theory: Approaches, Scholars, Terms* (Toronto: University of Toronto Press, 1993), pp. 558-60.

Stade, B., 'Bemerkungen über das Buch Micha', *ZAW* 1 (1881), pp. 161-72.

—'Weitere Bemerkungen zu Micha 4.5', *ZAW* 3 (1883), pp. 1-16.

—'Streiflichter auf die Entstehung der jetzigen Gestalt der alttestamentlichen Prophetenschriften', *ZAW* 23 (1903), pp. 153-71.

Stansell, G., *Micah and Isaiah: A Form and Tradition Historical Comparison* (SBLDS, 85; Atlanta: Scholars Press, 1988).

Stoebe, H.J., 'חאד', in *THAT*, I, pp. 599-622.

Stolz, F., 'בוש', in *ThWAT*, I, pp. 269-72.

Sweeney, M.A., 'Concerning the Structure and Generic Character of the Book of Nahum', *ZAW* 104 (1992), pp. 364-77.

—'Formation and Form in Prophetic Literature', in J.L. Mays, D.L. Petersen and K.H. Richards (eds.), *Old Testament Interpretation: Past, Present, and Future* (Festschrift Gene Tucker; Nashville: Abingdon Press, 1995), pp. 113-21.

—*Isaiah 1–39: With an Introduction to Prophetic Literature* (FOTL, 16; Grand Rapids: Eerdmans, 1996).

Thrall, W.F., and A. Hibberd, *A Handbook of Literature* (New York: Odyssey, 1960).

Tompkins, J.P. (ed.), *Reader-Response Criticism: From Formalism to Post-Structuralism* (Baltimore: The Johns Hopkins University Press, 1980).

Tov, E., *The Greek Minor Prophet Scrolls From Nahal Hever (8Hev XIIgr)* (DJD, 8; Oxford: Clarendon Press, 1990).

Tucker, G.M., 'Prophetic Superscriptions and the Growth of a Canon', in G.W. Coats and B.O. Long (eds.), *Canon and Authority: Essays in Old Testament Religion and Theology* (Philadelphia: Fortress Press, 1977), pp. 56-70.

Vaux, R., de, *Ancient Israel: Social Institutions* (New York: McGraw–Hill, 1966).

Vuilleumier, R., 'Michée', in C.-A. Keller (ed.), *Michée, Nahoum, Habacuc, Sophonie* (CAT, 11b; Neuchâtel: Delachaux & Niestlé, 1971), pp. 1-92.

Wagner, S., 'דרש', in *TDOT*, III, pp. 293-307.

Waltke, B., 'Micah', in T.E. McComiskey (ed.), *The Minor Prophets: An Exegetical and Expository Commentary* (Grand Rapids: Baker Book House, 1993), II, pp. 591-764.

Waltke, B., and M. O'Connor, *An Introduction to Biblical Hebrew Syntax* (Winona Lake, IN: Eisenbrauns, 1990).

Wehmeier, G., 'סתר', in *THAT*, II, p. 175.

Weinfeld, M., *Social Justice in Ancient Israel and in the Ancient Near East* (Minneapolis: Fortress Press; Jerusalem: Magnes Press, 1995).

Weiser, A., *The Old Testament: Its Formation and Development* (trans. D.M. Barton; New York: Association Press, 1961).

—*Das Buch der zwölf kleinen Propheten* (Göttingen: Vandenhoeck & Ruprecht, 1963).

Wellhausen, J., *Die Kleinen Propheten* (repr.; Berlin: W. de Gruyter, 1963).

Wenham, G.J., T*he Book of Leviticus* (NICOT, 3; Grand Rapids: Eerdmans, 1979).

Westermann, C., *Basic Forms of Prophetic Speech* (trans. H.C. White; Louisville, KY: Westminster/John Knox Press, 1991).

—*Isaiah 40–66: A Commentary* (trans. D.G. Stalker; OTL; Philadelphia: Westminster Press, 1969).

White, W., 'רצה', in *TWOT*, II, p. 859.

Wijngaards, J., 'הוציא and העלה: A Twofold Approach to the Exodus', *VT* 15 (1965), pp. 98-101.

Wildberger, H., *Jesaja* (BKAT, 10.1-3; Neukirchen–Vluyn: Neukirchener Verlag, 1972–82).

—'שאר', in *THAT*, II, p. 847.

Willi-Plein, I., *Vorformen der Schriftexegese innerhalb des Alten Testaments* (BZAW, 123; New York: W. de Gruyter, 1971).

Williams, R., *Hebrew Syntax: An Outline* (Toronto: University of Toronto Press, 2nd edn, 1976).

Willis, J.T., 'The Structure, Setting, and Interrelationships of the Pericopes in the Book of Micah' (unpublished PhD dissertation, Vanderbilt University, 1966).

—'Micah IV 14–V 5: A Unit', *VT* 18 (1968), pp. 529-47.

—'A Note on ואמר in Micah 3.1', *ZAW* 80 (1968), pp. 50-54.

—'Some Suggestions on the Interpretation of Micah 1.2', *VT* 18 (1968), pp. 372-79.

—'The Structure of the Book of Micah', *SEÅ* 34 (1969), pp. 5-42.

—'The Structure of Micah 3–5 and the Function of Micah 5.9-14 in the Book', *ZAW* 81 (1969), pp. 191-214.

—'Fundamental Issues in Contemporary Micah Studies', *ResQ* 13.2 (1970), pp. 77-90.

Wilson, M.R., 'נסה', in *TWOT*, II, p. 581.

Wolfendale, J., *A Homiletic Commentary on the Minor Prophets* (The Preacher's Complete Homiletic Commentary on the Old Testament, 20; New York: Funk & Wagnalis).

Wolff, H.W., 'Das Zitat im Prophetenspruch', in *idem*, *Gesammelte Studien zum Alten Testament* (Munich: Chr. Kaiser Verlag, 1964), pp. 36-121.

—*Joel and Amos* (Hermeneia; Philadelphia: Fortress Press, 1977).

—*Micha* (Neukirchen–Vluyn; Neukirchener Verlag, 1982).

—'Schwerter zu Pflugscharen—Missbrauch eines Prophetenwortes? Praktische Fragen und exegetische Klärungen zu Joël 4, 9-12, Jes 2, 2-5 und Mic 4, 1-5', *VT* 44 (1984), p. 280.

—*Micah: A Commentary* (trans. G. Stansell; Minneapolis: Augsburg, 1990 [German original 1982]).

Wood, L.J., 'חשב', in *TWOT*, I, pp. 329-30.

Woude, A.S., van der, 'Micah in Dispute with Pseudo-Prophets', *VT* 19 (1969), pp. 244-60.

Yee, G.A., *Composition and Tradition in the Book of Hosea: A Redactional Investigation* (SBLDS, 102; Atlanta: Scholars Press, 1987).

Youngblood, R., 'רעב', in *TWOT*, II, p. 976.

Ziegler, J., *Duodecim Prophetae* (Septuaginta: Vetus Testamentum Graecum; Göttingen: Vandenhoeck & Ruprecht, 2nd edn, 1967 [1943]), XIII, pp. 205-27.

Zobel, K., *Prophetie und Deuteronomium* (Berlin: W. de Gruyter, 1992).

INDEXES

INDEX OF REFERENCES

OLD TESTAMENT

INDEX OF AUTHORS

JOURNAL FOR THE STUDY OF THE OLD TESTAMENT
SUPPLEMENT SERIES